YO-BPY-672

DISCARD

mela

multi-ethnic literatures of the americas

AMRITJIT SINGH, CARLA L. PETERSON, C. LOK CHUA, SERIES EDITORS

*The MELA Series aims to expand and deepen our sense of American litera-
tures as multicultural and multilingual and works to establish a broader
understanding of "America" as a complex site for the creation of national,
transnational, and global narratives. Volumes in the series focus on the recov-
ery, consolidation, and reevaluation of literary expression in the United States,
Canada, and the Caribbean as shaped by the experience of race, ethnicity,
national origin, region, class, gender, and language.*

Pauline E. Hopkins
DAUGHTER OF THE REVOLUTION:
THE MAJOR NONFICTION WORKS OF PAULINE E. HOPKINS
EDITED AND WITH AN INTRODUCTION BY Ira Dworkin

Lin Yutang
CHINATOWN FAMILY
EDITED AND WITH AN INTRODUCTION BY C. Lok Chua

Claude McKay
A LONG WAY FROM HOME
EDITED AND WITH AN INTRODUCTION BY Gene Andrew Jarrett

SHADOWED DREAMS: WOMEN'S POETRY
OF THE HARLEM RENAISSANCE,
2ND EDITION, REVISED AND EXPANDED
EDITED AND WITH AN INTRODUCTION BY Maureen Honey

shadowed
Dreams

THE CRISI

SEPTEMBER '27   15¢

shadowed *Dreams*

Women's Poetry of the Harlem Renaissance

SECOND EDITION,
REVISED AND EXPANDED

EDITED AND WITH AN INTRODUCTION BY
Maureen Honey

RUTGERS UNIVERSITY PRESS
NEW BRUNSWICK, NEW JERSEY, AND LONDON

Library of Congress Cataloging-in-Publication Data

Shadowed dreams : women's poetry of the Harlem Renaissance / edited and with an introduction by
Maureen Honey.— 2nd ed., rev. and expanded.

   p. cm. — (Multi-ethnic literatures of the Americas)

   Includes bibliographical references.

   ISBN-13: 978–0–8135–3885–3 (hardcover : alk. paper)

   ISBN-13: 978–0–8135–3886–0 (pbk. : alk. paper)

   1. American poetry—African American authors. 2. American poetry—New York (State)—New
York. 3. American poetry—Women authors. 4. American poetry—20th century. 5. African
American women—Poetry. 6. Harlem Renaissance. 7. Women—Poetry. I. Honey, Maureen,
1945– II. Series.

PS591.N4S54 2006

811′.520809287—dc22

2005035688

A British Cataloging-in-Publication record for this book is available from the British Library.

This collection copyright © 2006 by Rutgers, The State University

Introduction © Maureen Honey

Foreword © Nellie Y. McKay

All rights reserved

No part of this book may be reproduced or utilized in any form or by any means, electronic or
mechanical, or by any information storage and retrieval system, without written permission from
the publisher. Please contact Rutgers University Press, 100 Joyce Kilmer Avenue, Piscataway, NJ
08854–8099. The only exception to this prohibition is "fair use" as defined by U.S. copyright law.

Book design by Adam B. Bohannon

Manufactured in the United States of America

**Frontispiece: "The Burden of Black Womanhood," Aaron Douglas,
cover of *The Crisis*, September 1927.**

To the Memory of Mae V. Cowdery

CONTENTS

* These poems are new to this edition.

ILLUSTRATIONS

PREFACE TO THE SECOND EDITION

When *Shadowed Dreams* was first published in 1989, little informa-
tion existed on women poets from the Harlem Renaissance despite
their central role in creating that artistic movement. In the interven-
ing seventeen years, important recovery work has occurred that ne-
cessitates a major revision of this anthology, which remains the only
one to focus exclusively on black women poets from the era. With
new writers having come to light and new poetry by those I included
in the first edition being uncovered in the course of my own and oth-
ers' research, the volume has been expanded to include eighteen new
poets and a doubling of the original number of poems. In addition,
I have expanded the original biographical sketches included in the
first edition to cover the new information on these poets that has
been excavated by Lorraine Elena Roses, Ruth Randolph, Cheryl
Wall, Venetria Patton, and myself, as well as others.

While the addition of this creative and biographical material ex-
pands significantly our understanding of African American women
writers participating in the New Negro Movement, I have also re-
arranged the material to bring the poets more clearly into focus.
Originally, I elected to organize *Shadowed Dreams* thematically in or-
der to highlight the subjects common to this generation, but in this
edition I have arranged the poetry by writer, introducing each with a
biographical sketch, and put the writers in alphabetical order for
easy reference. This schema allows us to see and hear more clearly
the individual poetic voice of each woman so that we can better ap-
preciate her artistic vision. Since I decided to abandon the thematic
format of the original anthology, I took care to arrange each poet's
section in a thematic order that invites the reader to move meaning-
fully from poem to poem. Each poet's section begins with poetry that
declares her artistic goal or defines her voice in some important way
and then moves through pieces focused on heritage or New Negro
militancy, love and nature poetry, and, finally, poems concerned
with aging and death. Not every poet left us enough poems to cover
all these topics, but those who did tell a story of birth, awakening,
defiance, pain, joy, intimacy, and their imagined legacy.

Although we now realize that women poets played a major role in the Harlem Renaissance and that their sensibility was more radical than we had thought, we have still to remove them from the shadows of literary history. When I ask people to name a woman poet from the era, I am generally confronted with silence. This needs to change, and I am hoping that by showcasing each poet in her own section and introducing her with a biographical sketch, she will acquire a stronger identity for contemporary readers. Gwendolyn Bennett, Mae Cowdery, Alice Dunbar-Nelson, Jessie Fauset, Helene Johnson, Georgia Douglas Johnson, Angelina Weld Grimké, Gladys May Casely Hayford (Aquah Laluah), Anne Spencer—these are names that should immediately spring to mind when we think of women poets from the Harlem Renaissance. As well, we need to get to know Anita Scott Coleman, Blanche Taylor Dickinson, Virginia Houston, Effie Lee Newsome, Esther Popel, and others whose poetry speaks to us over the decades with surprising force and richness.

In rethinking *Shadowed Dreams,* I realized that another major issue was my original time frame for the Harlem Renaissance, which I have decided was too small (nearly all the poems from the first edition were published in the 1920s). As we have revisioned the period, it has become clear that temporal and geographical expansion brings more women writers into the picture since many of them lived outside of New York City and continued to publish in journals during the Great Depression. Just where one identifies the beginning and end of the Harlem Renaissance is, of course, open to debate, and valid disagreement over dates abounds; however, I see the writing during the period between the wars (1919–1941) as distinctly different from African American creative writing that came before or after, so I have included poems that appeared in the late 1930s. Before World War I, we can detect traces of what would become hallmarks of work produced in the New Negro Movement—avoidance of a southern rural vernacular that had been ridiculed on the minstrel stage, portrayal of modern urban characters, identification with Africa, foregrounding of art as a political weapon, and militant resistance to racism—but the full flowering of these qualities would only occur after the war. Similarly, while the depression had a huge impact on black writers in various ways, poetry of the 1930s continues to reflect major themes of the Harlem Renaissance. African American creative writing in this decade does exhibit an emerging urban realism that became a form of literary naturalism through the 1950s and beyond. This evolution mirrors the stark economic realities of a population largely disillusioned with the North and battered by massive levels of unemployment and poverty, but writers continued to be influenced by the preceding decade in fundamental ways, and that shows up in women's poetry. World War II would prove to be a defining event for black Americans; it profoundly altered their rhetoric and political thinking. The wartime Double Victory campaign fought by the NAACP (National Association for the Advancement of Colored People) and the National Urban League used the image of black people in uniform fighting for democracy abroad as a wedge against segregation on the home front, sparking the opening salvos of the Civil Rights Movement that would follow. Creative writers became increasingly blunt in their depiction of life as a black American and virtually abandoned the Harlem Renaissance idea that art could bring African Americans and whites together.

I have kept the wonderful foreword by the late Nellie Y. McKay and my original introduction from the 1989 edition (with minor revision) as they frame the most important themes appearing in women's poetry and lay out issues that continue to confront us today as we move forward with recovery of these lost texts. I have also retained most of the poetry that appeared in the first edition for purposes of continuity, eliminating only those writers whose small output or doubtful ethnicity did not seem to warrant their inclusion here. Although the poets appear in alphabetical order, this method of organization serendipitously yields a reading order that is aesthetically satisfying, given that many of the strongest poets appear at the beginning of the anthology.

One final element I have added to the revised edition is original artwork from period journals and anthologies. The Harlem Renaissance was artistically multidimensional—music and art were as much in the mix as literature—and these illustrations are meant to evoke a larger aesthetic context from which the poetry emerged. There are nine illustrations by Aaron Douglas, Gwendolyn Bennett, Laura Wheeler, Richard Bruce Nugent, Winold Reiss, and Lois Jones. All but Reiss are African American. These illustrations are paired with poems that speak to the artwork's subject and visually animate it. I am hoping the illustrations in this anthology bring even more vividly to life the poetic voices that convey to us the dreams, hopes, pain, ecstasy, and anger of women who entered the twentieth century as modern women with new things to say. It is time we let the light of our attention fall on their words and hearts and bring them out of the shadows, where they have remained protected but invisible for decades. Their time is now.

In the late 1960s and early 1970s, with the exciting rediscovery of fig-
ures like Countée Cullen, Jean Toomer, Langston Hughes, and Rich-
ard Wright (to name a few of the most well known), many young
black women writers and scholars wondered aloud, at first mostly
among themselves, and then to the larger world: "Where were the
women who put pen to paper and gave voice to their creative im-
pulses?" Of course, almost everyone knew of Gwendolyn Brooks, the
first black poet to receive a Pulitzer prize, and radical contempo-
raries like June Jordan, Carolyn Rodgers, Nikki Giovanni, and Sonia
Sanchez, who made impolite and even outrageous claims for black-
ness, on paper, on street corners, in local bars, and in demonstra-
tions on college campuses and elsewhere, and they called themselves
poets. But for most of us then, if there was an identifiable tradition
in Afro-American literature, it was a man's world. Some of us, even
as we ventured out to search for black female literary models, con-
soled ourselves with the idea that the women had been too busy
keeping the "race" alive over its three-hundred-year-old Ameri-
can history to have found the time to write. Now we know that was
not so.

Given such an inauspicious beginning to the search for black
women writers, however, the pioneers who excavated the rich mine
of which we are now aware—the tradition of black women writing
in America—richly deserve all the credit we can give them. And as
the thirty-one volumes (with one more to come) of the recent
Schomburg Library of Nineteenth-Century Black Women Writers
reveal, in spite of how difficult it must have been, black women wrote
prolifically in all of the most popular forms—poetry, novels, short
fiction, and autobiography. The first task was discovering the tradi-
tion; the second, and equally challenging, has been making the ma-
terials available to students and teachers.

Maureen Honey's fine volume, *Shadowed Dreams: Women's Poetry
of the Harlem Renaissance,* makes a strong response to that second
challenge. Although scholarship on the Renaissance has burgeoned
in recent years, work on women remains to be done. At the same
time, most of what has already been published on women writers,

including on those who wrote during the Renaissance, has been on the novelists. Work in other fields lags behind. Consequently, *Shadowed Dreams* will occupy a significant place in the body of recovered Afro-American women's poetry, one equal to that of Erlene Stetson's 1980 landmark anthology, *Black Sister: Poetry by Black American Women, 1746–1980*. In addition, *Shadowed Dreams* comes at a most propitious time, following on the heels of Gloria Hull's *Color, Sex, and Poetry: Three Women Writers of the Harlem Renaissance* (1987), a text that focuses close attention on the lives and writings of a select group of women poets of that era. Both Stetson's and Hull's works set the stage for Honey's book, which gives a comprehensive view of the poetic achievements of the most important women poets of the period. This is the first time that anyone has attempted to do such a study of Harlem Renaissance women writers. Because of its timeliness, the text will be of immense interest to everyone interested in the Renaissance, offering a splendid resource for both general readers and those doing research on women in the Renaissance and black women poets in general.

    Shadowed Dreams contains the work of a number of poets, many of whose names are familiar to scholars of the Renaissance, and, just as importantly, many who are obscure even among the informed. Honey divides the poems into four groups [in the 1989 edition]: Protest, Heritage, Love and Passion, and Nature, revealing the wide individual and collective interests of the writers. The majority of the women are included in more than one section. Honey claims that poetry was the preferred form of creative expression for the women writers of the 1920s, and from her text we see that these women made the widest possible use of the form. Scholars already familiar with some of these writers, and who are aware of their other writings, will observe that in specific instances, such as in the poetry of Angelina Weld Grimké and Georgia Douglas Johnson, the themes and motifs they employ here are also present in their plays. In choosing to include several selections from each writer and, for the better-known writers, to print examples of their lesser-known work, Honey's collection gives us an expanded appreciation of the intellectual concerns of black women in the 1920s. This has been especially important among those of us who have interests in black women's lives from the nineteenth to the middle of the twentieth century.

While nature is a common motif in much of this poetry, more interestingly, Honey identifies the ease with which some women, even those who were heterosexual, wrote about their love of female beauty. In this she suggests that the writers identified strongly with women as a whole and "affirmed that bond in their work," although not many were willing to explore erotic love for women in this public way. In the more recent work on the Harlem Renaissance we have come to realize that gay culture was part of the artistic circles of the time. This perhaps made it easier for the subject to appear, at least in a limited way, in women's poetry.

With limited opportunities to have their work appear in traditional (white) anthologies of American poetry, or to publish single volumes of their own, much of what Harlem Renaissance women wrote appeared in the leading black journals of their day, especially in *The Crisis* (the journal of the NAACP) and *Opportunity* (the journal of the National Urban League). Since these were the most widely circulated and read of black media, these women, and the men whose work was published in the same places, were the most visible and widely read of the literary figures of their day. That these women appeared as often as they did in these journals indicates how well respected their work was by their peers, and how popular they must have been with readers.

The introduction to *Shadowed Dreams* will be particularly useful for students and those less familiar with the writings of women of the period. There is much here to learn about the Renaissance in general. Honey sets the tone for a largely historical understanding of her writers, and her brief survey of the social events and important literary and artistic figures of the time will serve the uninitiated well. One striking similarity among the women poets is their membership in the educated black middle class of the time. As a result, many wrote what appears only as conventional, genteel verse. At the same time, Honey makes it clear that they were imaginative artists, and among them, there were a few who entertained ideological agendas and produced striking metaphors and poems of high aesthetic quality. Unquestionably, all believed in art, and this group of women took advantage of the temper of the times to participate in the cultural life of their group.

Black women poets of the Harlem Renaissance fully deserve the attention that Maureen Honey gives them in her book. Given the male domination of the New Negro Movement, these were women who overcame many barriers in order to participate in the literary life of their time. With the high interest in all areas of women's lives at this time, this book is not only useful, it is vital to our understanding of a major area of Afro-American cultural history. And equally important, no longer will anyone be able to claim that the only major poets of the Renaissance were the men whose names have become the signatures for that movement over the past three decades. The women were there, too!

—Nellie Y. McKay
University of Wisconsin, Madison
December 1988

ACKNOWLEDGMENTS

I would like to thank several people without whom it would not have been possible to put together this revised anthology. Of course, without the generous copyright permission of the National Urban League and the NAACP, this project would not have been possible. I thank both from the bottom of my heart. All poems and illustrations from *Opportunity* and *Ebony and Topaz: A Collectanea* (1927) are reprinted by permission of the National Urban League; I wish to thank the Crisis Publishing Company, Incorporated, the magazine of the National Association for the Advancement of Colored People, for authorizing the use of all poems and illustrations from *The Crisis*, including the cover image by Laura Wheeler. All other material is in the public domain.

First on the list of individuals to thank is my editor at Rutgers, Leslie Mitchner, whose encouragement has been invaluable. Without her enthusiasm, the project never would have come together. Leslie was instrumental in bringing into being the first edition of *Shadowed Dreams* in 1989, when she worked hard to have Rutgers be its publisher in the midst of keen competition for the project. She read the poems, fell in love with them, and is the perfect editor for this revised edition. I cannot thank her enough for supporting me in my feeling that a revised edition was both appropriate and necessary. As well, the scholarly work of Cheryl Wall, Deborah McDowell, Gloria Hull, Hazel Carby, Ann Allen Shockley, Erlene Stetson, Mary Helen Washington, Lorraine Elena Roses, and Ruth Randolph, among others, made it possible for me to move forward with adding new writers to this volume and dedicating myself to recovering their poetry. Roses and Randolph, in particular, have done incredible work in unearthing biographical and literary information about African American women writers from the Harlem Renaissance era, and we who are doing recovery work in the period owe them a great debt of gratitude. Of course, the contributions of David Levering Lewis, Houston Baker Jr., Arnold Rampersad, Henry Louis Gates Jr., Amritjit Singh, John Lowe, George Chauncy, Darlene Clark Hine, Thadious Davis, Yemisi Jimoh, and others have moved our understanding of the Harlem Renaissance a great distance, and I have benefited immeasurably from their insight and historical/cultural recovery work, as well as from the kind words of many of them. I am especially grateful for the support of Amritjit Singh and John Lowe, whose conversations with me have boosted my spirits many a time. A note from Henry Louis Gates Jr. praising *Shadowed Dreams* when it first came out is one of my most treasured mementos.

Of further inspiration to me are scholars and poets who value this poetry and contribute to the tradition that created it. These would include Cheryl Clarke, whose lesbian poetry recalls the best of these early writers and whose encouragement when *Shadowed Dreams* first appeared has stayed with me all these years. The late June Jordan was a personal friend who visited my campus when I was putting the first edition together and whose vibrant poetic voice echoes the political and searingly honest verse of many Renaissance women writers. Her passing has cost us all dearly. My gratitude to poets and colleagues Grace Bauer, Hilda Raz, Stephen Behrendt, Greg Kuzma, and Ted Kooser, who create crystalline poetry and value the work I do in recovering women's poetic voices. My treasured friend, fiction writer Marly Swick, is also someone whose high regard means everything to me, as does that of Joy Ritchie, Gerald Shapiro, Judith Slater, Gwendolyn Foster, Wheeler Winston Dixon, Oyekan Owomoyela, Linda Pratt, Sherry Harris, Barbara DiBernard, and Kwakiutl Dreher. Joyce A. Joyce is a valued friend and supporter as well. Her trenchant insights into literature of the period and beyond are a continual source of insight. As well, the late Barbara Christian paved the way for those of us working in African American women's writings, and her glowing review of my early manuscript meant more to me than I can express. The late Nellie Y. McKay's generous foreword has also provided me with fundamental encouragement and affirmed my vision of what recovery of these poets means. Hers was a hugely important voice in African American studies and she will be sorely missed.

I could not have put this revised edition together without the assistance of Kris Gandara, Julie Iromuanya, Jackie Cruikshank, and Amber Harris Leichner, graduate students who typed many of the poems and helped me with library research on the writers. Their enthusiasm for the project was a great motivation for me to complete it, and their professionalism is much in evidence here. I also wish to thank the University of Nebraska Research Council for its grants to pay permissions fees and cover other expenses associated with the project as well as the English Department for providing me with the research assistants I depended on throughout.

There are three people I need to mention with special affection and gratitude. Venetria Patton, a former colleague and close friend, provided the impetus for getting this revised edition off the ground when she and I worked on gathering material for *Double-Take: A Revisionist Harlem Renaissance Anthology* (2001). We uncovered many poems that were not part of the first *Shadowed Dreams,* and she encouraged me to add them to the volume while helping me collect information on several of the writers. Without her collaborative expertise and invitation to work on *Double-Take,* I may never have tackled this revision; her ongoing friendship, professional respect, and endless enthusiasm have made it possible for me to continue working in the Harlem Renaissance period. My brother, Michael Honey, whose prize-winning scholarship in African American labor history has won my undying admiration, has been a stalwart supporter through the years. We have a special bond, professionally and personally, that is immensely rare and precious. Last but certainly not least, I wish to thank my loving partner, Tom Kiefer, for supporting me through thick and thin, being so understanding of the time it takes to complete a scholarly project of this size, and picking up the slack when that needed to be done despite his own demanding research and teaching program. He is at the center of my work and life in ways I cannot begin to list, as they are infinite.

This is the only anthology to be devoted exclusively to women poets of the Harlem Renaissance. Since many critical works, until recently, do not mention them at all, it is partly intended to balance the picture.[1] Furthermore, it is becoming apparent that poetry was the preeminent genre of the era for African American writers, and since women published relatively few collections, bringing together in a single volume the scattered pieces dispersed among several journals and anthologies helps us see literary patterns not evident otherwise. We can also see these women in dialogue with each other across region and time. The particular blend of romanticism, sensuality, anger, and faith in the capacity of art to effect change marks the Harlem Renaissance as a special time, one that has lessons for us today about the nature of racism and the black artist's relationship to political change. For black women, especially, the era after World War I was a time of expansion, renewal, and promise, the collapse of which demands careful study if we are to understand the many challenges faced by African American women writers yesterday and today.

Well known in intellectual circles of their day and widely published in African American journals and anthologies, women poets achieved the respect of their peers as well as popularity with a middle-class audience during their own era.[2] Scholars who lived through the Renaissance generally wrote favorably of them. Sterling Brown, for instance, compares Anne Spencer to Emily Dickinson and calls Georgia Douglas Johnson's poetry "skillful and fluent" (62–65). James Weldon Johnson praises Gwendolyn Bennett for her "delicate, poignant" lyrics while calling attention to Jessie Fauset's "light and neat" touch (205, 243). Later critics, however, tended to see women's verse as conventional and sentimental, out of step with the militant, rebellious race consciousness of the period. Those who accorded it some artistic value nevertheless agreed that most women poets remained within the genteel school of "raceless" literature, having largely confined themselves to the realm of private experience and the natural world (Davis and Peplow). Known primarily for their lyrical pastoral verse, women have been judged as imitating European traditions and contributing little that was useful to the creation of a black aesthetic. Hampered by devotion to a theory of art not drawn from their own experience, so the consensus was, whatever talent some of them exhibited was imprisoned by conformity to inappropriate models.

Any reappraisal of the women who participated in the Harlem Renaissance must begin with these twin misperceptions. In fact, much of their poetry exhibits the qualities of New Negro writing: identification with the race, a militant proud spirit, anger at racism, determination to fight oppression, rejection of white culture, and an attempt to reconstruct an invisible heritage. Even predominantly lyric poets produced verse concerned with protest and heritage. Anne Spencer, for instance, addressed lynching, female subordination, and racism, while Georgia Douglas Johnson reflected often on prejudice and cultural imperialism. Indeed, fully half of the poetry by women published in the two major journals of the Harlem Renaissance, *Opportunity* and *The Crisis,* dealt explicitly with race issues, and nearly as many women's poems were published as those by men.[3] Lynching, prejudice, stereotyping, white cultural imperialism, the assertion of rights, the strength of African ancestors, black culture, and the beauty of their color were all popular subjects during the decade for both men and women. Yet, as time went on, the image of women's poetry grew to be that of the pastoral or romantic lyric with only occasional reference to the vast number of race poems produced.[4]

Erlene Stetson, Gloria Hull, Deborah McDowell, and Cheryl Wall have broken new ground in criticism of women writers from this era by asserting that their art alludes, in a subversive way, to an oppressive social framework. McDowell has identified feminist, antiracist themes in Jessie Fauset's and Nella Larsen's work, for instance, two writers rather harshly judged as conventional and bourgeois ("Neglected"). Gloria Hull connects the verse of Angelina Weld Grimké, Alice Dunbar-Nelson, and Georgia Douglas Johnson to a larger framework of political writing and social activism in their personal lives (*Color*). Erlene Stetson maintains that black women's poetry is distinguished by subversive perception of the world and the use of subterfuge as a creative strategy. That their exploration takes place in a personal landscape, she asserts, should not detract from its radical implications (*Black Sister*). Cheryl Wall calls attention to the burden women of the era carried regarding stereotypes of them in the dominant culture; the poets chose verse forms that would allow them to explore forbidden territory safely.

I subscribe to the critical models described above, and this anthology is intended to demonstrate that the full import of these poets' imaginative choices has been obscured for modern readers by their seemingly anachronistic style and subject matter. When placed in historical context, however, their poetry comes alive, and its significance as an expression of the first modern black female voice becomes clear. A new reading reveals that it is animated, not by an imitative impulse, but rather by a defiant sensibility reflective of the rebellious women who wrote it. Because the total work of each writer was small (with the exception of Georgia Douglas Johnson), the pattern of metaphors and themes characteristic of women's writing is not evident when looking at individual poets. The impulse behind their poetry, therefore, is unclear since the framework from which it emerged is invisible. Nevertheless, artistic choices were made repeatedly that give definition to individual poems seemingly divorced from a black sensibility. Rather than representing a split consciousness, one that denies the African American heritage of the writer, we can see how this poetry, when collected in an anthology, uses the landscape of nature and romantic love, for instance, to affirm the humanity of women rendered invisible by the dominant culture. It forges a new consciousness hospitable to black female aspirations and culture.

Jessie Fauset is one of the writers who concentrated on the private world of romantic love in her poetry, yet she was a fervent supporter of Pan-Africanism and one of the prime movers of the Harlem Renaissance. In 1922, she stated, in fact, that the issue of race was always with her: "I cannot, if I will, forget the fact of color in almost everything I do or say" (quoted in Sylvander 83). Anne Spencer, who excelled at lush descriptions of her garden, fought against racial discrimination in her small Virginia town and declared in a headnote to her poems for Countee Cullen's *Caroling Dusk,* "I proudly love being a Negro woman" (47). Angelina Weld Grimké chose to write imagistic nature poems and, at the same time, produce plays and short stories about lynching and sexual oppression. The seeming contrast between these women's personal struggles against racism and the nonracial quality of much of their poetry is a characteristic shared by many female poets of the time and can be properly understood only by reference to the political context in which the Harlem Renaissance occurred.

At the time of the Great Migration northward, blacks found themselves under siege during an upsurge of terrorism in both the South and North in the World War I era. In the summer of 1919 alone, there were vicious attacks on black communities in twenty-five cities, and seventy people were lynched, with fourteen burned alive.[5] The Ku Klux Klan had been founded in 1915; D. W. Griffith had just made a film glorifying the Klan, *Birth of a Nation;* and the blackface minstrel show was a standard act in vaudeville. With the breakdown of Progressivism after the war, blacks found little political support, and this, added to the reverses after Reconstruction, left them extremely vulnerable and isolated.[6]

The racial violence, political disenfranchisement, and racist propaganda of the post-Reconstruction period produced a movement among blacks to educate white Progressives about the extent of reactionary violence against them and to upgrade the formal education of blacks themselves, a development that had particular impact on women's poetic forms. Bettina Aptheker has suggested that the focus on education, begun before Emancipation, grew out of a desire to fashion an informed leadership cadre that could spearhead moves toward legal, political, and economic power. Communities were in desperate need of black teachers, doctors, nurses, and lawyers. Furthermore, literacy and formal education, especially in the liberal arts, promised to demystify the defeated slaveholding class and dismantle the ideology of white supremacy, which held that blacks were genetically incapable of intellectual activity or exercise of the "higher faculties," i.e., reason and a cultured sensibility. Literacy posed a real threat to white supremacists because it not only opened avenues toward retrieving African American history but also demolished the lie of black intellectual inferiority with its corollary of white paternalism.[7]

The artists who came of age shortly before or during the Harlem Renaissance were raised by a generation newly emancipated, committed to education, and hungry for tangible accomplishments. They were well aware of the value of good, sound schooling and its capacity to uplift the race, while sensing their importance as inheritors of the struggle for equality and opportunity. Nathan Huggins argues that individual achievement in the arts symbolized dramatic progress from slavery and connoted more than personal accomplishment. To the masses, it was a source of power: "What may appear to us to be attitudes of bourgeois naiveté were very often highly race-conscious and aggressive" (Huggins, *Harlem* 6). The "Talented Tenth," as they were called by W.E.B. Du Bois, could serve as living examples that black inferiority was a myth serving to justify segregation and oppression. The Renaissance generation, therefore, conceived of itself as carrying on the struggle through attaining the highest possible level of literary accomplishment and surpassing the boundaries that a racist society tried to impose. Writers saw no contradiction between social activism and the production of nonracial literature because the two were fused in their minds: artistic achievement moved the race upward.

Operating within the reactionary political climate after World War I, with black people largely uneducated in a formal sense and unable to vote in the South, the vanguard of the African American community had few options before it. Marcus Garvey's immensely appealing nationalistic call for Pan-African unity was aborted by Garvey's deportation in 1927 and seriously weakened by his imprisonment during the previous four years. In addition, the limitations of Booker T. Washington's entrepreneurial approach to rural poverty were being recognized. Meanwhile, racist parodying of black folk culture in the minstrel show was in full sway. These factors pushed artists closer to classical forms as they reached for tools that promised to transcend a bleak political situation. The emotional need for a meaningful artistic tradition dovetailed with a narrowing of options in the 1920s to produce what Nathan Huggins correctly identifies as naive assumptions about the centrality of art to social change. It is predictable, however, that this largely urban middle-class group of artists would view artistic production as a liberating force.

Huggins alludes to another impetus for the welding of politics and art typical of this generation: a belief in the reconstructive, transformative power of culture, a holdover from the Progressive movement. He suggests that most considered art a bridge between the races. They believed that artists were more likely to be free of prejudice because sensitivity and rationality could transcend political conflict.[8] Intellect could overcome ignorance, break down alienation, and provide a bond between like-minded people of vastly different social castes. It was a position seemingly verified by the racial mixing that occurred in the salons of Harlem, Greenwich Village, and Paris and by the very real support for black artists by whites like Carl Van Vechten, H. L. Mencken, Zona Gale, and others.[9]

The conventional verse for which Renaissance poets have been criticized was a logical outgrowth of this focus on literary achievement and the Western humanistic tradition. If mastering the poetic forms of a literature forbidden to their parents or grandparents was a political act, then viewing those forms as timeless and universal invested the act with even greater power. The sonnet, the ode, the elegy, and classical allusion, when viewed platonically—as ideal forms—promised to provide a meeting ground, a common tongue, to which all might have access and by which all might be spiritually enlightened. There is no evidence that Harlem artists were conscious of the relationship between Western cultural domination (of which they had quite a sophisticated understanding) and their adoption of European literary forms. Even writers as innovative as Langston Hughes or Sterling Brown failed to comment on the contradiction in form and intent that characterized most of their peers' work. Certainly, poets of the Renaissance did not consider the models they followed to be the province or reflection of the conqueror. Instead, they viewed white Romantic poets of the nineteenth century as providing poetic forms appropriate for their own critiques of American society and through which black culture could be made visible.

The predominance of nature and love poetry is tangentially related to the appeal of Western literary forms, for in looking to the classical tradition poets were drawn to these subjects as expressions of a higher, more sublime plane than the problematic reality of daily life. Nineteenth-century Romantics were particularly compelling as models because they shared this generation's alienation from modern society, although not in a fully realized, articulated way. Byron, Wordsworth, Keats, Shelley, and Browning were important inspirational sources for Renaissance poets because the Romantics saw art and truth as connected, a viewpoint that echoed their own sense that the ills of modern life stemmed from a coarsening of the human spirit due to acquisitive, aggressive domination by a white ruling class. Nature offered an Edenesque alternative to the corrupted, artificial environment created by "progress."

In this way, Harlem intellectuals shared in the revulsion of many contemporary white artists toward what they believed to be a world run by morally bankrupt leaders. Similarly, they looked to the body and sensuality for vitality, as did other writers of the 1920s who, influenced by Freud, rebelled against Victorian prudery.[10] While African Americans were skeptical of the phenomenon that came to be known as "primitivism," they, too, were drawn to a vision of releasing creative energy through plumbing one's natural drives, particularly the erotic. When Virginia Houston writes about "the ecstacy / Of soft lips covering mine, / Dragging my soul through my mouth" in her poem "Ecstasy," she is expressing the notion that erotic impulses are connected to liberation of the self, a commonly held idea in the 1920s.

Pastoral Imagery and Black Women's Identity

As African Americans, women poets were sensitive to the political and artistic currents affecting black men of their day, but as women they drew special meaning from them. Alienated by a technological, urban world that excluded blacks and operated for self-interest rather than social justice, women also saw the cityscape as manmade. Although Harlem is celebrated in their poetry, the urban environment is primarily represented as alien and intrusive. Nature, in contrast, is presented as nurturing, life-giving, a haven from strife. It is also personified as female. Effie Lee Newsome refers to dew as "Night's pregnant tears" in "Morning Light (The Dew-Drier)"; Mae Cowdery speaks of "the sable breast / Of earth" in "Longings"; and Helene Johnson apotheosizes "a strong tree's bosom" in "Fulfillment."

Sharing the pastoral vision of male poets like Countée Cullen and Claude McKay, women had added reason to locate the self in natural settings. Nature provided an objective correlative through which they could articulate their gender oppression as well as that of race, for nature, like them, had been objectified, invaded, and used by men seeking power and wealth. At times, nature is brought to life as a woman, and the poet evokes for her our sympathy or admiration.

The river in Ethel Caution-Davis's poem of the same name, for instance, is described as "a decrepit old woman / Shivering in her sombre shawl of fog," while the moon is a woman searching for her children in Esther Popel's "Theft."

The connection between male domination, white supremacy, and the destruction of nature is evident in Anne Spencer's "White Things." She begins with a statement that most things on this earth are "colorful" but that the single race without color is the one that dominates: "Most things are colorful things—the sky, earth, and sea. / Black men are most men; but the white are free!" In a sophisticated analysis of power lust, Spencer likens the colonization process to a draining of nature's vitality when she says that white men "blanched with their wand of power" all with which they came in contact. Abruptly, Spencer shifts her focus to terrorism against blacks in the second stanza, ending with a chilling image of one member of a lynch mob laughingly swinging a skull "in the face of God," enjoining his deity to turn the world white.

While the poem mentions neither Native Americans nor women, it concerns both. Spencer wrote these lines after reading about a woman, pregnant at the time, tortured by a Georgia lynch mob in 1918. She had been trying to protect her husband, who had killed his employer, a farmer known for his vicious treatment of black laborers (Greene 130). The reference to colonization of Native Americans can be found in the first stanza, where the arrival of Europeans is described in line four: "They stole from out a silvered world—somewhere." The poet then metaphorically places the original inhabitants of these "earth-plains" in the landscape by referring to "hills all red," which the colonizer paradoxically turned white with his bloody attack. The metaphor is extended in lines ten and eleven, where we are told whites "turned the blood in a ruby rose / To a poor white poppyflower." Spencer identified strongly with Native Americans (her father was half Seminole, and she frequently wore her long, straight hair in braids). Here, she makes a connection between their defeat and terrorism against African Americans, linking both to the mad desire of a minority race to destroy everything of color—indigenous people, black people, and nature itself.

When Spencer first submitted this poem in 1923 to *The Crisis*, she was told by the editors that they would publish it only if she would delete a stanza referring to "white men" which appeared in the original version because they could not afford to alienate white publishers (Greene 140). This incident sheds light on the veiled references to race and gender oppression that appear in women's poetry of the Harlem Renaissance. Black artists were vulnerable in a political situation where African Americans were still struggling to form a power base. Not only could women identify with a natural landscape that men dominated and violated, but the identification afforded them metaphors for describing their oppression in ways subversive of white male power yet indirect enough not to offend that very group.

Whiteness, for instance, is a malevolent force in their poetry, associated with invisibility, suffocation, and death. The white light of the moon is portrayed as a demon that will steal the soul of a mother's baby in African writer Gladys Casely Hayford's poem "Lullaby": "Close your sleepy eyes, or the pale moonlight will steal you, / Else in the mystic silence, the moon will turn you white. / Then you won't see the sunshine, nor smell the open roses, / Nor love your Mammy anymore, whose skin is dark as night. / . . . Wherever moonlight stretches her arms across the heavens, / You will follow, . . . till you become instead, / A shade in human draperies." Here Hayford creates an allegory for the process by which black people can become separated from their roots through using the moon as a symbol of white culture. If you gaze too long at images of whiteness, the mother warns her child, you will reject your racial heritage and conform to alien standards, thereby becoming a shadow self.

A more complicated use of white metaphors appears in Esther Popel's "Theft." The moon is described as an old woman looking in vain for her children, afraid of and taunted by the elements as she hurries home. She creeps along, huddled in an old black cape, and tries to escape the wind that pelts her with snowballs, "filling her old eyes with the flakes of them." Suddenly she falls and is buried by the snow while jewels fall from her bag onto earth, whereupon they are seized by tall trees, which then sparkle with their "glittering plunder." The trees are uncharacteristically ominous in this poem, but the usage of moon and snow are typical. The snow blinds this old woman, trips and envelops her; it causes her to lose a small treasure carefully guarded. Finally, its companion, the wind, laughs at her piteous moans and turns her own children against her when they are found. Negative white elements are present in a double sense here: the desperate mother is defeated by them, and she is herself white, or rather yellow, the color of old white paint. Popel's central figure is ambiguous in that she evokes pity, modifying the image of the moon as dangerous. At the same time, she represents weakness, debilitation, and devastating loss.

Allusions to white domination and danger abound in women's poetry, yet the predominant message encourages resistance and survival. Alice Dunbar-Nelson's reflections on a snow-covered autumn tree in "Snow in October," for instance, focus on its resilience under a heavy burden: "Today I saw a thing of arresting poignant beauty: / A strong young tree, brave in its Autumn finery / . . . Bending beneath a weight of early snow, / Which . . . spread a heavy white chilly afghan / Over its crested leaves. / Yet they thrust through, defiant, glowing, / Claiming the right to live another fortnight." While Dunbar-Nelson's ostensible subject is aging, the notion of defying a deathly white power is at the core of the poem.

Angelina Weld Grimké's piece "Tenebris" echoes this subtle assertion of self against white control. Likening the branches of the poem's tree to a hand "huge and black," whose shadow rests against "the white man's house," Grimké invites us to find in her image a statement about the relationship of blacks to white society. One reading of the poem is that it sees black struggle as a subterranean, persistent chipping away at white structures. The black hand "plucks and plucks" at the bricks, which are "the color of blood and very small," at night when the occupant is sleeping, falsely secure that the image on his house is the shadow of a harmless tree. Yet the last line asks, "Is it a black hand, or is it a shadow?" and we are left sensing that the white man's house is in danger. The portrait of a house built with blood-colored bricks evokes memories of the big house on a plantation maintained by the blood and sweat of slave labor. It is also haunted by the ghosts of people whose anguish and anger are growing shadows on the white man's power, gathering force while he basks in his privilege.

Furthermore, allusive images of entrapment, masking, and burial appear regularly in these poems, at times explicitly in conjunction with references to men. Blanche Taylor Dickinson, for instance, in "Four Walls" protests having her existence limited to a room that keeps her from wandering freely through life. The speaker longs for the strength of Samson so she can break her bondage to "this conscious world with guarded men" but fears that she has internalized their rules to a point where freedom would have no meaning. Another poem of Dickinson's that implies women are constrained by a male force is "To an Icicle," which warns against having a false sense of security in a world governed by those who are physically stronger: "Chilled into a serenity / As rigid as your pose / You linger trustingly, / But a gutter waits for you / Your elegance does not secure / You favors with the sun. / He is not one to pity fragileness / He thinks all cheeks should burn / And feel how tears can run." Allusion to the home as imprisoning is made as well in Georgia Douglas Johnson's "Wishes," where the speaker complains: "I'm tired of pacing the petty round of the ring of the thing I know / I want to stand on the daylight's edge and see where the sunsets go." The image of a wedding ring is evoked to demonstrate the confinement of marriage with its petty tasks and movement toward nowhere while the world lies waiting for exploration. In like fashion, Effie Lee Newsome chides men for denying women their freedom in "The Bird in the Cage": "I am not better than my brother over the way, / Only he has a bird in the cage and I have not."

Restlessness pervades poetry of the decade along with laments about the inability to move or travel very far away from home. Horizons beckon, roads appear, yet the speaker is rooted to one spot.[11] Some critics have suggested that these poets relied on imagination, dream, and rumination to extricate them from a painful reality. Ronald Primeau, for example, identifies this impulse as central to Georgia Douglas Johnson's work. He believes she exalts creativity because it can fashion a world that does not exist, one where it is possible to imagine freedom and beauty even when they cannot be realized (Bontemps, *Harlem* 266). This theme can be found in the poetry of Angelina Weld Grimké, too, as her speakers sit at the edge of an ocean and dream of sailing to unknown places or gaze out a window at twilight, reflecting on the emerging stars. As Gloria Hull notes, Grimké's personae are often submerged, diminished; yet, their mind's eye is focused on intense images that hint at infinite spaces (*Color* 144). Anne Spencer's verse is also characterized by marked contrast between the sordidness of the material plane and the speaker's imaginary world of love and natural beauty. Lyric poetry, then, became a vehicle for movement, since it transported both poet and reader to a place where women could feel safe, unbound, and powerful.

The use of trees in these poems is common, for trees are stationary, as women are immobilized by confining roles. Symbolic of paralysis, they are nevertheless viewed positively. In Grimké's "The Black Finger," a tree's silhouette is highlighted by sunset: "I have just seen a most beautiful thing: / Slim and still, / Against a gold, gold sky, / A straight, black cypress / Sensitive / Exquisite / A black finger / Pointing upwards." Leading the eye toward a vast open space where the soul can soar, the tree in this poem can in some sense stand for the miraculous survival of black aspiration as the poet ends by asking: "Why, beautiful still finger, are you black? / And why are you pointing upwards?" Helene Johnson employs the same metaphor in "Trees at Night," where she draws an image of vibrant wonder crystallized by the interplay of light and shadow on a moonlit night: "Slim sentinels / Stretching lacy arms / About a slumbrous moon; / Black quivering / Silhouettes, / Tremulous, / . . . And printed 'gainst the sky.— / The trembling beauty / Of an urgent pine." It is the silhouette of the tree that attracts the poet's eye, the intricate pattern of branches against a sky, the stillness of a solid trunk anchored by sure roots and pushing against the force of gravity. The trunk's rich brownness is starkly highlighted in silhouette, devoid of obscuring foliage and beautiful in its hardy survival of harsh conditions. The poetic tree transcends its condition of immobility to stand for quiet endurance, pride, dignity, and aspiration. Like women, it has a delicate beauty under the toughness that enables it to survive.

An even more pronounced poetic strategy allowing for metamorphosis is the personification of night as a woman whose powers are both protective and liberating. While night in its color offers an obvious parallel as a source of self-imagery, it is conventionally feared as a time of danger, a space inhabited by frightening supernatural beings. Night symbolizes the unknown, the absence of reason and control, the antithesis of conscious awareness. These are also properties assigned to black people and to women. Having felt the sting of "otherness," poets identified with night's dark power, feared and maligned. In rescuing night from negative fantasies and imbuing it with creative force, the writer could subvert the stigma of distorted perceptions.

"What do I care for morning," asks Helene Johnson in her poem of the same name, "For the glare of the rising sun . . . ? / . . . Give me the beauty of evening, / The cool consummation of night." The preference for nighttime over day, expressed in Johnson's poem, is marked in women's poetry and served a variety of functions. One of these was to assert the primacy of blackness in a world that favored white things. Quieter, calmer, less dramatic than the day, night is nevertheless an essential force in life, the contemplation of which brings serenity to a restless, discontented spirit. Gwendolyn Bennett's imagist portrait "Street Lamps in Early Spring" is typical in its elegiac tone: "Night wears a garment / All velvet soft, all violet blue . . . / And over her face she draws a veil / As shimmering fine as floating dew." Overlooked by the insensitive, the beauty of blackness and femaleness is here brought from the background to center stage and admired for its steady, subtle force.

Bennett's poem captures another aspect of night's usefulness as an image for black women. Night is said to draw over her face a veil "shimmering fine as floating dew." Cast as a goddess whose features are hidden, night stands for the masked self, obscured by the fears and projected fantasies of gazers with the power to define. Although night is veiled in mystery, in this poetry she escapes the distorted negative images of those who fail to see her clearly. Self-assured, she parades through poetry of the Harlem Renaissance with regal grace. The donning of a mask for self-protection, then, does not forever submerge the vital, beautiful person underneath, who possesses powers unrecognized by the world.

Not only a vibrant woman of great spirit who rules her domain wisely, night offers respite from the daily struggle to survive, for in a dark world, blackness cannot be used as a marker of difference. Since there is no need to dissemble, the poet can come alive in her presence: "Last night I danced on the rim of the moon, / Delirious and gay, / Quite different from the mood / I wear about by day. . . / . . . And oh! my feet flew madly! / My body whirled and swayed! / My soul danced in its ecstasy, / Untrammeled, unafraid!" (from Ethel Caution-Davis's "Last Night"); "To dance— / In the light of the moon, / A platinum moon, / Poised like a slender dagger / On the velvet darkness of night" (from Mae Cowdery's "Longings"). The images of movement here contrast sharply with the references to deathlike stillness that appear elsewhere, and the poets celebrate the activation of their creative and erotic energy. While women looked to natural settings in general for space in which to savor the freedom from confining roles, night was sought most frequently, as it was a time when the objectifying eye was closed in sleep and the freedom to be at one with the soul could be safely enjoyed.

It is also to night that the poet turns for solace and restoration. In "Want," Mae Cowdery makes use of this convention when she soothes herself through communing with the stars and moon: "I want to take down with my hands / The silver stars / That grow in heaven's dark blue meadows / And bury my face in them. / I want to wrap all around me / The silver shedding of the moon / To keep me warm." The reference to night as comforter transforms it from a setting of terror, a time when black people were tormented by white vigilantes, into one of peace. Poems centered on lynching victims, for instance, commonly close on a note of relief as night mercifully descends to remove a man's soul from his tortured body. The images of softness linked to night indicate association with a mother's comforting embrace. Consoler of the bruised and even broken spirit, guardian of the soul at rest, night serves as a metaphor for the restorative powers within, to which the poet can turn when feelings of despair overwhelm her. Just as the death of each day is followed by a healing period of quiet repose, so too does the battered spirit find sustenance in womblike suspension of interaction with the outside world.

The impulse to protect oneself from a hurtful reality is not an admission of defeat, but rather an acknowledgment that the forces arrayed against a black woman's dignity and development of her powers are formidable. Anne Spencer's poem "Letter to My Sister" develops this idea and provides insight into the motif of retreat found in poetry about night. Though the gods Spencer mentions are not identified as male, it is made clear that women battle a common enemy and share a kind of bondage that sets them apart from men. "It is dangerous for a woman to defy the gods," she begins, "To taunt them with the tongue's thin tip . . . Or draw a line daring them to cross." The speaker adds, however, that appeasement will not protect women from harm: "Oh, but worse still if you mince timidly— / Dodge this way or that, or kneel or pray." Instead, she recommends deftly removing one's treasured secrets from view and revealing them only in strict privacy: "Lock your heart, then quietly, / And, lest they peer within, / Light no lamp when dark comes down / Raise no shade for sun." Although the day's piercing light destroys, it can be thwarted by guarding the innermost recesses of the self.

Michael Cooke has identified self-veiling as a major stage in the development of African American literature, one that occurred in the early part of this century and extended through the 1920s. His terminology aptly describes women's nature poetry—indirect, coded, wrung free of overt anger. Yet it would be a mistake to view this verse as divorced from issues of race, gender, or oppression. The theme of regeneration through retreat and disguise echoes the actual practice of poets searching for a way to make themselves heard without facing annihilation. It also suggests avoidance of more frontal assaults on an overwhelmingly powerful enemy. This would have been a realistic strategy in the early twentieth century, particularly for women whose formative years occurred in the terrible repression that followed Reconstruction.

Another Spencer poem, "Lady, Lady," brings to the surface the three major themes of women's poetry (equation of blackness and femaleness with strength, resistance to white male oppression, and survival of the core self) and illustrates how they are intertwined with nature metaphors. Typical of much Renaissance poetry, it studies a member of the working class, a launderer, made invisible by racism and classism. The washerwoman bears the stamp of her oppressor. Her face has been chiseled by pain from carrying "the yoke of men"; her hands are twisted "like crumpled roots" by the labor she does for white people, symbolizing the stunting of her growth and crippling of her true posture. They are also "bleached poor white," a sign of her consignment to a draining, exploited existence controlled by whites. Despite the harsh life she has led, however, there remains a sacred, inviolable place within her where a spirit burns brightly, "altared there in its darksome place," host to a transcendent guiding force.

Women's search for roots and identity led inward, moved backward to an imaginary Eden where sensitivity could survive and even flourish. For writers who largely could not travel to Europe or Africa, the concept of a hidden self, rich with wisdom, offered an attractive substitute for an unknown, removed history. Moreover, it was accessible and consistent with the Romantic notion that truth lies within, uncorrupted by one's external circumstances.[12] Bernard Bell suggests, in fact, that the Romantic pastoral aspect of literature during the Harlem Renaissance might be best understood as ancestralism, arising from a desire to reconcile the urban present with a rural past: "Out of a sense of loss, a feeling that the times were out of joint and the soul was under siege, . . . a romantic longing for a freer, more innocent time and place was born . . . where the rhythms of life were closely linked to nature and one's essential humanity was unquestioned . . . [and] that fostered a feeling of harmony . . . with one's ancestors [and] one's self" (114). It is possible, then, to detect an affirmation of the poet's own gender and race in pastoral lyrics, for retreat to the pre-industrial past or the self within furnished ties to a heritage dimly glimpsed and a locale more hospitable to the emergence of female power.

Love Lyrics and Erotic Verse

Women's pastoral verse is indirect and masked, but their love poetry is an attempt to speak in a straightforward and authentic manner. It, too, grows out of a preoccupation with the Romantics in that passionate attachments were thought to elevate one's spirit above the plane of normal existence to a sublime state of intensified experience. Here the uncorrupted soul could fully express the self. Even heartache was viewed as purifying because it proved that the poet had dared to share a real part of herself with someone; it was evidence of an unmasked encounter.

Seemingly unconnected to social issues, this love poetry appears at first glance to be an anomalous feature of a literary movement to break free of stereotypes and record the African American experience. Yet it reverberates with emotions that implicitly challenged the dehumanizing caricatures of black people found in American culture. For instance, one of the many misconceptions held by white people at the time was that blacks were a happy race, perpetually childlike in their ability to laugh at woe and shrug off cares. Such an image served important psychological functions for whites, among them relief from guilt, the allaying of fears about rebellion, and escape from a sober model of propriety.[13] A laughing black face put whites at ease and seemingly offered a world where troubles could be left behind. New Negro writers addressed this issue by making public their rage at having to hide so much of themselves in order to fulfill white fantasies. When read in this context, the love poetry takes on added significance, for in it the poet reveals her pain, her human capacity to be vulnerable and suffer deep disappointment. She possesses the gift of laughter, but it is clear that sadness has shaped her as much as joy, that suffering is a part of her life.

The heartbreak over unrequited love that runs through this poetry also asserts that the personal realm of the poet need not be uplifting in order to be a proper subject for public verse. All feelings are worthy of poetic expression. This claiming of the despondent self represented an important departure from nineteenth-century African American poetry, which followed that era's conception of art as something that should inspire and instruct. It was, therefore, incumbent on the poet at that time to be optimistic and end poems on a forward-looking note.[14] Insisting on the full range of human emotions for their province, poets of the Harlem Renaissance expanded the boundaries of acceptable subjects to include despair and woeful yearning after something lost.

The right, indeed, the necessity, to recognize anguish as a consequence of being fully alive is a theme often struck in this poetry of the heart. Refusing to take the safer yet diminished path of a life without dreams or large emotional risks, the poet proclaims that her suffering produces growth. Emotional transport, whether toward joy or sorrow, is heralded as a life force that brings the speaker into contact with her humanity and the world around her. It is both her route to self-actualization, as she is willing to encounter life directly, and her announcement that she is multidimensional, a woman of sensitivity and passion.

In evaluating the significance of Renaissance love poetry, it is important to keep in mind that a fundamental tenet of white supremacy was that African Americans were not capable of fine romantic feelings. Lindsay Patterson is careful to point this out in his anthology of love poetry by black writers from Angelina Weld Grimké to

Sonia Sanchez, stating that denigration of bonding among slaves was one of the primary forms of control exerted by slaveholders over their property. He believes it is affirming, therefore, to make visible an African American tradition of love poetry and to see it as a form of resistance (Patterson). One way to dehumanize an oppressed group, of course, is to strip it of the capacity to form meaningful attachments, and black writers of the period were well acquainted with caricatures that implied they were an unromantic people.

Furthermore, the frankly erotic dimension of women's poetry negated desexed images of the plantation mammy, immensely popular at the time with a white audience. The mammy was a safe figure for the white female imagination because she wanted only to take care of her employer (mystifying the exploitative relationship between them) and posed no sexual competition.[15] Divorced from sexuality, the mammy, like her Uncle Tom counterpart, was identified solely with her role as caretaker. To bring their bodies into public view under their own terms was to state that black women were sentient, complex beings deserving sexual pleasure, a statement also being made by jazz and blues singers of the 1920s, who were expanding the boundaries of female sexual expression as well as African American music.[16]

Amplifying women's choice of erotic poetry is the African American context in which they operated, for women as mothers were glorified by male artists of the Harlem Renaissance. The frontispiece to Alain Locke's influential *The New Negro* (1925), for example, is a Winold Reiss portrait of a young woman cradling a baby, entitled "The Brown Madonna" (see fig. 5). Indeed, one of the primary metaphors of the New Negro Movement was that of the young mother leading the race to a brighter day. As a representation of rebirth, such an image was irresistible, and women too made use of it but more ambivalently. Often, for instance, birth is distanced in their poetry by embedding it in a natural landscape described as pregnant or maternal. Though mothers appear in their verse, child-rearing or nurturing roles are not favored topics. In turning so often in poems to moments of erotic passion, women highlighted those relationships they could enter as autonomous persons and from which they could fashion adventurous lives. Many of these poets were, in fact, single or childless. Those who were married often refused to assume domestic burdens and were social activists as well as writers.[17] These were women in flight from Victorianism, and their verse claims sexual independence. The refusal of Harlem poets to hide female erotic passion was resistance to being defined as selfless nurturers or as anyone's property. Romantic passion existed outside the boundaries of marriage and Victorian conceptions of womanhood as well as beyond racist stereotypes of the mammy or the "African primitive."

The romantic eroticism found in verse of the Harlem Renaissance not only made visible the hunger of black women for unrestricted, self-defining experience, but also brought to the surface feelings for women that had been previously invisible. After World War I, black women's verse began to explore the forbidden territory of explicit passionate attraction between women. Only two female writers from this era have been thus far identified by scholars as lesbian or bisexual: Alice Dunbar-Nelson and Angelina Weld Grimké. Gloria Hull brought to light both Dunbar-Nelson's diary entries concerning her attachments to women and Grimké's overtly lesbian, unpublished poetry.[18] There are others, however, who published romantic or erotic poetry addressed to women about whom not enough information exists to make a determination of their actual intimate liaisons but yet whose poetry participates in a lesbian sensibility.

Gladys May Casely Hayford's "Rainy Season Love Song," for instance, is addressed to a woman referred to as "my love" in the first stanza. The persona of the poem describes making love to this figure in a rainstorm that shares the speaker's desire. Rain kisses her "everywhere," flows between her breasts, while lightning and thunder move inside her body. The speaker kisses her beloved's "dusky throat," feels electricity wherever she touches, and finally lies in her lover's arms. While not as overtly sexual, Hayford's "The Serving Girl" creates a similarly erotic milieu as the speaker describes an encounter with the woman of the title, who brings fish "peppered, and golden fried for me" along with palm wine "that carelessly slips / From the sleeping palm tree's honeyed lips." The poem then ends with a provocative question: "But who can guess, or even surmise / The countless things she served with her eyes?" Mae Cowdery wrote love poems to women also. In her 1936 collection, *We Lift Our Voices*, she included "Insatiate," which concerns the speaker's intense jealousy over her female lover, while three other published pieces suggest a lesbian relationship. In one, the poet says the onset of dusk is "Like you / Letting down your / Purple-shadowed hair / To hide the rose and gold / Of your loveliness." "Farewell" is subtler but implies the loss of a female lover when the speaker refers to "the rumpled softness" of her lost love's hair and "the lush sweetness" of her lips, "like dew / On new-opened moonflowers." Finally, in "Poem . . . for a Lover," the speaker's object of longing is said to possess "gay little songs" and "lips . . . redder / Than bitter-sweet berries."

The appearance of such poetry was made possible in part by the support of Alain Locke and Countée Cullen, who are now thought to have been themselves gay and who were committed to frank expression of sexuality in verse.[19] An important anthology of the period was Cullen's 1927 *Caroling Dusk,* which included the most comprehensive array of female poets assembled to that date and featured Hayford's two most suggestive woman-centered pieces. Cullen's own verse, of course, shared many of the features found in women's writing, including a reverence for nineteenth-century Romantics, most notably Keats, and a tendency to focus on love. His sensibility was in tune with theirs, and he has been subjected to similarly harsh contemporary criticism.[20] Alain Locke's intellectual leanings were perhaps even more instrumental in creating a tolerant atmosphere for poems with a lesbian sensibility. While by no means a friend to women artists (he often pointedly neglected them), his philosophical leadership in the New Negro Movement fostered acceptance of the kind of writing they were doing. An openness toward lesbian themes in poetry specifically is suggested in his foreword to Georgia Douglas Johnson's collection *An Autumn Love Cycle* (1928), where he praises the poet for joining that group of women "rediscovering the Sapphic cult of love" (xviii). Locke also thought highly of Mae Cowdery's poetry.

Renewed attention to the Harlem Renaissance is revealing, in fact, that gay and lesbian culture was very much a part of Harlem artistic circles. Lesbian and bisexual singers Bessie Smith, Ma Rainey, and Gladys Bentley, for instance, were star performers during the 1920s, and their lesbianism was known to those who frequented jazz clubs.[21] In addition, the primary organizers of Harlem social life, A'Lelia Walker and Carl Van Vechten, routinely sought the company of lesbians and gay men and invited them to their parties.[22] Harlem writer Bruce Nugent came out as gay in the 1960s and was a close friend of Wallace Thurman, a major gay black writer of the period. George Chauncey documents the huge gay balls that drew thousands of spectators at Harlem's Hamilton Lodge in the 1920s and 1930s, while Lillian Faderman describes the vibrant lesbian scene of both Harlem and Greenwich Village at the time (*Odd Girls*).

It is, perhaps, this atmosphere that allowed women to explore female-to-female love so unself-consciously in their poetry. Even poets who were evidently heterosexual, such as Anne Spencer, Gwendolyn Bennett, and Georgia Douglas Johnson, wrote freely about loving women, suggesting that these writers identified strongly with women as a whole and affirmed that bond in their work. It took courage to write about woman-love in a period when psychologists were developing modes of illness for lesbians.[23] Although only a handful of poems dating from this era overtly expressed erotic attraction for women, their existence marks the earliest body of literature to deal with this subject by black women. It would take another forty years for such poetic voices to be heard again.

Anne Spencer, Mae Cowdery, and Helene Johnson: Three Lost Poets

The characteristics and significance of women's poetry during the Harlem Renaissance can perhaps best be understood by closely examining three representative figures. Anne Spencer is the first of these, arguably the most polished of the women poets. Typical of most women's low output, she published less than thirty poems between 1920 and 1931, in spite of enthusiastic responses from leading figures of the period, such as her mentor James Weldon Johnson. In addition, Spencer's poetry conforms to contemporary notions about women's writing of the time. It is pastoral, convoluted, and heavily influenced by the classical training Spencer received at the seminary in Lynchburg, Virginia, where she spent her teenage years. Her favorite poet was Robert Browning. It is the lyric poetry of Spencer, Grimké, and Dunbar-Nelson that was most likely to be included in later anthologies of African American verse, and, thus, their poems have had to bear the weight of all those excluded.

Anne Spencer's life and publishing history explode the mythology that has developed around writers conceived of as bourgeois, apolitical artists who failed to produce innovative work. While Spencer and her husband led a comfortable life in rural Virginia, her roots were in poverty. Spencer's parents were former slaves who left their plantation birthplace to establish independent lives. Determined not to work for a white man, her father, Joel, opened a saloon in Martinsville, Virginia, where he frequently had Anne perform for his customers as she was a bright, attractive child. Anne's mother, Sarah, left her husband when he refused to stop taking his daughter to the bar and supported them both with difficulty, becoming a cook in a West Virginia mining town. Unable to look after her child while at work, Anne's mother placed her with the family of a black barber in nearby Bramwell.

Spencer's childhood, therefore, was marked by disruption and financial hardship. Although she was well cared for, she had no formal education until age eleven, when Sarah sent her to Virginia Seminary, apparently to get her away from the white men of Bramwell before she hit adolescence. She acquired a keen sense of how it felt to live on the periphery of American society, identifying at an early age with outcasts and rebels. She refused to be "a lady," resisting rules at the seminary, wearing pants as an adult, and protesting the exclusion of blacks from the library in Lynchburg, among other things. In short, Anne Spencer the woman was unconventional, politically active, and passionate in her opposition to injustice.

These qualities are reflected in her writing, although not in pieces for which she is best known. An unpublished poem, for instance, written during the Renaissance era, reveals her commitment to social justice and the far-reaching nature of her political vision. "The Sévignés" was prompted by an article Spencer read in a 1930 issue of *National Geographic* describing a new monument that had just been erected of an "old-time darkey" in Natchitoches, Louisiana, to commemorate Harriet Beecher Stowe's *Uncle Tom's Cabin.* Spencer was offended by the servility of the statue and the slaveholding history it uncritically recalled. Her poem parallels the racism of twentieth-century America with the callousness of seventeenth-century aristocrat Marquise de Sévigné, whose letters reveal gross insensitivity to sufferings of the poor. The poem not only connects a corrupt aristocracy with a supposed democracy but also points out the hypocrisy of French immigrants who left Europe to escape oppression and then enslaved people themselves: "No penance, callous beyond belief, / For these women who had so lately fled from the slavery of Europe to the great wilds of America."

As well, the nature poetry at which Spencer excelled was animated frequently by subtle references to racism or sexism. J. Lee Greene, for example, interprets "Grapes: Still-Life" as an allegorical portrait of people of color and tells us that "Creed," a poem with no reference to race, was inspired by the poet's visit to Harper's Ferry, scene of the slave revolt led by John Brown (134). Spencer also wrote feminist poems, such as "Before the Feast at Shushan," which concerns the rebellious Persian queen Vashti, chronicled in the Old Testament, who tries to establish an egalitarian relationship with her husband, the speaker of the poem. Significantly, the poem's metaphors are drawn from flora and fauna: King Ahasuerus compares kissing Queen Vashti to crushing a grape and declares his right to rape her when he boasts, "And I am hard to force the petals wide." Indeed, the setting for Ahasuerus's monologue about the resisting Vashti's charms is a garden which, he says, "enspells the brain." Pastoral beauty is a backdrop against which the ugliness of prejudice, hatred, and domination is effectively juxtaposed. Dividing her time between cultivating a splendid garden in Lynchburg and discussing politics with out-of-town guests from the NAACP, Spencer blended her two passions in lyrics whose import may not be clear to those unaware of their context.

Blunt and politically astute, Spencer reported in her last years that she was discouraged from writing racial protest poems by editors, critics, and friends and that the prose she wrote but never published was "topical and controversial" (quoted in Greene 129). We can only speculate on the degree to which other women writers, too, were steered away from political poetry, but Spencer's experience hints at the difficulties they all had in breaking out of the formats considered acceptable for women's verse.

Helene Johnson is in many ways Anne Spencer's opposite. She was one of the period's youngest writers, whereas Spencer did not publish until she was nearly forty. Although Spencer's rural home in Lynchburg was a frequent stopping-place for writers, musicians, and NAACP organizers, she never set foot in New York, while Johnson planted herself squarely in Harlem. Finally, Johnson's best poetry is as street-smart and proletarian as Spencer's is staidly traditional. In fact, the vibrant cadence and daring language of Helene Johnson's verse is reminiscent of Langston Hughes, writing as she often did in the vernacular of Harlem street life and striking original metaphorical notes. In "Poem," for example, the persona boldly flirts with the subject of her mind's eye: "Gee, boy, I love the way you hold your head, / High sort of and a bit to one side, / . . . Gee, brown boy, I loves you all over. / . . . I'm glad I can / Understand your dancin' and your / Singin', and feel all the happiness / And joy and don't-care in you." One of her best poems, "Bottled," recapitulates the fractured grammar of everyday talk while reclaiming the derogatory epithets of racists. Indeed, the thrust of the poem is a turning-inside-out of racism. The speaker, to mention one example, sees black people in a positive light once she stops identifying with white culture: "And yesterday on Seventh Avenue / I saw a darky dressed to kill / In yellow gloves and swallowtail coat / And swirling a cane. And everyone / Was laughing at him. Me too, / At first, till I saw his face / When he stopped to hear a / Organ grinder grind out some jazz." The radical nature of this poetry lies not only in its employ of what was considered non-poetic language, but also in Johnson's praise of those aspects of black culture most despised by whites. She loved insouciance, sensuality, vivacity, and celebrated them. She also made clear her preference for black American and African life over what she presented as the oppressive qualities of white ways. "Bottled," for instance, compares a geological specimen of brown sand collected from the Sahara desert to the dancing man on Seventh Avenue, declaring that he, like it, was stolen, labeled, and put on display for the enjoyment of his captors. His African roots are recalled in the speaker's imagination as she restores to him the splendor of an environment that does not denigrate black people, one that is compatible with his spontaneity.

Similarly, in "Magalu," the speaker warns a young African woman not to be seduced by a missionary to whom she is eagerly listening: "Do not let him lure you from your laughing waters, / Lulling lakes, lissome winds. / Would you sell the colors of your sunset and the fragrance / Of your flowers, and the passionate wonder of your forest / For a creed that will not let you dance?" Johnson's imagination was clearly activated by the sights and sounds of jazz age Harlem. Often when she strays from that idiom, her writing tends to be flat and labored, though much of it is very good. Although she could compose good lyric verse, some of it neither sings nor moves the heart. She produced little of the avant-garde poetry on which she could have established a considerable literary reputation, however.

Helene Johnson belonged to the inner circle of renegade artists who brought to life experimental periodicals such as *Fire!!* whose single issue in 1926 ignited a storm of controversy; and she contributed to every major anthology and journal of her day, but in spite of her talent and energy, she virtually disappeared from the historical record.[24] We know Johnson was born in 1906 and grew up in Boston, attended Boston University, and entered Columbia University in 1927, when she moved to New York at age nineteen with her cousin, Dorothy West. She joined a group of young black intellectuals who started a literary journal called *The Saturday Evening Quill* (1928–1930). She last appears in print in March 1935, when West, editor of the magazine, published her work in the Boston journal *Challenge* (1934–1937). Arna Bontemps reported in the late 1960s that Johnson was living in Brooklyn with her husband, whom she later divorced, and daughter, but no one seems to know much about what happened to her after the Renaissance ended. The literary fate of this promising poet is instructive, for it underscores the invisible forces operating against distinctive female voices from the era. Even with an excellent ear, disciplined writing, and far-reaching social connections, Helene Johnson disappeared into literary obscurity until current efforts to recover her work.[25]

Mae Cowdery, like Johnson, hit the New York scene at a very young age, captured the attention of prominent scholars and editors, and then vanished. She was one of the few women to publish a volume of verse. The only child of a prosperous Philadelphia caterer and a social worker, Cowdery gravitated quickly to the Greenwich Village crowd when she arrived in New York after graduating from high school in 1927, by which early age she had already won first prize in a poetry contest run by *The Crisis*. Her writing reportedly was heavily influenced by Edna St. Vincent Millay, and she is said to have worn tailored suits, bow ties, and kept her short hair "slicked down to patent leather" (Kellner, *Harlem* 84).

This arresting personal portrait is enough to attract the attention of modern readers, but it is Cowdery's writing that is the most compelling thing about her. Her forte was the poetry of passion—anguished, fierce, and erotic. While some of her work is clumsy, there is a spark of originality that makes it stand out from other poetry of her day, a modern quality of spareness and physical directness. She refers, for instance, to her speaker's "lust," "tempestuous ardor," and "carnal anticipation" in "Lines to a Sophisticate." The speaker assures her lover that she does not want to possess her but to "savor and sip slowly / That I might know each separate scent / Of your elusive fragrance." "Insatiate" examines a lesbian's contradictory feelings about sexual infidelity, and the speaker longs for a lost lover's touch in "Farewell," moaning: "No more / The feel of your hand / On my breast / Like the silver path / Of the moon / On dark heaving ocean." The personae of Cowdery's poems gaze upon lovers with open desire, recall exquisite moments of intimacy, and indulge themselves in the heat of passion, as in "Exultation," where the speaker shouts: "O night! / With stars burning— / Fire falling / Into a dark and whispering sea!"

This was unusually frank poetry for the 1920s, and it is remarkable that Cowdery published as much as she did. Though her output was impressive, the content of more than passing interest, and her aesthetic decidedly modern, many of today's readers know nothing of Mae Cowdery's work, although she is steadily gaining fans as her poetry is recovered. This is partly explained by her omission from most of the period's anthologies, which were published when she was still a high school student in Philadelphia, and partly by the fact that her poetry collection did not appear until 1936. In addition, she seems to have been curiously distant from other black women poets, who tended to know each other, and so is not mentioned in their personal papers. Dependent on men for visibility (most notably William S. Braithwaite, Langston Hughes, and Arthur Huff Fauset), Cowdery possibly arrived on the Harlem literary scene too late to forge the links with other women that might have at least marked her as one of the era's promising women writers for future readers and, more poignantly, that might have saved her life (she died by suicide in New York in 1953).

Cowdery's invisibility, the silencing of Helene Johnson's remarkable voice, and Anne Spencer's failure to publish after 1931 suggest to us how women poets, who played such a key role in the Harlem Renaissance, disappeared not only from popular but from historical view. All black writers suffered from the impact of the Great Depression on the publishing industry, of course, and the proletarian sensibility of the 1930s was out of tune with the jazz-age rhythms and romantic leanings of 1920s poetry. Nevertheless, women endured greater reverses than the men in their subsequent scholarly treatment, which in part illustrates how dependent they were on male mentors who understood and shared in their poetic vision. Once the male scholars of their generation left the scene, they had no advocates. This, combined with their failure to leave many published collections, made them vulnerable to later sexist appraisals of their part in this historic cultural movement.

Moreover, we can see from the fact that many women stopped writing by the mid-1930s that the existence of a female support system was crucial for their work as well. The community that pulled together women from Philadelphia, Boston, New York, Washington, D.C., and small towns began to disintegrate toward the end of the decade when several got married, moved, or experienced personal losses.[26] In addition, important gatekeepers disappeared at this time: Jessie Fauset left *The Crisis* in 1926, where she had been literary editor for many years; Gwendolyn Bennett was forced out of her teaching post at Howard University for dating a medical student, subsequently stepping down as assistant editor at *Opportunity*.[27] There were those who went against this trend, such as Georgia Douglas Johnson and Alice Dunbar-Nelson, who wrote until the end of their lives, but even they favored prose over poetry in their later years. Although not always in positions to further each other's careers, women poets received emotional support from socializing together, reviewing each other's work, and having female role models. All these things helped them deal with the pressures that flowed from being a black woman artist. We can speculate that once this fragile network fell apart they had a hard time holding onto their identities as poets.

Finally, it is clear that the New Negro Movement was male dominated, both in terms of access to resources and in the kind of writing that garnered the highest praise. One has only to compare the exuberant writing of Claude McKay and Langston Hughes as they rambled through Europe with the frightened, homesick diary entries of Gwendolyn Bennett in Paris to get a glimpse of how problematic bohemian adventure was for women.[28] While sexual sophistication and international travel distinguished Harlem Renaissance artists from the previous generation, women were largely excluded from these experiences, which hurt their artistic careers. In addition, there is plenty of evidence that the close personal ties of male writers to Alain Locke gave them an inside track for acquiring grants and other aids (Hull, *Color* 7–10). Anne Spencer, for example, reported that she was held back by Locke because he wanted to promote Countée Cullen (Greene 140). Even though some men were supportive of women's writing, the lion's share of attention went to other men, establishing a historical trajectory not easily reversed.

Legacy of Women's Poetry

When measured against the historical role Renaissance artists claimed for themselves as creators of a new African American sensibility, much of the women's work apparently fails. To be fair, so does much of the men's. Nathan Huggins, for example, considers Claude McKay and Countée Cullen flawed poets because they embraced a European artistic tradition at odds with their own experience. Crippled by their notion that art should be universal and not focus on race alone and unable or unwilling to depart from traditional structures, they fell short of the greatness they sought, he believes (Huggins, *Harlem*). J. Saunders Redding also faults Cullen for being inhibited by verse modeled after nineteenth-century Romantic lyricists and concludes he contributed little to African American literature, standing aloof as he did from revolutionary currents of his time (Redding, *To Make*). Finally, in his discussion of Renaissance novelists, Addison Gayle Jr. concludes that black writers were not able to develop fully their questioning and rebellious vision because they were limited by white patronage (Gayle). All of these things can be said of women as well, with the additional constraints imposed by a male-dominated setting. Their failure to challenge a literary tradition built by the very culture that oppressed them resulted at times in a rather awkward fusion of radical sentiment and sentimental form, just as the movement toward affirming things distinctly African American conflicted with an impulse to define their sensibility in Romantic or classical terms. In many ways, these poets failed to provide the kind of legacy they aspired to create, and the contradictions under which they labored produced at times curiously stilted pieces.

Yet although some of the women's poetry collected here is clichéd, there is a body of work that speaks with a distinctly modern cadence, artfully expressing messages of substance. Many poems of high aesthetic quality were left to us by Anne Spencer, Angelina Weld Grimké, Alice Dunbar-Nelson, Gladys Casely Hayford, Gwendolyn Bennett, Mae Cowdery, Helene Johnson, Lucy Mae Turner, Anita Scott Coleman, and others who collectively helped expand the boundaries of poetry to include imagism, blank verse, erotic sensuality, and the African American vernacular. Moreover, Carrie Williams Clifford, Georgia Douglas Johnson, and Effie Lee Newsome were solid composers of popular verse, an important component of any artistic movement.

We can see today the class and gender barriers that kept most women from exploring the new frontiers being opened up by Langston Hughes, Sterling Brown, Zora Neale Hurston, and others, but if we are to comprehend the sensibility of these poets we must be sensitive to the difficulties under which they wrote and the historical conditions that shaped their thinking. As women, they were comfortable with the arena of private poetry, and it reflects the circumscribed conditions in which they lived. It is possible to see them remaining within a female as well as a white tradition, therefore, as they explored their inner selves, intimate relations with lovers, and private connections to the natural world. They found congenial poetic models in the imagists and English Romantics because these forms allowed them access to a core self. Communing with nature in spontaneous, associative ways or unself-consciously exploring the intensity of their most intimate connections with lovers furnished a markedly female strategy for claiming an African American worldview.

The current revival of interest in women writers from this pivotal era is revising our notion of what the Harlem Renaissance was about, and the debt modern black writers owe to these pioneers of self-expression is increasingly being recognized. Gloria Hull (*Color*) and Barbara Christian, for instance, conclude that contemporary African American women writers have been able to achieve a liberating, self-oriented perspective in part because their forerunners adopted the lyric "I" persona. Likewise, Bernard Bell credits the lyricism of the New Negro Movement with stimulating a similar artistic awakening among Third World writers. It may be that the way in which Renaissance poets will prove most influential is the road they paved toward a distinctly twentieth-century sensibility based on intimacy, frank espousal of feelings, and the search for personal empowerment in a world intent on denying black people their humanity. If so, we will come to see these poets as the daring people they were, appropriating a cultural heritage they were told was beyond their grasp and blazing a path for those who would follow.

Notes

1. Studies that omit women altogether include Redding; Jackson and Rubin; Wagner; and Thurman. A. P. Davis discusses women fiction writers but no poets; Davis and Redding include two women poets, Frances E. W. Harper and Anne Spencer.

2. Brown 62, 65. See also Brawley 111–113; J. W. Johnson 243, 205; Cullen; Calverton; Braithwaite; and Kerlin.

3. Omitting names whose gender was not clearly marked (e.g., first name omitted in favor of initials), there are 347 poems by men in both journals from 1918 through 1931 and 277 by women. The numbers are nearly even for *The Crisis*, where Jessie Fauset was literary editor.

4. Exceptions to this trend are Davis and Peplow, who include poems by women under the category "Race Pride." Bontemps anthologizes many women's poems concerning race; Huggins's *Voices from the Harlem Renaissance* is another anthology with poetry of this kind; Adams, Conn, and Slepian reprint racial poetry by Bennett, Helene Johnson, and Frances Harper.

5. A comprehensive overview of this period is provided by Lewis. See also Henri; Osofsky; Meier and Rudwick; and Giddings.

6. Black women were frustrated, for instance, by the insensitivity of white feminists to their political agenda, although the National American Woman Suffrage Association did condemn lynching in 1917. The racism of the Woman Movement is well documented by Stetson, "Black Feminism"; and Terborg-Penn.

7. An exposition of this racist ideology is provided by Wood. See also Woodward; Higham; Jackson; and Newby.

8. Agreeing with this perspective is Singh.

9. A good treatment of the patron roles played by whites during the Harlem Renaissance is Kellner's *Carl Van Vechten and the Irreverent Decades*.

10. May describes the beginning of this movement.

11. Wall describes this theme (14–16).

12. For amplification of the connection between self and nature made by Romantic poets, who served as role models for Renaissance poets, see Abrams.

13. See Huggins (*Harlem* 244–301) and Osofsky (184) on the psychological importance of such a caricature for whites.

14. Sherman explicates this idea.

15. A good description of this stereotype appears in Cripps.

16. Jazz and blues singers from this era are described by Harrison; see also Angela Davis.

17. Both Alice Dunbar-Nelson and Anne Spencer were married, but they lived with female relatives who relieved them of many household responsibilities, allowing them to write and do political work. Jessie Fauset and Gwendolyn Bennett did not marry until the end of the decade and were childless. Helene Johnson remained single throughout this period.

18. Hull, *Give Us Each Day* and "Under the Days."

19. Hull discusses the sexual preference of both men in *Color* (8).

20. Cullen has come under similarly harsh criticism as a result. Redding, for example, has called Cullen "a genteel school-poet" whose poetry is "effete" and "bloodless": "It is as if he saw through the eyes of a woman" ("The New Negro Poet" 18–33).

21. See, for instance, Garber, "Gladys Bentley"; Lieb; and Albertson. Studies of lesbian, gay, and bisexual figures in the Harlem Renaissance include Chauncey; Faderman, *Odd Girls;* Garber, "Spectacle in Color"; Schwartz; and Cobb.

22. Hull, *Color* 9, 11, 187; see also Weinberg.

23. Faderman discusses this homophobic reaction as a backlash against women's rights in *Surpassing the Love of Men*.

24. This circle included Langston Hughes, Zora Neale Hurston, Gwendolyn Bennett, Wallace Thurman, Bruce Nugent, Dorothy West, and Alain Locke, among others.

25. A recent reprinting of Helene Johnson's poetry is Mitchell's *Helene Johnson*.

26. Jessie Fauset married Herbert Harris in 1929; Gwendolyn Bennett married a medical student at Howard and moved to Florida with him in 1928; Angelina Weld Grimké was traumatized by the death of her father in 1930 and by 1933 had gone into seclusion in New York City; and Clarissa Scott Delany, a close friend of Grimké's, died in 1927.

27. On Jessie Fauset's key role in the Harlem Renaissance, see A. Johnson; and Mc-Dowell, "Neglected Dimension."
28. Personal papers of Gwendolyn Bennett (Box 1, Folder 1), New York Public Library, Schomberg Center for Research in Black Culture, New York City.

Works Cited

Abrams, M. H., ed. *English Romantic Poets.* New York: Oxford University Press, 1975.

Adams, William, Peter Conn, and Barry Slepian, eds., *Afro-American Literature.* Boston: Houghton Mifflin, 1970.

Albertston, Chris. *Bessie.* New York: Stein & Day, 1972.

Aptheker, Bettina. *Woman's Legacy: Essays on Race, Sex, and Class in American History.* Amherst: University of Massachusetts Press, 1982.

Bell, Bernard. *The Afro-American Novel and Its Tradition.* Amherst: University of Massachusetts Press, 1987.

Bone, Robert. *The Negro Novel in America.* New Haven: Yale University Press, 1965.

Bontemps, Arna, ed. *American Negro Poetry.* New York: Hill & Wang, 1963.

——, ed. *The Harlem Renaissance Remembered.* New York: Dodd, Mead & Co., 1972.

Braithwaite, William S., ed. *Anthology of Magazine Verse for 1928 and 1929.* New York: Harold Vinal, 1928 and 1929.

Brawley, Benjamin. *The Negro in Literature and Art in the United States.* New York: Duffield & Co., 1930.

Brown, Sterling. *Negro Poetry and Drama.* Washington, D.C.: Associates in Negro Folk Education, 1937.

Calverton, V. F., ed. *Anthology of American Negro Literature.* New York: Modern Library, 1929.

Chauncey, George, Jr. *Gay New York: Gender, Urban Culture, and the Making of the Gay Male World, 1890–1940.* New York: Basic Books, 1994.

Christian, Barbara. *Black Women Novelists: The Development of a Tradition, 1892–1976.* Westport, CT: Greenwood Press, 1980.

Cobb, Michael L. "Insolent Racing, Rough Narrative: The Harlem Renaissance's Impolite Queers." *Callaloo* 23, no. 1 (winter 2000): 328–351.

Cooke, Michael. *Afro-American Literature in the Twentieth Century.* New Haven: Yale University Press, 1984.

Cowdery, Mae V. *We Lift Our Voices and Other Poems.* Philadelphia: Alpress Pubs., 1936.

Cripps, Thomas. *Slow Fade to Black: The Negro in American Film, 1900–1942.* New York: Oxford University Press, 1977.

Cullen, Countée, ed. *Caroling Dusk: An Anthology of Verse by Negro Poets.* New York: Harper Brothers, 1927.

Davis, Angela. *Blues Legacies and Black Feminism.* New York: Random House, 1998.

Davis, Arthur P. *From the Dark Tower: Afro-American Writers, 1900–1960.* Washington, D.C.: Howard University Press, 1974.

Davis, Arthur P., and Michael Peplow, eds. *The New Negro Renaissance: An Anthology.* New York: Harper & Row, 1975.

Davis, Arthur P., and J. Saunders Redding, eds. *Cavalcade: Negro American Writing from 1760 to the Present.* Boston: Houghton Mifflin, 1971.

Faderman, Lillian. *Odd Girls and Twilight Lovers: A History of Lesbian Life in Twentieth-Century America.* New York: Columbia University Press, 1991.

———. *Surpassing the Love of Men: Romantic Friendship and Love between Women from the Renaissance to the Present.* New York: William Morrow & Co., 1981.

Garber, Eric. "Gladys Bentley: The Bulldagger Who Sang the Blues." *Outlook* 1 (spring 1988): 52–61.

———. "A Spectacle in Color: The Lesbian and Gay Subculture of Jazz Age Harlem." In *Hidden from History: Reclaiming the Gay and Lesbian Past,* eds. Martin Duberman, Martha Vicinus, and George Chauncey Jr. New York: New American Library, 1989.

Gayle, Addison, Jr. *The Way of the New World: The Black Novel in America.* Garden City, NY: Anchor Books, 1975.

Giddings, Paula. *When and Where I Enter: The Impact of Black Women on Race and Sex in America.* New York: William Morrow & Co., 1984.

Greene, J. Lee. *Time's Unfading Garden: Anne Spencer's Life and Poetry.* Baton Rouge: Louisiana State University Press, 1977.

Harley, Sharon, and Rosalyn Terborg-Penn, eds. *The Afro-American Woman: Struggles and Images.* Port Washington, NY: Kennikat Press, 1978.

Harrison, Daphne Duval. *Black Pearls: Blues Queens of the 1920s.* New Brunswick: Rutgers University Press, 1988.

Henri, Florette. *Black Migration: Movement North, 1900–1920.* Garden City, NY: Anchor Books, 1975.

Higham, John. *Strangers in the Land: Patterns of American Nativism, 1860–1925.* New York: Atheneum Press, 1963.

Huggins, Nathan. *The Harlem Renaissance.* New York: Oxford University Press, 1971.

———, ed. *Voices from the Harlem Renaissance.* New York: Oxford University Press, 1976.

Hull, Gloria. *Color, Sex, and Poetry: Three Women Writers of the Harlem Renaissance.* Bloomington: Indiana University Press, 1987.

———, ed. *Give Us Each Day: The Diary of Alice Dunbar-Nelson.* New York: W. W. Norton, 1984.

———. "'Under the Days': The Buried Life and Poetry of Angelina Weld Grimké." *Conditions* 2 (autumn 1979): 17–25.

Jackson, Blyden, and Louis Rubin, eds. *Black Poetry in America.* Baton Rouge: Louisiana State University Press, 1974.

Jackson, Kenneth. *The Ku Klux Klan in the City, 1915–1930.* New York: Oxford University Press, 1967.

Johnson, Abby Arthur. "Literary Midwife: Jessie Redmon Fauset and the Harlem Renaissance." *Phylon* 39 (June 1978): 143–153.

Johnson, Georgia Douglas. *An Autumn Love Cycle.* Freeport, NY: Books for Libraries Press, 1928.

Johnson, James Weldon, ed. *The Book of American Negro Poetry.* New York: Harcourt Brace and World, 1922, 1931.

Kellner, Bruce. *Carl Van Vechten and the Irreverent Decades.* Norman: University of Oklahoma Press, 1968.

———, ed. *The Harlem Renaissance: An Annotated Bibliography.* Westport, CT: Greenwood Press, 1984.

Kerlin, Robert T., ed. *Negro Poets and Their Poems.* Washington, D.C.: Associated Publishers, 1923.

Lewis, David Levering. *When Harlem Was in Vogue.* New York: Alfred A. Knopf, 1981.

Lieb, Sandra. *Mother of the Blues: A Study of Ma Rainey.* Amherst: University of Massachusetts Press, 1981.

May, Henry F. *The End of American Innocence: A Study of the First Years of Our Own Time, 1912–1917.* New York: Alfred A. Knopf, 1959.

McDowell, Deborah. "The Neglected Dimension of Jessie Fauset." In *Conjuring: Black Women, Fiction, and the Literary Tradition,* eds. Hortense Spillers and Marjorie Pryse. Bloomington: University of Indiana Press, 1985.

———, ed. Introduction to *Plum Bun: A Novel without a Moral,* by Jessie Redmon Fauset. New Brunswick: Rutgers University Press, 1985.

———, ed. Introduction to *Quicksand and Passing,* by Nella Larsen. New Brunswick: Rutgers University Press, 1986.

Meier, August, and Elliot Rudwick. *From Plantation to Ghetto: An Interpretive History of American Negroes.* New York: Hill & Wang, 1966.

Mitchell, Verner D., ed. *Helene Johnson: Poet of the Harlem Renaissance.* Amherst: University of Massachusetts Press, 2000.

Newby, I. A. *Jim Crow's Defense: Anti-Negro Thought in America, 1900–1930.* Baton Rouge: Louisiana State University Press, 1965.

Osofsky, Gilbert. *Harlem: The Making of a Ghetto, Negro New York, 1890–1930.* New York: Harper & Row, 1963.

Patterson, Lindsay, ed. *A Rock Against the Wind: Black Love Poems.* New York: Dodd, Mead & Co., 1973.

Perry, Margaret. *Silence to the Drums: A Survey of the Literature of the Harlem Renaissance.* Westport, CT: Greenwood Press, 1976.

Primeau, Ronald. "Frank Horne and the Second Echelon Poets of the Harlem Renaissance." In *The Harlem Renaissance Remembered,* ed. Arna Bontemps. New York: Dodd, Mead & Co., 1972.

Redding, J. Saunders. "The New Negro Poet in the Twenties." In *Modern Black Poets,* ed. Donald Gibson. Englewood Cliffs, NJ: Prentice-Hall, 1973.

———. *To Make a Poet Black.* Chapel Hill: University of North Carolina Press, 1939.

Schwartz, A. B. Christa. *Gay Voices of the Harlem Renaissance.* Bloomington: Indiana University Press, 2003.

Sherman, Joan, ed. *Invisible Poets: Afro-Americans and the Nineteenth Century.* Urbana, University of Illinois Press, 1974.

Shockley, Ann Allen, ed. *Afro-American Writers, 1746–1933: An Anthology and Critical Guide.* Boston: G. K. Hall, 1988.

Singh, Amritjit. *The Novels of the Harlem Renaissance.* University Park: Pennsylvania State University Press, 1976.

Stetson, Erlene. "Black Feminism in Indiana, 1893–1933." *Phylon* 44 (December 1983): 292–298.

———, ed. *Black Sister: Poetry by Black American Women, 1746–1980.* Bloomington: Indiana University Press, 1981.

Sylvander, Carolyn. *Jessie Redmon Fauset, Black American Writer.* Troy, NY: Whitson Pub. Co., 1981.

Terborg-Penn, Rosalyn. "Discrimination against Afro-American Women in the Women's Movement, 1830–1920." In *The Afro-American Woman: Struggles and Images,* eds. Sharon Harley and Rosalyn Terborg-Penn. Port Washington, NY: Kennikat Press, 1978.

Thurman, Wallace. "Negro Poets and Their Poetry." In *Black Expression: Essays by and about Black Americans in the Creative Arts,* ed. Addison Gayle Jr. New York: Weybright & Talley, 1969.

Wagner, Jean. *Black Poets of the United States.* Urbana: University of Illinois Press, 1973.

Wall, Cheryl. *Women of the Harlem Renaissance.* Bloomington: Indiana University Press, 1995.

Weinberg, Jonathan. "'Boy Crazy': Carl Van Vechten's Queer Collection." *Yale Journal of Criticism* 7, no. 2 (1994): 25–49.

Wood, Forrest G. *Black Scare: The Racist Response to Emancipation and Reconstruction.* Berkeley: University of California Press, 1968.

Woodward, C. Vann. *The Strange Career of Jim Crow.* New York: Oxford University Press, 1966.

A NOTE ON THE REVISED TEXT

These poems for the revised edition of *Shadowed Dreams* first appeared in journals of the New Negro Movement or in anthologies and collections from the period. The journals include *The Crisis,* founded by the National Association for the Advancement of Colored People (NAACP) in 1910 and edited by W.E.B. Du Bois; *Opportunity,* established by the National Urban League in 1923 and edited by Charles S. Johnson; *The Messenger,* spanning the years 1917–1928 and edited by A. Philip Randolph and Chandler Owen; the single issue of *Fire!!* edited by Wallace Thurman in November 1926; *The Saturday Evening Quill,* founded by a group of African American writers in Boston (1928–1930) and edited by Eugene Gordon; a special issue of *Palms* edited by Countée Cullen in 1926; *Black Opals,* a short-lived 1927 journal edited by Arthur Huff Fauset in Philadelphia; and *Challenge,* edited by Dorothy West from 1934 to 1937. Material from *Negro World,* published by Marcus Garvey's Universal Negro Improvement Association from 1918 to 1933, is not represented because so little poetry by black women appears in its pages.

Anthologies of the day include James Weldon Johnson's *The Book of American Negro Poetry* (1922, 1931); Robert T. Kerlin's *Negro Poets and Their Poems* (1923); Alain Locke's touchstone text *The New Negro* (1925); the National Urban League's *Ebony and Topaz* (1927); Countée Cullen's ground-breaking *Caroling Dusk* (1927); *Readings from Negro Authors,* edited by Otelia Cromwell, Lorenzo Dow Turner, and Eva B. Dykes (1931); Victor Calverton's *An Anthology of American Negro Literature* (1929); William Stanley Braithwaite's *Anthology of Magazine Verse* (1927, 1928); and Beatrice M. Murphy's *Negro Voices* (1938). These are anthologies in which significant numbers of poems by women appear and which arguably were the most influential.

Although relatively few poetry collections were published by women, those that were furnished the remaining material for this volume: Georgia Douglas Johnson's *The Heart of a Woman and Other Poems* (1918), *Bronze: A Book of Verse* (1922), and *An Autumn Love Cycle* (1928); Sarah Lee Brown Fleming's *Clouds and Sunshine* (1920); Carrie Williams Clifford's *The Widening Light* (1922); Sarah Collins

Fernandis's *Poems* (1925); Clara Ann Thompson's *A Garland of Poems* (1926); Mae V. Cowdery's *We Lift Our Voices and Other Poems* (1936); Lucy Mae Turner's *'Bout Culled Folkses* (1938); Anita Scott Coleman's *Small Wisdom* (1937); Esther Popel's *A Forest Pool* (1934); and Ida Rowland's *Lisping Leaves* (1939). These are not all the collections published by women of the Harlem Renaissance (those published after 1940 are not included), but most of them are represented here.

All publication venues of a particular poem are listed in order of appearance to indicate how well distributed it was. The only changes that have been made to the original pieces are silent corrections of typographical, spelling, and punctuation errors or lengthening of lines that were obviously limited by the width of columns in the original typescript.

The selection process was governed by a number of factors. One of these was that I wanted to represent all the major poets with a good number of pieces, their lesser-known works as well as those that have been reprinted, in order to give a sense of their range. I felt it was important, too, to include writers who never made it into the major anthologies or journals. Most women had neither the resources nor social contacts to compile a significant body of work, and many remained outside Harlem Renaissance publishing networks, yet they played a key role in the cultural awakening within African American communities of the time while suggesting their broadly based nature. Artistic value was another factor I considered in making the final selection. Admittedly relying on subjective judgment, I looked for pieces that have held up over time and that contain striking metaphors or well-composed lines to underscore the contemporary as well as historical value of this poetry. I eliminated, for instance, verse that seemed to me derivative or awkwardly rendered. Finally, I chose poems representative of the subjects and themes that appear most frequently during this period and provide a glimpse into the concerns and sensibility of the Renaissance generation. These poems reverberate with notes commonly struck, and their meaning is enriched by the threads that weave them together. This literary generation shared a voice as well as a historical era.

Finally, it should be noted that during the Harlem Renaissance, journals published poetry by many white writers without identifying their ethnicity. In the case of those poets in this anthology for whom I could not find biographical information, therefore, it is possible that they are not African Americans. As we retrieve more information about women writers from the past, we will, I hope, be able to more accurately attribute authorship to women of color.

Oh Magalu, come! Take my hand
and I will read you poetry . . .
    —*Helene Johnson, "Magalu" (1927)*

shadowed
Dreams

Gwendolyn B. Bennett (1902–1981)

One of the most important movers and shakers of the Harlem Renaissance, Gwendolyn Bennett was a talented painter, poet, essayist, and editor. Her distinguished painting career was overshadowed by her literary activity, and she remains best known for her poetry, especially "Hatred" and "Heritage," and for her editorial work at *Opportunity* magazine from 1926 to 1928, when she wrote a column called "The Ebony Flute." She was born on July 8, 1902, in Giddings, Texas, to Maime and Joshua Bennett, who became teachers on a Nevada Indian reservation. The family moved to Washington, D.C., when Gwendolyn was a child; shortly afterward her parents divorced. At age seven, she was taken from her mother to Harrisburg, Pennsylvania, by her law student father, then Brooklyn, New York, where she attended high school from 1918 to 1921. She did not see her mother again until 1924. Bennett studied fine arts at Columbia University and graduated from the Pratt Institute. In 1924, she became an instructor of fine art at Howard University in Washington, D.C. In December of that year, Bennett won a Delta Sigma Theta Sorority scholarship to Paris, where she studied art until 1926, when she returned to the United States and moved to D.C., where she resumed her teaching position at Howard. Bennett's poems and artwork appeared in *The Crisis, Opportunity,* and other journals from 1922 to 1934, and her poems were included in all the major anthologies of her day. After her marriage to Howard University medical student Alfred Jackson in 1928, Bennett's career changed markedly, for after Jackson's graduation they moved South, to Tennessee and then Florida. The couple moved to Hempstead, Long Island, in 1932. When her husband died in 1936, Bennett moved back to Harlem. Here she joined the Harlem Artists Guild and helped direct the Harlem Community Art Center with sculptor Augusta Savage from 1938 to 1941. Among her students were the influential African American painters Jacob Lawrence and Romare Bearden. After World War II, Bennett became secretary for the Consumers Union until her retirement in 1968. She and her second husband, Richard Crosscup, whom she married in 1940, then ran an antiques shop in Kutztown, Pennsylvania, where she died in 1981. Bennett's poetry ranges from imagistic in form to more extended meditations on her cultural heritage as an African American woman; she excelled at descriptions of nature and portraits of black women.

OPPORTUNITY
JOURNAL OF NEGRO LIFE

JULY 1926

1. Gwendolyn B. Bennett, cover of *Opportunity,* July 1926

To a Dark Girl

I love you for your brownness
And the rounded darkness of your breast.
I love you for the breaking sadness in your voice
And shadows where your wayward eye-lids rest.

Something of old forgotten queens
Lurks in the lithe abandon of your walk
And something of the shackled slave
Sobs in the rhythm of your talk.

Oh, little brown girl, born for sorrow's mate,
Keep all you have of queenliness,
Forgetting that you once were slave,
And let your full lips laugh at Fate!

► *Opportunity,* October 1927; *Caroling Dusk,* ed. Countée Cullen, 1927; *Anthology of American Negro Literature,* ed. V. F. Calverton, 1929; *The Book of American Negro Poetry,* ed. James Weldon Johnson, 1931.

Heritage

I want to see the slim palm-trees,
Pulling at the clouds
With little pointed fingers. . . .

I want to see lithe Negro girls
Etched dark against the sky
While sunset lingers.

I want to hear the silent sands,
Singing to the moon
Before the Sphinx-still face. . . .

I want to hear the chanting
Around a heathen fire
Of a strange black race.

I want to breathe the Lotus flow'r,
Sighing to the stars
With tendrils drinking at the Nile. . . .

I want to feel the surging
Of my sad people's soul,
Hidden by a minstrel-smile.

► *Opportunity,* December 1923; *The Book of American Negro Poetry,* ed. James Weldon Johnson, 1931.

Song

I am weaving a song of waters,
Shaken from firm, brown limbs,
Or heads thrown back in irreverent mirth.
My song has the lush sweetness
Of moist, dark lips
Where hymns keep company
With old forgotten banjo songs.
Abandon tells you
That I sing the heart of a race
While sadness whispers
That I am the cry of a soul. . . .

A-shoutin', in de ole camp-meetin' place,
A-strummin' o' de ole banjo.
Singin' in de moonlight,
Sobbin' in de dark.
Singin', sobbin', strummin' slow . . .
Singin' slow; sobbin' low.
Strummin', strummin', strummin' slow . . .

Words are bright bugles
That make the shining for my song,
And mothers hold brown babes
To dark, warm breasts
To make my singing sad.

A dancing girl with swaying hips
Sets mad the queen in a harlot's eye.
> Praying slave
> Jazz-band after
> Breaking heart
> To the time of laughter . . .
Clinking chains and minstrelsy
Are welded fast with melody.
> A praying slave
> With a jazz-band after . . .
> Singin' slow, sobbin' low.
Sun-baked lips will kiss the earth.
Throats of bronze will burst with mirth.
> Sing a little faster,
> Sing a little faster,
> Sing!

► *Opportunity,* October 1926.

Hatred

I shall hate you
Like a dart of singing steel
Shot through still air
At even-tide,
Or solemnly
As pines are sober
When they stand etched
Against the sky.
Hating you shall be a game
Played with cool hands
And slim fingers.
Your heart will yearn
For the lonely splendor
Of the pine tree;
While rekindled fires
In my eyes

Shall wound you like swift arrows.
Memory will lay its hands
Upon your breast
And you will understand
My hatred.

The object of the poet's hatred is presumably white racism. At the time it was published, the poem
was viewed as a militant rejection of racist views.

► *Opportunity,* June 1926; *Caroling Dusk,* ed. Countée Cullen, 1927; *The Book of American Negro
Poetry,* ed. James Weldon Johnson, 1931.

Advice

You were a sophist,*
Pale and quite remote,
As you bade me
Write poems—
Brown poems
Of dark words
And prehistoric rhythms. . . .
Your pallor stifled my poesy
But I remembered a tapestry
That I would some day weave
Of dim purples and fine reds
And blues
Like night and death—
The keen precision of your words
Wove a silver thread
Through the dusk softness
Of my dream-stuff. . . .

*This poem probably refers to Alain Locke, a professor of philosophy at Howard University, where
Bennett taught fine art. Locke was a mentor to several poets of the Harlem Renaissance and a key
leader of the New Negro Movement.

► *Caroling Dusk,* ed. Countée Cullen, 1927.

To Usward

Dedicated to all Negro Youth known and unknown who have a song to sing, a story to tell or a vision for the sons of earth. Especially dedicated to Jessie Fauset upon the event of her novel, *There Is Confusion.**

Let us be still
As ginger jars are still
Upon a Chinese shelf.
And let us be contained
By entities of Self. . . .
Not still with lethargy and sloth,
But quiet with the pushing of our growth.
Not self-contained with smug identity
But conscious of the strength in entity.
If any have a song to sing
That's different from the rest,
Oh let them sing
Before the urgency of Youth's behest!
For some of us have songs to sing
Of jungle heat and fires,
And some of us are solemn grown
With pitiful desires,
And there are those who feel the pull
Of seas beneath the skies,
And some there be who want to croon
Of Negro lullabies.
We claim no part with racial dearth;
We want to sing the songs of birth!
And so we stand like ginger jars
Like ginger jars bound 'round
With dust and age;
Like jars of ginger we are sealed
By nature's heritage.
But let us break the seal of years
With pungent thrusts of song,
For there is joy in long-dried tears
For whetted passions of a throng!

There Is Confusion, by Jessie Fauset, was published in 1924 to great fanfare by the NAACP and
The Crisis, where Fauset was literary editor under W.E.B. Du Bois. Bennett composed this poem for
a dinner at Manhattan's Civic Club in Fauset's honor on March 21, 1924, and read it on that occasion.
➤ *The Crisis,* May 1924; *Opportunity,* May 1924.

Secret

I shall make a song like your hair . . .
Gold-woven with shadows green-tinged,
And I shall play with my song
As my fingers might play with your hair.
Deep in my heart
I shall play with my song of you,
Gently. . . .
I shall laugh
At its sensitive lustre . . .
I shall wrap my song in a blanket,
Blue like your eyes are blue
With tiny shots of silver.
I shall wrap it caressingly,
Tenderly. . . .
I shall sing a lullaby
To the song I have made
Of your hair and eyes . . .
And you will never know
That deep in my heart
I shelter a song of you
Secretly. . . .

➤ *Caroling Dusk,* ed. Countée Cullen, 1927.

Quatrains

1.
Brushes and paints are all I have
To speak the music in my soul—

While silently there laughs at me
A copper jar beside a pale green bowl.

2.
How strange that grass should sing—
Grass is so still a thing . . .
And strange the swift surprise of snow—
So soft it falls and slow.

► *The Crisis*, December 1923; *Caroling Dusk*, ed. Countée Cullen, 1927.

Street Lamps in Early Spring

Night wears a garment
All velvet soft, all violet blue . . .
And over her face she draws a veil
As shimmering fine as floating dew . . .
And here and there
In the black of her hair
The subtle hands of Night
Move slowly with their gem-starred light.

► *Opportunity*, May 1926.

Nocturne

This cool night is strange
Among midsummer days . . .
Far frosts are caught
In the moon's pale light,
And sounds are distant laughter
Chilled to crystal tears.

► *The Crisis*, November 1923; *The Book of American Negro Poetry*, ed. James Weldon Johnson,
1931.

Moon Tonight

Moon tonight,
Beloved . . .
When twilight
Has gathered together
The ends
Of her soft robe
And the last bird-call
Has died.
Moon tonight—
Cool as a forgotten dream,
Dearer than lost twilights
Among trees where birds sing
No more.

► *The Gypsy,* October 1926; *Anthology of Magazine Verse,* ed. William S. Braithwaite, 1927.

Fantasy

I sailed in my dreams to the Land of Night
Where you were the dusk-eyed queen,
And there in the pallor of moon-veiled light
The loveliest things were seen. . . .

A slim-necked peacock sauntered there
In a garden of lavender hues,
And you were strange with your purple hair
As you sat in your amethyst chair
With your feet in your hyacinth shoes.

Oh, the moon gave a bluish light
Through the trees in the land of dreams and night.
I stood behind a bush of yellow-green
And whistled a song to the dark-haired queen. . . .

► *Caroling Dusk,* ed. Countée Cullen, 1927.

Wind

The wind was a care-free soul
    That broke the chains of earth,
And strode for a moment across the land
    With the wild halloo of his mirth.
He little cared that he ripped up trees,
    That houses fell at his hand,
That his step broke calm on the breast of seas,
    That his feet stirred clouds of sand.

But when he had had his little joke,
    Had shouted and laughed and sung,
When the trees were scarred, their branches broke,
    And their foliage aching hung,
He crept to his cave with a stealthy tread,
    With rain-filled eyes and low-bowed head.

➤ *Opportunity,* November 1924.

Lines Written at the Grave of Alexander Dumas

Cemeteries are places for departed souls
And bones interred,
Or hearts with shattered loves.
A woman with lips made warm for laughter
Would find grey stones and silent thoughts
Too chill for living, moving pulses . . .
And thou great soul, would shiver in thy granite shroud,
Should idle mirth or empty talk
Disturb thy tranquil sleeping.

A cemetery is a place for shattered loves
And broken hearts . . .
Bowed before the crystal chalice of thy soul,
I find the multi-colored fragrance of thy mind
Has lost itself in Death's transparency.

Oh, stir the lucid waters of thy sleep
And coin for me a tale
Of happy loves and gems and joyous limbs
And hearts where love is sweet!

A cemetery is a place for broken hearts
And silent thoughts . . .
And silence never moves, nor speaks
Nor sings.

Alexander Dumas was a black French novelist of the nineteenth century.

► *Opportunity,* July 1926; *Caroling Dusk,* ed. Countée Cullen, 1927.

Purgation

You lived
And your body
Clothed the flames of earth.

Now that the fires have burned away
And left your body cold,
I tremble as I stand
Before the chiseled marble
Of your dust-freed soul.

► *Opportunity,* February 1925.

Epitaph

When I am dead, carve this upon my stone:
Here lies a woman, fit root for flower and tree,
Whose living flesh, now mouldering round the bone,
Wants nothing more than this for immortality,
That in her heart, where love so long unfruited lay
A seed for grass or weed shall grow,
And push to light and air its heedless way;

That she who lies here dead may know
Through all the putrid marrow of her bones
The searing pangs of birth,
While none may know the pains nor hear the groans
Of she who lived with barrenness upon the earth.

► *Opportunity,* March 1934.

Ethel Caution-Davis (1880 –1981)
(a k a Ethel M. Caution)

Ethel Caution was born in Cleveland, Ohio, in 1880, to parents who died
while she was very young. Adopted by a married woman with the surname
of Davis, who died when Ethel was only a teenager, she was raised in Boston
and educated there at Girls Latin School and Wellesley College, from which
she graduated in 1912. Having taken the name Ethel Caution-Davis during
these years, the intrepid young educator moved out of the Northeast to take
teaching jobs in Durham, North Carolina, and then Kansas City, Kansas, before
becoming a dean of women at Talladega College in Alabama. Self-supporting,
unmarried, and evidently without family, Caution-Davis then moved back East
to New York City, where she was employed with a public assistance program
and then as director of a residence club for single women until her retirement
several years later. At the age of 101, she died in New York City in 1981. Caution-
Davis's output of poetry was small, but it is interesting for its loving focus on
women as well as for its accessibility. Her best-known poem, "Long Remem-
bering," is unusual for her in that its rhyme scheme is more complex than her
other work, and it reveals the love Caution-Davis had for travel as well as her
knowledge of diverse landscapes around the globe.

Last Night

Last night I danced on the rim of the moon,
      Delirious and gay,
Quite different from the mood
      I wear about by day.

Athwart my vibrant body
      A chiffon cloud I flung,
Diaphanous and azure,
      With starpoint brilliants hung.

And oh! my feet flew madly!
      My body whirled and swayed!
My soul danced in its ecstasy,
      Untrammeled, unafraid!

Last night I danced on the rim of the moon,
      Delirious and gay,
Then slipped into my sober self
      Just ere the break of day.

► *The Crisis*, February 1929.

To . . .

Out of the hush of night,
Out of the sob of morn,
Out of the sigh of noon,
Thy soul was born.

Part of the gentle tears
That dim fair April's eyes,
Part of the gladsome smiles
That warm her skies;

Grace of the violet shy,
Fragrance of new-born rose,
Beauty of every flower
That woodland grows;

Softness of mild May winds,
Sweetness of days in June;
Lilt from a melody
Of heavenly tune;

Out of the ages past,
Out of the years to be,
Out of his vast unknown,
God fashioned thee.

► *The Crisis*, December 1927.

To E.J.J.

Sparkling eyes of diamond jet;
Willful hair a-curling yet;
Rounded cheeks and lips well set—
Lips a-smiling, smiling yet;
Slender fingers quick to do
Gracious things for me and you;
Feet that never weary grow
Lightening of another's woe;
Heart a-bubbling o'er with love
From the Fountain-head above;
Life all laughter, words of cheer
Echoing down and down the year;
Loved her well when first we met,
And I love her, love her yet.

► *The Crisis*, August 1930.

The River

The river is a decrepit old woman
Shivering in her sombre shawl of fog.
Stray wisps of gray foam cling to her dank temples.
Now and then she mutters sitting there
Huddled like a shadow against the wall.
And I cannot tell
Whether she repents some folly of her youth
Or whether she bemoans her children
Who could not pace their restless steps
To her age-tempered tread.

► *The Crisis,* March 1930.

Long Remembering

If I should go to sleep tonight
Knowing I ne'er should waken,
I would not be dismayed.
My soul, glad for release,
Would wing its way unto a long remembering

Of mornings spent upon the Siasconsett strand
Watching the sun rise
Dripping red spray from the ocean's eastern rim.
Of hours on Narragansett's craggy coast*
When, perched in solitude upon a rock,
Feet dipping in the spray,
I listened to the waves
Beat their high sounding paean on the shore.

Of evenings in mid-ocean when the moon
Laddered its path of gold
From sky down o'er the waves
To where I stood ship-bound

Trying to quench undying thirst
With wonder of the night.

Of dusk in distant balsam wood
When nature poured her evensong
From thrushes' throat.

Of moments with a cardinal—
He perched upon a swaying pine,
I tip-toe on the sod—
Talking to each other of happiness and God.

Of blue flags by a Carolina stream,
Of dogwood tracing petals pink
Against a silver sky.
Of flowers peeping through June snow at Scheideg;
Of Spietz reflected in the Thuner See;[†]
Of English gardens
And purple heather hemming in the Scottish lochs.
Of Capri's grotto blue[‡]
And cedars silhouetted against the Carmel sea.[§]
Of lacy spires etched against the sky
Of Chartres and Senlis, St. Patrick's and Milan.[‖]
Of music in a child's unstudied laughter;
Of unexpected handclasps by the way.

If I should go to sleep tonight
Knowing I ne'er should waken,
I would not be dismayed.
My pagan soul, if thus it be,
Clothed only in such robes as these
Would wing its way into Eternity
Asking that afterlife be long enough
For such remembering.

*The Siasconsett is a body of water in New England; Narragansett Bay is an inlet of the Atlantic
Ocean in East Rhode Island.

†Scheidegg and Spiez are Swiss cities; Thuner See is a lake in central Switzerland formed by the Aar River and near the city of Thun.

‡Capri is an island in the Bay of Naples, Italy.

§Carmel, California.

‖Chartres is a cathedral in northern France; St. Patrick's is a Catholic church in England; Milan, Italy.

► *The Crisis,* October 1928.

Carrie Williams Clifford (1862–1934)

Carrie Williams was born in Chillicothe, Ohio, in 1862 and spent her early life in Ohio before moving from Columbus to Washington, D.C., with her husband, William H. Clifford, a lawyer and state politician, and their two sons. While in Ohio, Clifford founded the first chapter of the Federation of Colored Women's Clubs, an important national organization promoting suffrage and women's rights. Clifford was also a member of the Niagara Movement, progenitor of the NAACP. These political activities inform much of her poetry, published in *Race Rhymes* (1911) and *The Widening Light* (1922), which is imbued with a militant determination to end racial discrimination and usher in a new era of black pride. Clifford became a leading member of the Washington, D.C., black artistic and political community, where she hosted weekly gatherings attended by notables such as Alain Locke, W.E.B. Du Bois, Georgia Douglas Johnson, and others. A woman proud of her race and gender, Carrie Williams Clifford has left a body of verse that speaks to the highly political nature of the Harlem Renaissance era. She died in 1934.

To Phyllis Wheatley (First African Poetess)

No! Not like the lark, didst thou circle and sing,
High in the heavens on morn's merry wing,
But hid in the depths of the forest's dense shade,
There where the homes of the lowly were made,
Thou nested! Though fettered, thou frail child of night,
The melody trilled forth with naïve delight;
And all through the throes of the night dark and long,
Earth's favored ones harkened thy ravishing song,
So plaintive and wild, touched with Africa's lilt;
Of wrong small complaint, sweet forgiveness of guilt—
Oh, a lyric of love and a paean of praise,
Didst thou at thy vespers, Dark Nightingale, raise;
So sweet was the hymn rippling out of the dark,
It rivaled the clear morning song of the lark.

Phyllis Wheatley (ca. 1753–1784) was the first African American poet to publish a volume of verse, *Poems on Various Subjects, Religious and Moral* (1773). She was forcibly brought to America from Africa as a child and sold to a Boston merchant named John Wheatley. Taught to read Latin and English by her owners, Phyllis was sent by them to England for health reasons, where she published a poetry collection at the age of twenty. After her return to Boston, she married and had three children, all of whom died. Her life was hard due to ill health and poverty, one she describes in *Memoirs and Poems of Phyllis Wheatley, A Native African and A Slave,* published posthumously in 1838.

► *The Widening Light,* Carrie Williams Clifford, 1922.

A Toast to Africa

(Christmas, 1920)
From a goblet of rarest and richest red gold,
Encrusted with jewels of value untold,
All flowing and glowing with nectar of wine,
Distilled from the spirits of souls sweet and fine
As these sons and daughters whose deeds I rehearse,
With zeal all-consuming, though halting my verse—
I drink to my Race on this epochal morn,
Remembering the Christ-child who came lowly-born,—

Was despised, crucified and rejected of men,
But *now* to whom honor and glory—Amen!

► *The Widening Light,* Carrie Williams Clifford, 1922.

The Widening Light

A sound of muttering, faint and far and low—
A sound of stirring restlessly about—
A harsher note and frequently a shout—
Of red defiance? Not of peace I trow;*
Oh, self-deceived and blind who do not know
The meaning of this unaccustomed rout!
Do you not feel the frenzy? Can you doubt
The triumph of Race Hatred's overthrow?
The moving millions of the darker clan
Have wakened to Jehovah's ancient cry—
Not stunted, greedy, boastful, pale-faced man
Omnipotent is—"verily none save I!"
And piercing the dark clouds of dreadful night
Behold! They greet the light, the light, The Light!

*Trust.
► *The Widening Light,* Carrie Williams Clifford, 1922.

For the New Year

The New Year comes! Fling wide, fling wide the door
Of opportunity! the spirit free
To scale the utmost height of hopes "to be,"
To sit on peaks ne'er reached by man before.
The boundless infinite let us explore
To search out undiscovered mystery
Undreamed of in our poor philosophy!
The bounty of the gods upon us pour!

Nay! in the New Year, we shall be as gods;
No longer ape-ish puppets, or dull clods
Of earth! but poised, empowered to command,
Upon the Etna* of new worlds we'll stand;
This scant earth-raiment to the winds we'll cast,
Full richly robed as supermen at last!

*Mount Etna is an active volcano in Sicily.

► *The Crisis*, February 1920.

An Easter Message

Now quivering to life, all nature thrills
At the approach of that triumphant queen,
Pink-fingered Easter, trailing robes of green
Tunefully o'er the flower-embroidered hills,
Her hair perfumed of myriad daffodils:
Upon her swelling bosom now are seen
The dream-frail lilies with their snowy sheen,
As lightly she o'er-leaps the spring-time rills.
To black folk choked within the deadly grasp
Of racial hate, what message does she bring
Of resurrection and the hope of spring?
Assurance their death-stupor is a mask—
A sleep, with elements potential, rife,
Ready to burst full-flowered into life.

► *The Crisis*, April 1920; *Negro Poets and Their Poems*, ed. Robert T. Kerlin, 1923.

The Flight

Away down south in Dixie-land
The place where they were born,
Where grows the cotton, silver-white
Tobacco, cane and corn—

I see your beauty, feel your charm;
I knew your ancient lure
For those dark earth-sprites, who for you
Did pain untold endure!

But now the cabin lonely stands
Beneath the spreading tree;
The old plantation echoes not
The weird slave-melody!

Gone! All are gone! How strange it seems!
I miss their gleaming eyes—
Their loud guffaws, whose hearty ring
Floats lightly to the skies.

What do they seek? Where have they fled?
Why do they roam afar?
They go to find the Promised Land,
With gates of Hope ajar.

Where schools stand ready to impart
The precious Rule of Three;
And high ambition may be served
To even the last degree.

Where aspiration soars aloft,
And self-respect may grow;
Where none would limit nor confine
The man who wants *to know.*

O Southland that they loved so well,
The time will come when you
Wishing them back, will learn the truth
That faithful friends are few!

This poem refers to the Great Migration of black people from the South to cities of the North from
1915 through the 1920s. This exodus was prompted by drought, the boll weevil infestation of cotton,
the extreme poverty of tenant farming, and recruitment activities by northern industries that needed

workers for their expanding plants. Thousands of migrants went to Chicago, Detroit, Harlem, and elsewhere to make a better living and to escape the often brutal slave mentality of whites in the South.

▶ *The Widening Light,* Carrie Williams Clifford, 1922.

Little Mother

(Upon the lynching of Mary Turner) *
Oh, tremble, Little Mother,
For your dark-eyed, unborn babe,
Whom in your secret heart you've named
The well-loved name of "Gabe."

    For Gabriel is the father's name,
    And the son is sure to be
    "Just like his father!" as she wants
    The whole, wide world to see!

But tremble, Little Mother,
For your unborn baby's fate;
The father tarries long away—
Why does he stay so late?

    For dark the night and weird the wind,
    And chilled the heart with fear!
    What are those hideous sounds and cries
    Each instant drawing near?

Oh, tremble, dark-faced mother,
At the dreadful word that falls
From lips of pale-faced demons,
As the black man pleads and calls.

    For they're dragging Gabe, at a stout rope's end,
    And they say, "She is bound to tell!"
    Something she knows not a thing about,
    Or they'll "Give her the same as well!"

Oh, tremble, helpless mother!
They're beating down the door,
And you'll never feel the father's kiss,
Or the stir of the baby more.

Oh, the human beasts were ruthless,
And there upon the ground,
Two bodies—and an unborn babe—
The ghastly morning found.

*Mary Turner and her husband were lynched by a white Georgia mob in 1918. Gabriel Turner, a tenant farmer, had killed his employer, known for his cruel treatment of black laborers. Their unborn baby was cut out of Mary's womb during the lynching. Anne Spencer's poem "White Things" was also prompted by this lynching.

► *The Widening Light,* Carrie Williams Clifford, 1922.

Sorrow Songs

Oh, haunting melodies of grief and pain;
Oh, heart-wrung agonies distilled in song;
Oh, moving minors—weird, pathetic strain;
Oh, trembling cries forced by the cruel thong
Of Hate! Oh, whisperings of hope and faith,
Breathing fidelity to Unseen Love,
From bleeding, bruised souls lashed to the earth;
Oh, soft appealing moans, potent to move
Upon the calloused hearts of world-worn men;
Sweet voices of my brothers from the past
Dark night of slavery, dread era when
These little ones were in its power held fast;
Sad Sorrow Songs, you yet shall come to be
Brave shouts of victory from Souls set free!

► *The Crisis,* June 1927.

Silent Protest Parade

(On Fifth Avenue, New York, Saturday, July 28, 1917, protesting against the St. Louis riots) *

Were you there? Did you see? Gods! Wasn't it fine!
Did you notice how straight we kept the line,
As we marched down the famous avenue,
Silent, dogged and dusky of hue,
Keeping step to the sound of the muffled drum,
With its constantly recurring *tum—tum, tum—*
Tum—Tum—Tum—Tum—Tum;
Ten thousand of us, if there was one!
As goodly a sight as this ancient sun
Has ever looked upon!

Youth and maid
Father, mother—not one afraid
Or ashamed to let the whole world know
What he thought of the hellish East St. Louis "show,"
Orgy—riot—mob—what you will,
Where men and e'en women struggled to kill
Poor black workers, who'd fled in distress from the South
To find themselves murdered and mobbed in the North.

We marched as a protest—we carried our banner,
On which had been boldly inscribed every manner
Of sentiment—all, to be sure, within reason—
But no flag—not that we meant any treason—
Only who'd have the heart to carry Old Glory,
After hearing all of the horrible story,
Of East St. Louis? And never a word,
From the nation's head, as if he'd not heard†
The groans of the dying ones here at home,
Though 'tis plain he can hear even farther than Rome.

Oh, yes, I was there in the Silent Parade,
And a man (he was white) I heard when he said,

"If they had music now, 'twould be great!"—
"We march not, sir, with hearts elate,
But sad; we grieve for our dark brothers
Murdered, and we hope that others
Will heed our protest against wrong,
Will help to make our protest strong."

Were you there? Ah, brothers, wasn't it fine!
The children—God bless 'em—headed the line;
Then came the mothers dressed in white,
And some—my word! 'twas a thrilling sight—
Carried their babies upon their breast,
Face tense and eager as forward they pressed,
With never a laugh and never a word,
But ever and always, the thing they heard
Was the *tum—tum—, tum, tum,*
Of the muffled drum—*tum, tum, tum!*

And last the black-coated men swung by,
Head up, chest firm, determined eye—
I was so happy, I wanted to cry.
As I watched the long lines striding by,
(Ten thousand souls if there was one)
And I knew that "to turn, the worm had begun,"
As we marched down Fifth Avenue unafraid
And calm, in our first Silent Protest Parade!

*This parade of ten thousand, conducted in silence with everyone dressed in white, was held in New York to protest the July 2, 1917, East St. Louis, Illinois, race riot in which nearly two hundred African Americans were killed and six thousand burned out of their homes. It remains one of the worst race riots in American history. This was one of the first mass protests ever organized by African Americans.

†A reference to President Woodrow Wilson.

► *The Widening Light,* Carrie Williams Clifford, 1922.

Phantom (The Lure of Nature)

My sweetheart is a phantom!
Tho' I search for her everywhere, I cannot find her!
When I go into the wood,
I hear her laughter like the sound of running water;
And the swish of her silken skirts
As the wind blows them over the tall grasses.
But nowhere can I find her!

My sweetheart is a phantom!
She eludes me,
Tho' I search for her everywhere;
In the morning I hear her singing
Like a lark in the sky!
I hie me to the temple of the grove—
But nowhere find her.

When I walk abroad thro' the fields,
I follow the gleam of the gold of her hair
As she plays hide and seek
Between the long rows of the corn-stalks;
But when I pursue, she flees;
Tho' I search for her everywhere,
I cannot find her!

Her blood-red lips entreat me—
Passionately I press them to my mouth,
When, lo! Within my hand,
There lie the petals of a rose.
My sweetheart is a phantom,
She eludes me,
Tho' I search for her everywhere.

Faint with my futile search,
I fling myself upon the greensward
Yearning for my beloved.

Suddenly upon the air
A far, faint, fluting floats.
It is the voice of my phantom sweetheart,
Lulling me to the realm of dreams.

I sleep—anon I wake!
Her violet breath is in my nostrils,
Upon my face, a flower dropped from her,
Sweet in my ears the music of her voice,
And all my senses steeped in ecstasy!
Ah! Then I know my love has lain with me.
But when I seek for her,
I cannot find her.
My sweetheart is a phantom.

► *The Widening Light,* Carrie Williams Clifford, 1922.

Ecstasy

Your eyes star-worlds of beauty are,
My long road blazing from afar,
    Sweet Emily!

The essence of the rose's musk
Bathes your wine-lips as through the dusk
    They summon me!

The downy pillows of your breast,
Sweet Eden where my soul would rest
    Eternally!

► *The Widening Light,* Carrie Williams Clifford, 1922.

Anita Scott Coleman (1890–1960)

The daughter of a Cuban father who purchased his wife as a slave, Anita Scott Coleman was born in Guaymas, Mexico, in 1890 and raised in New Mexico, where she became a teacher. She later married, had four children, and lived in Los Angeles, where she and her husband established a children's boarding home. Coleman published numerous short stories and poems from 1920 to 1939, some of them prize-winning, in *The Messenger, Opportunity, The Crisis,* and *Half-Century Magazine.* She is one of the few African American women of her era to publish poetry collections: *Small Wisdom* (1937, under the pseudonym Elizabeth Stapleton Stokes); and *Reason for Singing* (1948). In 1961, she published a short children's story, *The Singing Bells.* Coleman was a gifted poet and fiction writer whose prolific output and literary talent deserve greater recognition. In two photos that appear in the January 1926 issue of *The Crisis* and the June 1926 *Opportunity,* Coleman appeared to be dark in color, and her poetry is animated by love of dark-skinned people as well as the beauty of blackness. She attacks racism directly in her poems, such as the kaleidoscopic "Impressions from a Family Album," in which a former slave curses his master and a little black girl whacks her white doll. Coleman's uncompromising voice is at the same time lyrical, vibrant, and profoundly visual, qualities that are most on display in her 1937 collection of fifty-three poems, most of which are meditations on aging, children, old friends, and artistic immortality. Coleman's keen intelligence and exquisite sensitivity to nature coexisted with race pride in her substantial poetic legacy. Anita Scott Coleman died in 1960.

Black Faces

I love black faces. . . .
They are full of smould'ring fire.
And Negro eyes, white—with white desire,
And Negro lips so soft and thick,
Like rich velvet within
Fine jewelry cases.
I love black faces. . . .

► *Opportunity,* October 1929.

Negro Laughter

Negro laughter . . .
    is not the laughter of those others
Who force their distrait mirth
    through thin pale lips.

Negro laughter . . .
    is a stem of joyousness, a hardy tendril
Thrusting through the moraines
    of long distress.

► *The Crisis,* March 1930.

Black Baby

The baby I hold in my arms is a black baby.
    Today I set him in the sun and
    Sunbeams danced on his head.
The baby I hold in my arms is a black baby.
    I toil, and I cannot always cuddle him.
    I place him on the ground at my feet.
    He presses the warm earth with his hands,
    He lifts the sand and laughs to see

It flow through his chubby fingers.
I watch to discern which are his hands,
Which is the sand. . . .
Lo . . . the rich loam is black like his hands.

The baby I hold in my arms is a black baby.
Today the coal-man brought me coal.
Sixteen dollars a ton is the price I pay for coal.
Costly fuel . . . though they say:—
Men must sweat and toil to dig it from the ground.
Costly fuel . . . 'Tis said:—
If it is buried deep enough and lies hidden long enough
'Twill be no longer coal but diamonds.
My black baby looks at me.
His eyes are like coals,
They shine like diamonds.

► *Opportunity,* February 1929.

The Shining Parlor

It was a drab street
A white man's street . . .
Jammed with automobiles
Streetcars and trucks;
    Bee-hived with fruit vendors' stalls,
    Real estate concerns, meat shops,
Dental clinics, and soft drink stands.

It was a drab street
A white man's street . . .
But it held the shining parlor—
A boot-black booth,
    Commandeered by a black man,
    Who spent much time smiling out
Upon the hub-bub of the thoroughfare.

Ever . . . serenely smiling . . .
With a brush and a soiled rag in his hands.
Often . . . white patrons wait for
Their boots to be "shined,"
   Wondering the while
   At the wonder—
Of the black man's smile.

► *The Crisis*, September 1929.

Portraiture

Black men are the tall trees that remain
Standing in a forest after a fire.
Flames strip their branches,
Flames sear their limbs,
Flames scorch their trunks.
Yet stand these trees
For their roots are thrust deep
In the heart of the earth.
Black men are the tall trees that remain
Standing in a forest after a fire.

► *The Crisis*, June 1931.

Idle Wonder

My cat is so sleek and contented;
   She is a real house-cat.
She has not seen any other cat
Since she came to live with me.

   I wonder does she think,
   I wonder does she dream,
   I wonder does she ever imagine

Herself out, among cats,
I wonder is she like poor Agnes.

Agnes lives with the white folk
And they think she is contented
And actually delighted with being
    Their house-maid.

► *Opportunity,* May 1938.

Impressions from a Family Album

Grand-Pap
Grandpap was very old,
When this was struck. So old!
But he could recollect . . .
The way 'twas told
That Annie was the p'utt'est gal
On ol' Marse Tom's plantation,
And Annie was his mammy.
        'Could recollect . . .
How he was allus kept
To wait 'pon ol' Marse Tom
To shoo off flies, while ol' Marse slept
And when ol' Marse woke
Go fetch his pipe and bring his book
And mix the mint-julep. . . .
        'Could recollect
The w'uppin's Master gin him
'Lowing fo' to teach him how to show
The proper 'spec's where 'spec's* were due. . . .
'Lawsy! Ol' Marster sure insisted
Wid a great big strop
That he say: — "Thank-ee, Yessuh . . .
Yessuh, Thank-ee," in de proper way,
        'Could recollect . . .

The w'uppin's sure enuff
And all the times he said:—
"Thank-ee," and cussed ol' Marster . . .
Underneath his breaf.

Old Praying Sue
My man is black . . .
God . . . You alone, know why.
Shed but one briny tear
For all the drops of sweat
That fall from off his brow
Merciful God . . . mark one little smile
That wreathes his trembling lips
See but the mite of faith and courage
In his eyes . . .
That I might learn with blest humility
Even though, my man is black
It is not he, but Christ
They crucify.

Melissa—Little Black Girl
Dolly, my dear . . .
A kind lady gave you to me
I'm grateful too . . . 'um, yes,
Cause you're pretty and sweet
And you're dressed up neat.
But I don't love you . . . I positively don't . . .
'Cause the man that made you
Gave you long flaxen hair.
And God made me . . . But look at my hair.
The man that made you, didn't put any feel
Inside your cold little breast.
He left the feel out
From your head to your heels,
But he gave you blue eyes, instead.
Now suppose you were me . . .
Oh . . . my doll-baby Rose . . .

And you knew how it felt
To be lonely and black
And I . . . just sat on a chair
And gave you . . . a cold stare . . .
Wouldn't you . . . give my head
A hard whack . . . Just like that!

Oh . . . oh . . . My dolly . . .
     My doll-baby Rose. . . .

Jim—A Weary Traveler
I been a weary traveler
But I ain't goin'er be no more . . .
I'm 'bout to take my chance at lovin'
'Cause my heart tells me to.
I been a weary traveler
But I ain't goin'er be no more.
When a man's dry, he wants licker
When he's weary, he takes his rest.
When he finds a sweet woman . . .
To please her . . . he tries his best.

Little Samson—Philosopher
Some white folks are anglers
     They throws the bait. . . .
Some white folks are fishes
     They swallows bait.
Us, black folks?
     Go 'long, don't bother me.
     We is bait.

*Respects.

► *The Crisis*, February 1930.

Wash Day

The rain has hung her washing out
The earth is cool and dry
Dirty faces are descried in silver pools
Of water as men go by.

➤ *Opportunity* April 1927.

Definition

Night is a velvet cloak
Wrapped 'round a gay Lothario;
Day is a flash-light
In the hand of a prude.

➤ *Opportunity,* November 1927.

Deepening Night

I know no skill of healing to outweigh
　　This sure, dark miracle of quietness
　　Which night's cool fingers, in their brief caress,
Lay over the red scar of strident day;
Touching to silence all the loud display
　　Of restless movement, like some sorceress
　　Holding a fragile thread against the press
Of circumstance, to make it castaway.

This starlit stillness, where the wearied find
Truce with all insistent, futile things;
Stripping pretense from each small strutting mind
To leave it poised for lifting ultimate wings,
Beggars remembered music—and no light
Outwits the shadows of this deepening night.

➤ *Small Wisdom,* "Elizabeth Stapleton Stokes," 1937.

The Colorist

God is an Indian—He loves gay color so . . .
Red, yellow, purple, oranges and blue
Are in the sky at sunset, at the sunrise, too.
God is Irish–He likes green color best.
All the trees and grasses in green garments oft-times dress.
God is Saxon, stern and cold.
For snow is white and ice is cold.
The downy clouds are white. And a
White moon peeks when lovers pledge their troth.
Cotton is white and snowy lambkin's fleece.

God is African—for night is robed in black.
The twinkling stars are black men's eyes,
The black clouds, tempests tell.
While little seeds of flowers birthed are
Tans and browns and black. . . .

► *The Crisis*, September 1925.

Antidote

I think, sometimes,
The only poets are the ones
Who don't write poems in the spring:
Those blessed souls
Who find earth very fair, without the tense desire
To do a thing about it;
Knowing
That their few weak words
Are poorly matched with nature at her best;
In quiet contemplation
Quite content to leave
Their little egos unexpressed.

► *Small Wisdom*, "Elizabeth Stapleton Stokes," 1937.

Public Notice

"Held for exchange"—a transient tenure
  Of sunlight, sifted through tangled green,
Fretting the pool with restless shadows,
  Darkening it where the gold had been.

And a turn of road, with cool leaves lacing
  Across and back; and a whippoorwill
Calling his mate when the dusk has fallen;
  And starlight over a wooded hill.

These I offer, with tacit promise
  The pact endure through eternity
For a windy sky, and a long white shore,
  And a wide, untenanted space of sea.

► *Small Wisdom,* "Elizabeth Stapleton Stokes," 1937.

Fragment

Clumsy fingers fumble
  The sober thread
In wistful stitches dreaming
  It gold, instead.

Weaving, unaccustomed,
  A quiet cloak,
Lest some radiance dazzle
  Trusting folk.

I shall wear it gaily,
  That no one guess
How ill it warms the cold of
  My loneliness.

Close-wrapped, to hide my stumbling
  Down the years,
I shall go, flaunting laughter—
  Blind with tears.

► *Small Wisdom,* "Elizabeth Stapleton Stokes," 1937.

Wisdom

She never dreamed that happiness would trace
Its April self so clearly in her face
For him to see; nor doubted she could leave
So small a heart upon so sheer a sleeve
Unmarked. Now, wise too late, she tries to wear
Her adoration with a careless air—
Lest, grown so sure, he find it very dull:
Being eternally impeccable.

► *Small Wisdom,* "Elizabeth Stapleton Stokes," 1937.

On Being Taken for Granted

This casually tendered bit of flame—
  Think you, it scores my heart?
Or brands with certain passion there
  Its very counterpart?

Such flickering scarlet! Knew you not
  Some fiercer, candent light
For firing an intensity
  Immaculate and white?

► *Small Wisdom,* "Elizabeth Stapleton Stokes," 1937.

And So You Want a Poem—

And so, you want a poem. Can it be you're still believing
    Such small words as I know to fling across an empty page
Will match the iridescent gleam that threads your own wild
    weaving?
    Nor lose their frail integrity in your rich heritage?

I improvise a pattern; to find that you remember
    Tracing it on canvas bright with hues I never knew;
Or flaunt some brave new wisdom—and you recognize the ember
    Of radiant philosophies, long since grown old to you.

Maybe—my words touched deftly—there will be your quickened
    spirit
    Light enough, and beautiful, to see their twilight through;
And borrowed luster, shining in some common phrase, endear it.
    Maybe, in your enchantment, I shall make a verse for you.

► *Small Wisdom,* "Elizabeth Stapleton Stokes," 1937.

Denial

These shining years which cover by some grace
Each wistful moment with a warm content,
Must still go lightly, lest irreverent
Or careless passing leave them commonplace.
We must seem lusterless, who know the trace
Of rapture in each smallest incident—
Must casually note each dear intent,
To bear its wonder with a quiet face.
Yet, by serene avowal of my heart
I shall be marked from common folk, who go
In dull and dusty ways. Because I know
This blinding beauty and can have no part

With loneliness or sorrow very long—
My silence wears the ecstasy of song.

► *Small Wisdom*, "Elizabeth Stapleton Stokes," 1937.

Of Growing Older

Such grudge as one may bear these mounting years
Stems from their alphabet of trivial fears,
Potent to stay the spirit's slow disdain
Of hesitant flesh and fetter it again.
Youth knew its reasoned terror of the wide
Unfurrowed way its dreams had need to ride,
Feigning a gallantry until the last
Outpost of immaturity was past.
But mellowed wisdom, having learned to bear
The whims of fortune, should have done with fear;
And all the apprehension of the keen
Rapid precision of a great machine;
Or doubt for surety of brave essay
In swift new venturing, which mark the way
Of middle age—be one with childishness
Long since outworn. This, then, the strict assess
Of growing older. Would some god devise
A simpler journey—or a dearer prize!

► *Small Wisdom*, "Elizabeth Stapleton Stokes," 1937.

The Dust of the Streets

Out of the dust of the earth men are made,
Even now our feet tread on
The minute particles of forms of unborn men,
Here in the streets,
And men will come

To tread upon our breasts
When they are stilled,
After aeons of time have sifted us
Into the dust of streets.

► *The Crisis*, July 1929.

Plea for Immortality

For all the green young reach for sky
    From stubborn-rooted hold,
These trees fulfill their span—to lie
    Anonymous in mould;
Matrix for seed—nor all they knew:
    Bronzed memories of light,
Nor wrack of storms' dark interview,
    Outstays their gathering night.

But I—whose characters retrace
    A timeless palimpsest—*
Translate in halting paraphrase
    Wisdom the years attest,
Wistful that new transparency
    Luster my transient trust . . .
Must I, too, forfeit breath to be
    Undocumented dust?

*Something from which a text has been partially or entirely erased to make room for another text.

► *Small Wisdom*, "Elizabeth Stapleton Stokes," 1937.

Coveted Epitaph

This—my spirit: disciplined
    To haven no whimpering sound
Of flaccid pity or loose-lipped plaint
    That its wounds went long unbound.

Fired like old Damascus steel,*
Patterned to scrupulous vein;
Tempered to bend—tip to hilt—
Bend—and spring back again.

*Damascus steel, also called watered steel, is hand-wrought and made in various Asian countries. It is made of a heterogeneous material, repeatedly folded over and welded, then finally etched to reveal the resulting grain. It is used most often for sword blades.

► *Small Wisdom,* "Elizabeth Stapleton Stokes," 1937.

Marion Grace Conover (?–?)

There is no biographical information about this poet, who published only a handful of poems in *Opportunity* and Boston's *The Saturday Evening Quill*. She was one of the founding members of the Saturday Evening Quill Club. Conover's are economical poems, well composed and representative of the period's emphasis on romantic love.

Voices

In the secret silences of my soul songs are sung
And vague thoughts awaken, yet they slip from me
Elusively . . . .

And the silver echo of a bell has rung
Calls, like turbulent waves at sea—
Incessantly . . . .

▶ *The Saturday Evening Quill,* June 1928; *Opportunity,* August 1928.

Fancy

A roving wind from the West am I
And I want adventure before I die.
There's a candle light
Flick'ring bright—
I rush into the golden ray
And lo! I kiss the flame away!

▶ *The Saturday Evening Quill,* June 1928.

Comment

Perhaps you have forgotten
That a lotus flower
Pure, fragile, white,
May blossom in foul places
Far from the sun's pale light.

▶ *The Saturday Evening Quill,* June 1928.

You

A bit of Heaven
A bit of Hell
Blended together
Exceedingly well. . . .

► *The Saturday Evening Quill,* June 1928.

Mae V. Cowdery (1909–1953)

Born in Philadelphia on January 10, 1909, Mae Virginia Cowdery was the only child of a social worker mother, who was an assistant director of the Bureau for Colored Children, and a postal worker/caterer father, Lemuel Cowdery. She attended the Philadelphia High School for Girls. While she was only a high school senior in 1927, she published three poems in *Black Opals,* a Philadelphia journal, and won first prize in a poetry contest run by *The Crisis* for "Longings." That same year, she won the Krigwa Prize for "Lamps." After graduation, Cowdery came to New York in 1927 to attend the Pratt Institute, although the school records show no evidence of her attendance until 1931. She frequented the cabarets of Harlem and Greenwich Village, where she lived. A photograph of her published by *The Crisis* in 1928 reveals a young woman of unusual beauty, style, and originality, with a bow tie, tailored jacket, and very short hair. Widely published in the late 1920s in *The Crisis,* Cowdery was one of the few women of the Harlem Renaissance to bring out a volume of her own work, *We Lift Our Voices and Other Poems* (1936), with a glowing foreword by William Stanley Braithwaite, who termed her "a fugitive poet." Cowdery's poetry was said to be inspired by Edna St. Vincent Millay, whom she may have known during her years in the Village, and much of it recalls the imagism of Angelina Weld Grimké and other Modernist poets of her day. Above all, Cowdery's poems are sensual, erotic, and openly lustful, with several written to female lovers. Although her poetry from the mid-thirties suggests Cowdery had a daughter, no mention is made of a marriage or children in the scanty biographical material about her. In spite of winning honors at an early age and receiving encouragement from Langston Hughes, Alain Locke, Benjamin Brawley, and others, Cowdery fell into obscurity after 1936. Jessie Fauset's brother, Arthur Huff Fauset, who knew her in Philadelphia, called her "a flame that burned out rapidly . . . a flash in the pan with great potential who just wouldn't settle down." Critic Richard Long, who met her in the early 1950s, observed, "She seemed a bright intelligence made bored and restless by her surroundings" (Vincent Jubilee, "Philadelphia's Afro-American Literary Circle and the Harlem Renaissance" [PhD diss., University of Pennsylvania, 1980], 67). Mae Cowdery took her own life in New York City at the age of forty-four in 1953.

Goal

My words shall drip
Like molten lava
From the towering volcano,
On the sleeping town
'Neath its summit.

My thoughts shall be
Hot ashes
Burning all in its path.

I shall not stop
Because critics sneer,
Nor stoop to fawning
At man's mere fancy.

I shall breathe
A clearer freer air
For I shall see the sun
Above the crowd.

I shall not blush
And make excuse
When a son of Adam,
Who calls himself
"God's Layman,"
Slashes with scorn
A thing born from
Truth's womb and nursed
By beauty. It will not
Matter who stoops
To cast the first stone.
Does not my spirit
Soar above these feeble
Minds? Thoughts born
From prejudice's womb
And nursed by tradition?

I will shatter the wall
Of darkness that rises
From gleaming day
And seeks to hide the sun.
I will turn this wall of
Darkness (that is night)
Into a thing of beauty.

I will take from the hearts
Of black men—
Prayers their lips
Are 'fraid to utter.
And turn their coarseness
Into a beauty of the jungle
Whence they came.

The lava from the black volcano
Shall be words, the ashes, thoughts
Of all men.

► *Black Opals,* spring 1927; *Anthology of Magazine Verse,* ed. William S. Braithwaite, 1927.

The Young Voices Cry

(To Alice Dunbar-Nelson)
Oh you who bore us in pain and joy
To whom God entrusted our souls—
Be not deaf to our pleading
Nor blind to our silent weeping!
Look not down on us in condescending anger—
Lest tired of futile tears and prayers,
We blaze a new path into depths
You cannot enter—And only from afar
Will you see our loveliness of life
And the simple beauty of truth
To which time has blinded and deafened you!

► *We Lift Our Voices,* Mae V. Cowdery, 1936.

Lamps

Bodies are lamps
And their life is the light.
Ivory, Gold, Bronze and Ebony—
Yet all are lamps
And their lives the lights.

Dwelling in the tabernacles
    Of the most high—are lamps.
Lighting the weary pilgrims' way
    As they travel the dreary night—are lamps.
Swinging aloft in great Cathedrals
    Beaming on rich and poor alike—are lamps.
Flickering fitfully in harlot dives
    Wanton as they that dwell therein—are lamps.
Ivory, Gold, Bronze and Ebony—
    Yet all are lamps
And their lives the lights.

Some flames rise high above the horizon
    And urge others to greater power.
Some burn steadfast thru the night
    To welcome the prodigal home.
Others flicker weakly, lacking oil to burn
    And slowly die unnoticed.
What matter how bright the flame
    How weak?
What matter how high it blazes
    How low?
A puff of wind will put it out.

You and I are lamps—Ebony lamps.
Our flame glows red and rages high within
But our ebon shroud becomes a shadow
And our light seems weak and low.
    Break that shadow
    And let the flame illumine heaven

Or blow wind . . . blow . . .
And let our feeble lights go out.

► *The Crisis*, December 1927.

Heritage

It is a blessed heritage
To wear pain,
A bright smile on our lips.
Our dark fathers gave us
The gift of shedding sorrow
In a song.

► *We Lift Our Voices*, Mae V. Cowdery, 1936.

If I Must Know

If I must know sorrow
To live
Then burden my soul
With the frustrated dreams
Of good women!

If I must know torture
To live
Then bind me with vows
To complacency!

If I must know love
To live
Then be quick . . . !
Give me back this elusive thing
The Gods call love . . . !

► *The Crisis*, July 1930.

2. Richard Bruce Nugent, *Opportunity,* August 1927

Insatiate

If my love were meat and bread
And sweet cool wine to drink,
They would not be enough,
For I must have a finer table spread
To sate my entity.

If her lips were rubies red,
Her eyes two sapphires blue,
Her fingers ten sticks of white jade,
Coral tipped . . . and her hair of purple hue
Hung down in a silken shawl . . .
They would not be enough
To fill the coffers of my need.

If her thoughts were arrows
Ever speeding true
Into the core of my mind,
And her voice round notes of melody
No nightingale or lark
Could ever hope to sing . . .
Not even these would be enough
To keep my constancy.

But if my love did whisper
Her song into another's ear
Or place the tip of one pink nail
Upon another's hand,
Then would I forever be
A willing prisoner . . .
Chained to her side by uncertainty!

► *We Lift Our Voices*, Mae V. Cowdery, 1936.

Lines to a Sophisticate

Never would I seek
To capture you with tempestuous ardor
Nor hold you at arm's length
In carnal anticipation . . .
But like a wine of rare vintage
I would savor and sip slowly
That I might know each separate scent
Of your elusive fragrance.

Never would I seek to capture all your beauty
And imprison it in the mouldy bottle of my lust;
Rather would I pour it into the chalice of my love
And let its bouquet escape to mingle with the air
That I might breathe again your perfume
Long after you are gone. . . .

► *We Lift Our Voices*, Mae V. Cowdery, 1936.

Some Hands Are Lovelier

Two trees breathe
The same sweet air,
And sun, and rain—

And whisper
To the moonless night
The same dim prayer
Of star-wrought wonder.

Two trees stand
Above a red, red road
Whose branches touch
And now withdraw . . . and meet again
In undreamed ecstasy.

Some lips are sweeter
To capture in mad beauty
And then release—
Some hands are lovelier
To clasp awhile—
And then, let go!

► *We Lift Our Voices,* Mae V. Cowdery, 1936.

Denial

Though your love claims me
With tender ardent hands,
And desire is a soft sensuous song
Laving with its liquid fire
This eager body that would surrender
In swift reply—

Though the cold relentless savant
That guards the inner recess
Where my soul meditates
As great dream bells chime
A wild sweet flowing music—
Would listen and yield
To this eager body's plea—

Your songs are sounds
That ring against my ear
In discordant harmony
With your inner spirit's singing—
That vibrant sea that flows between
A man and woman's soul,
Surging and breaking upon their hearts
In the clear sounds of unheard music.

► *We Lift Our Voices*, Mae V. Cowdery, 1936.

Farewell

No more
The feel of your hand
On my breast
Like the silver path
Of the moon
On dark heaving ocean.

No more
The rumpled softness
Of your hair
Like wind
In leafy shadowed trees.

No more
The lush sweetness
Of your lips
Like dew
On new-opened moon flowers.

No more
The drowsy murmurings
Of your voice
Like the faint twitter
Of birds before dawn.

No more
The poignant melody
Of hours spent
Between moonlight
And sunrise
Like the song
Of a crystal river
Going out to sea . . .

Only the awful sound
Of silence
In that hour
Before dawn
When the moon has waned,
The stars died,
And the sun is buried in mist.

► *The Crisis*, February 1929.

Having Had You

Having had you once
And lost you,
It is too much to ask
For you again.

Having heard your voice,
The words of other lovers
Are stones . . . falling into an empty well.

Having known your kiss,
The lips of other lovers
Are withered leaves . . . upon the wind.

Were you a God
I could build a shrine
And worship you.

Ah . . . if you were but the moon,
I could snare you
In the branches of a tree!

Were you anything
But what you are . . .
A dream come true
And now a dream again . . .
I might have you back!

But having had you once
And lost you,
It is too much
To want you back again . . . !

► *The Crisis*, August 1930.

Poem . . . for a Lover

I would give you
The blue-violet dreams
Of clouds . . . forgotten
And left to grow old
In the sky.

I would give you
The dew-drenched hope
Of flowers . . . forgotten
By a long dead lover
And left in a garden to die.

But you have no need
Of my meagre gifts
With your gay little songs
And lips . . . redder
Than bitter-sweet berries

Left on a leafless bush
By the frost. . . .

► *We Lift Our Voices,* Mae V. Cowdery, 1936.

Dusk

Like you
Letting down your
Purple-shadowed hair
To hide the rose and gold
Of your loveliness
And your eyes peeping thru
Like beacon lights
In the gathering darkness.

► *Ebony and Topaz,* ed. Charles S. Johnson, 1927.

Longings

To dance—
In the light of moon,
A platinum moon,
Poised like a slender dagger
On the velvet darkness of night.

To dream—
'Neath the bamboo trees
On the sable breast
Of earth—
And listen to the wind.

To croon—
Weird sweet melodies
Round the cabin door

With banjos clinking softly—
And from out the shadow
Hear the beat of tom-toms
Resonant through the years.

To plunge—
My brown body
In a golden pool,
And lazily float on the swell,
Watching the rising sun.

To stand—
On a purple mountain
Hidden from earth
By mists of dreams
And tears—

To talk—
With God.

▶ *The Crisis*, December 1927.

Want

I want to take down with my hands
The silver stars
That grow in heaven's dark blue meadows
And bury my face in them.

I want to wrap all around me
The silver shedding of the moon
To keep me warm.

I want to sell my soul
To the wind in a song
To keep me from crying in the night.

I want to wake and find
That I have slept the day away.
Only nights are kind now . . .
With the stars . . . moon . . . winds . . . and me. . . .

► *The Crisis*, September 1928.

Exultation

O day!
With sun glowing—
Gold
Pouring through
A scarlet rustling tree!

O night!
With stars burning—
Fire falling
Into a dark and whispering sea!

► *We Lift Our Voices*, Mae V. Cowdery, 1936.

Four Poems

After the Japanese
Night turned over
In her sleep
And a star fell
Into the sea.

Earth was a beautiful
Snow woman
Until the rain
Washed her face one day.

I am the rain
Throbbing futilely
On the cold roof
Of your heart.

The moon
Is a madonna
Cradling in the crescent curve
Of her breast
A newborn star.

Of Earth
A mountain
Is earth's mouth . . .
She thrusts her lovely
Sun-painted lips
Through the clouds
For heaven's kiss.

A hill is earth's soul . . .
She raises her
Verdant joyous prayer
Unto the gods
On dawn-tinged thrones.

A river
Is earth's grief . . .
Tears from the hidden wells
Of her soul . . .

O Earth . . . why do you weep?

Poplar Tree
Ofttimes I wish that I could be
Like yonder rustling poplar tree,

And with green arms hold to my breast
Secrets the twittering birds confessed,

To have the winds blow thru my hands
Unsung melodies of far-off lands.

To sink my feet deep into earth
Down to the river that gave me birth,

And thrust my face into heaven's blue
To watch what all the angels do.

Oh ofttimes I wish that I could be
Like yonder rustling poplar tree,

But for today I'm satisfied
To share spring's magic by your side.

God Is Kind
God
Is kind,
He lets us dream
Of untarnished silver . . .
Of skies that have never known
The pain of a storm . . .
Of the peace and contentment
In a robin's even' song.

We dream of love
Without its aftermath
Of loneliness . . .

God
Is kind,
He lets us dream
Of unattainable things!

► *We Lift Our Voices*, Mae V. Cowdery, 1936.

Interlude

I like this quiet place
Of lawns and trees well kept
And bright geometric gardens
Where droning bees hover and lift
On pollen-burdened wings . . .
Where even sunlight is genteel
And birds are shy and swiftly scarlet.

I love this quiet place
Of sane and placid beauty,
But soon I shall return
To be torn anew
At the bold thrust of skyscrapers
Against a murky sky
And the strident song
Of cars and people rushing by.

At times I shall remember
This quietude of lawns and trees
And shy birds swiftly scarlet . . .
This place I love but not enough
To linger overlong . . .

Life must go on . . . and with it
Interludes like this. . . .

► *We Lift Our Voices*, Mae V. Cowdery, 1936.

A Prayer

I saw a dark boy
      Trudging on the road
('Twas a dreary road
      Blacker than night).

Ofttimes he'd stumble
   And stagger 'neath his burden
But still he kept trudging
   Along that dreary road.

I heard a dark boy
   Singing as he passed;
Ofttimes he'd laugh
   But still a tear
Crept thru his song,
   As he kept trudging
Along that weary road.

I saw a long white mist roll down
   And cover all the earth
(There wasn't even a shadow
   To tell it was night).
And then there came an echo . . .
   . . . Footsteps of a dark boy
Still climbing on the way.

A song with its tear
   And then a prayer
From the lips of a dark boy
   Struggling thru the fog.
Ofttimes I'd hear

The lashing of a whip
   And then a voice would cry to heaven:
   "Lord! . . . Lord!
   Have mercy . . . mercy!"
And still that bleeding body
   Pushed onward thru the fog.
Songs . . . Tears . . . Blood . . . Prayer
   Throbbing thru the mist.

The mist rolled by
   And the sun shone fair,
Fair and golden
   On a dark boy . . . cold and still
High on a bare bleak tree
   His face upturned to heaven,
His soul upraised in song,
    "Peace . . . Peace
    Rest in the Lord."

Ofttimes in the twilight
   I can hear him still singing
As he walks in the heavens,
   A song without a tear,
A prayer without a plea. . . .

Lord, lift me up to the purple sky
   That lays its hand of stars
Tenderly on my bowed head
   As I kneel high on this barren hill.
My song holds naught but tears,
   My prayer is but a plea.
Lord take me to the clouds
   To sleep . . . to sleep.

► *The Crisis*, September 1928.

I Sit and Wait for Beauty

(. . . to . . . John Lovell . . .)
Long have I yearned and sought for beauty
And now it seems a futile race
To strive to look upon the marvel
Of so fair a face.

She is not here with the trees
That bend to wind in endless grace,
Nor has she come from a blue sea
In the frothing lace
That breaks upon the shore in white ecstasy.

She did not come on the piercing call
Of wild birds in flight,
Nor in young love did I find her—
Nor in the wordless wonder of the night,
Or with yon' star that holds my breath
Upon a silver spear. Thus I know her to be more than all
These things . . . Than life or death—

And even tho' I become a God
With all magic secrets at my command
She will ever hide her face
And elude my grasping hand.

► *Challenge,* May 1935.

The Wind Blows

The wind blows—
My soul is like a tree
Lifting its face to the sun,
Flinging wide its branches
To catch the falling rain,
To breathe into itself a fragrance
Of far-off fields of clover,
Of hidden vales of violets,—
The wind blows,—
It is spring!

The wind blows—
My soul is like sand,
Hot, burning sand

That drifts and drifts,
Caught by the wind,
Swirling, stinging, smarting,
Silver in the moonlight
Soft breath of lovers' feet,—
Lulled to sleep by the lap of waves,—
The wind blows,—
It is summer!

The wind blows—
My soul is still
In silent reverie,
Hearing sometimes a sigh
As the frost steals over the land,
Nipping everywhere.

Earth is dead.
The woods are bare.
The last leaf is gone,
Nipped by death's bitter frost.

My youth grown grey
Awaits the coming of
The new year.
The wind blows,—
It is winter!

► *Opportunity,* October 1927; *Anthology of Magazine Verse,* ed. William S. Braithwaite, 1928.

I Look at Death

I looked into the face of death
And found it kind.
I looked at life that offered me
No more than before . . . a spilled cup
Of wine . . . My heart's own blood.

Death was friendly
And showed me pale gardens
And trees with silver fruit
And slender jade grass
With pearls for dew . . .

I am in a quandary—
There is something so strange
. . . So still . . . about this loveliness
Of death. . . .

► *We Lift Our Voices*, Mae V. Cowdery, 1936.

Clarissa Scott Delany (1901–1927)
(a k a Clarissa Scott)

C larissa Scott was born in 1901 and raised in Tuskegee, Alabama, where her father was secretary to Booker T. Washington at Tuskegee Institute and where she attended school. In 1916, she enrolled at the Bradford Academy for three years and then at Wellesley College, from which she graduated Phi Beta Kappa in 1923. After graduation, she taught at Dunbar High School in Washington, D.C., for three years, until late 1926, when she married Hubert Delany, a lawyer who became a New York City domestic-relations court judge. In New York, Clarissa Scott Delany gathered material on neglected black children for the Women's City Club and the National Urban League. A talented singer and pianist, Delany was also a fine writer, and by the mid-1920s she had begun publishing book reviews in *Opportunity.* In 1926, she published three poems after winning a prize in 1925 for her first poem "Solace." All four were included in Countée Cullen's *Caroling Dusk* the following year. Tragically, these would be the only poems Delany published, for she died suddenly in 1927 of kidney failure brought on by a prolonged bacterial infection at the young age of twenty-six.

The Mask

So detached and cool she is,
No motion e'er betrays
The secret life within her soul,
The anguish of her days.

She seems to look upon the world
With cold ironic eyes,
To spurn emotion's fevered sway,
To scoff at tears and sighs.

But once a woman with a child
Passed by her on the street,
And once she heard from casual lips
A man's name, bitter-sweet.

Such baffled yearning in her eyes,
Such pain upon her face!
I turned aside until the mask
Was slipped once more in place.

► *Palms*, October 1926; *Caroling Dusk*, ed. Countée Cullen, 1927; *Readings from Negro Authors*, ed. Cromwell et al., 1931.

Interim

The night was made for rest and sleep,
For winds that softly sigh;
It was not made for grief and tears;
So then why do I cry?

The wind that blows through leafy trees
Is soft and warm and sweet;
For me the night is a gracious cloak
To hide my soul's defeat.

Just one dark hour of shaken depths,
Of bitter black despair—
Another day will find me brave,
And not afraid to dare.

► *Palms*, October 1926; *Caroling Dusk*, ed. Countée Cullen, 1927.

Joy

Joy shakes me like the wind that lifts a sail,
Like the roistering wind
That laughs through stalwart pines.
It floods me like the sun
On rain-drenched trees
That flash with silver and green.

I abandon myself to joy—
I laugh—I sing.
Too long have I walked a desolate way,
Too long stumbled down a maze
Bewildered.

► *Opportunity*, October 1926; *Caroling Dusk*, ed. Countée Cullen, 1927.

Solace

My window opens out into the trees
And in that small space
Of branches and of sky
I see the seasons pass,
Behold the tender green
Give way to darker heavier leaves.
The glory of the autumn comes
When steeped in mellow sunlight.
The fragile, golden leaves
Against a clear blue sky

Linger in the magic of the afternoon
And then reluctantly break off
And filter down to pave
A street with gold.
Then bare, gray branches
Lift themselves against the
Cold December sky
Sometimes weaving a web
Across the rose and dusk of late sunset
Sometimes against a frail new moon
And one bright star riding
A sky of that dark, living blue
Which comes before the heaviness
Of night descends, or the stars
Have powdered the heavens.
Winds beat against these trees;
The cold, but gentle rain of spring
Touches them lightly.
The summer torrents strive
To lash them into a fury
And seek to break them—
But they stand.
My life is fevered
And a restlessness at times
An agony—again a vague
And baffling discontent—
Possesses me.
I am thankful for my bit of sky
And trees, and for the shifting
Pageant of the seasons.
Such beauty lays upon the heart
A quiet.
Such eternal change and permanence
Take meaning from all turmoil
And leave serenity
Which knows no pain.

► *Opportunity,* June 1925, November 1927; *Caroling Dusk,* ed. Countée Cullen, 1927; *Readings from Negro Authors,* ed. Cromwell et al., 1931.

Blanche Taylor Dickinson (1896 – ?)

Very little is known about this interesting poet whose publications span only a short period of time (1927–1929). Although her name suggests she was married, we, in fact, do not know her marital status, nor do we know her birth name. Dickinson reported that she was living in Sewickley, Pennsylvania, in 1926 and that she was born on a Kentucky farm. She attended Simmons University and then taught in Kentucky for several years, most likely when she was publishing her poetry in *Opportunity, The Crisis, American Poet, Ebony and Topaz,* and *Caroling Dusk.* Dickinson would only have been in her early thirties when she published in these prestigious venues, but after 1929, she disappears from view. A photo of Dickinson appears in the July 1927 issue of *Opportunity,* when she was awarded the Buckner Prize for "A Sonnet and a Rondeau" (published in September), in which she appears to be a beautiful young woman with sensitive eyes, well-coiffed hair, and a sensual mouth. Despite her attractiveness, Dickinson's poetry addresses the pain of women who feel invisible and ugly within the confines of white standards of beauty. The poetic personae she adopts are isolated and imprisoned but capable of passionate encounters. As with her imagined speakers, Blanche Taylor Dickinson bared her vulnerability as a black woman in a hostile environment—and, like them, she succumbed to silence.

Four Walls

Four great walls have hemmed me in.
Four strong, high walls:
Right and wrong,
Shall and shan't.

The mighty pillars tremble when
My conscience palls
And sings its song—
I can, I can't.

If for a moment Samson's strength
Were given me I'd shove
Them away from where I stand;
Free, I know I'd love
To ramble soul and all,
And never dread to strike a wall.

Again, I wonder would that be
Such a happy state for me . . .
The going, being, doing, sham—
And never knowing where I am.
I might not love freedom at all;
My tired wings might crave a wall—
Four walls to rise and pen me in
This conscious world with guarded men.

► *Caroling Dusk*, ed. Countée Cullen, 1927.

The Walls of Jericho

Jericho is on the inside
Of the things the world likes best;
"We want in," the dark ones cried,
"We will love it as the rest."

"Let me learn," the dark ones say.
They have learned that Faith must do
More than meditate and pray
That a boulder may fall through
Making one large man size entrance
Into wondrous Jericho.
They have learned: forget the distance,
Count no steps, nor stop to blow.

Jericho still has her high wall,
Futile barrier of Power. . . .
Echoed with the dark ones' footfall
Marching around her every hour;
Knowledge strapped down like a knapsack
Not cumbersome, and money
Not too much to strain the back. . . .
Dark ones seeking milk and honey.

Over in the city staring
Up at us along the wall
Are the fat ones, trembling, swearing
There is no room there for us all!
But there've been too many rounds
Made to give the trip up here.
Shout for joy . . . hear how it sounds . . .
The very walls echo with cheer!

► *Caroling Dusk,* ed. Countée Cullen, 1927.

A Dark Actress—Somewhere

They watched her glide across the stage,
Each one poised with breath a tip-toe,
Felt his soul strings link with hers,
Loosed his heart and let it go
To her brown and tapering fingers,

Crushing it into a ball,
Throwing it with accuracy,
Smiling as she saw it fall.
Bending willow-like to music,
As a bird in willows, singing
Of a love that's so much fancy
From a dream marsh ever springing.
"Art," the critic said next day,
And people flocked to see her play,
Laid their fair hearts at her feet—
But never saw her on the street.

► *The Crisis*, September 1928.

Fortitude

She screamed but no one heard her . . .
Her body was a silencer.
She cried and never moved a tear . . .
Her heart was broken, tears dripped there.

Silent, she seemed content to lay
Her soul awhile in fresh red clay.
Proud to stand, all grief defying . . .
We knew that she was all but dying.

► *Opportunity*, February 1927.

Revelation

1.
She walked along the crowded street
Forgetting all but that she
Was walking as the other girls
And dressed as carefully.

The windows of the stores were frilled
To lure femininity,
To empty little pocketbooks
And assuage queen vanity.

And so my walker liked a dress
Of silver and of gold,
Draped on a bisque mannequin
So blond and slim and bold.

She took the precious metal home
And waved her soft black hair;
Powder, rouge and lipstick made
Her very neat and fair.

She slipped the dress on carefully,
Her vain dream fell away. . . .
The mirror showed a brownskin girl
She hadn't seen all day!

2.
"You have classic features,
Something like Cleopatra.
Eyes like whirlpools
And as dangerous. . . .
Weeping willow eyelashes
Shade the mighty depth
Of your eyes. Your lips
Are danger signals
Which a fool like me
Will not regard . . .
But go dashing past them
To gain a kiss . . . or Death."
That is what he said to me.
I filled with a sweet and vain regret
That Beauty, the stranger, and I had met.
His praise was heat to drink me dry.
So I found a stream, and with a sigh

I stooped to drink . . . ah, to see
The cruel water reflecting me!
Dark-eyed, thick-lipped, harsh, short hair . . .
But Lucifer saw himself, too, fair.

▶ *Caroling Dusk*, ed. Countée Cullen, 1927.

A Sonnet and a Rondeau (Poem)

Ah, I know what happiness is . . .
It is a timid little fawn
Creeping softly up to me
For one caress, then gone
Before I'm through with it . . .
Away, like dark from dawn!
Well I know what happiness is . . .
It is the break of day that wears
A shining dew decked diadem . . .
An aftermath of tears.
Fawn and dawn, emblems of joy . . .
I've played with them for years,
And always they will slip away
Into the brush of another day.

Is a human heart more brazen
Than a floating, fleecy cloud
Pillowed on the sky's blue bosom,
Kissing stars before the crowd
Of earthly prudes, all forgiving
Secret passions of the earth
Seducing a virgin seed
Till a bastard tree makes birth?
Is a human heart immodest
More so than a cold steel pin
Staggering to a magnet, waiting,
Or a hen bird fluttering when
Her mate calls? Can it be sin?

Consummation of God's mating.
Proof that love needs no berating.

► *Opportunity,* September 1927; *Caroling Dusk,* ed. Countée Cullen, 1927.

Things Said When He Was Gone

My branch of thoughts is frail tonight
As one lone wind-whipped weed.
Little I care if a raindrop laughs
Or cries; I cannot heed

Such trifles now as a twinkling star,
Or catch a night-bird's tune.
My whole life is you, tonight,
And you, a cool distant moon.

With a few soft words to nurture my heart
And brighter beams following love's cool shower
Who knows but this frail wind-whipped weed
Might bear you a gorgeous flower!

► *Ebony and Topaz,* ed. Charles S. Johnson, 1927.

To an Icicle

Chilled into a serenity
As rigid as your pose
You linger trustingly,
But a gutter waits for you.
Your elegance does not secure
You favors with the sun.
He is not one to pity fr0ileness.
He thinks all cheeks should burn
And feel how tears can run.

► *Caroling Dusk,* ed. Countée Cullen, 1927.

Fires

The bonfire flutters to an ash
And quietens to attest
Its love of earth. A dash
Of mourning across the breast
That gulps its cool tears down
Sighing, "Now we'll have rest!"

And one by one mauve cinders fall
Past my grate's hot bars,
Settle, willingly give all
With not a curse for fate who mars
Continuity of love,
Die smiling to the one above.

But lately I have stood beside
A long grey box, grey as the ash
Of any fire I've seen subside,
And I have marked the long red dash
Of clay. Tears streamed, I turned,
Wondering why the fire still burned.

► *Opportunity,* June 1929.

That Hill

It crawled away from 'neath my feet,
And left me standing there;
A little at a time, went up
An atmospheric stair.

I couldn't go for watching it,
To see where it would stop;
A tree sprang out and waved to me
When it had reached the top.

The tree kept nodding friendly like,
Beckoning me to follow;
And I went crawling up and up,
Like it did from the hollow.

Then I saw why the thing would go
A-soaring from the dell—
'Twas nearing Heaven every bound,
And fleeing fast from Hell!

► *Caroling Dusk*, ed. Countée Cullen, 1927; *The Crisis*, January 1927.

To One Who Thinks of Suicide

Sometimes it seems that only cowards live
With weighted hearts each day;
It seems braver far to take life up and go
A solitary way.
It seems a self reliant soul should know
When life has palled,
And win applause for surprising God . . .
Going in . . . uncalled.

Poor vain, gallant hero,
If the journey ended at the grave
I would cheer you . . . or perhaps I'd go
And wear the laurels of the brave.

But no! I rather choose to stay
And trust the clouds to blow away.
I'll blink and peer through fog of doubt
Until God blows my candle out. . . .

► *The Crisis*, January 1928.

Alice Dunbar-Nelson (1875–1935)

Born Alice Ruth Moore in New Orleans on July 19, 1875, Dunbar-Nelson was the younger daughter of Patricia Moore, a Louisiana-born freed slave who became a seamstress, and Joseph Moore, a seaman. After graduating from Straight College (Dillard University) in 1892, she left a teaching career in New Orleans in 1898 to teach in Brooklyn, New York, when she met Paul Laurence Dunbar, the most famous African American poet of the day. They married in March 1898 and soon moved to Washington, D.C., where he worked at the Library of Congress and she again taught school. Theirs was a stormy marriage, and in 1902 they separated. Dunbar-Nelson began living with her mother, divorced sister, and nieces in Wilmington, Delaware, where she taught English and chaired the English Department at a public high school. When Paul Laurence Dunbar died from tuberculosis in 1906 at age thirty-four, she took it upon herself to help preserve his legacy and to use his fame as a springboard for social causes. A social activist as well as writer, Dunbar-Nelson accepted speaking engagements throughout the remainder of her life in this capacity. Beginning in 1904, she pursued her education by enrolling at Cornell University, the Pennsylvania School of Industrial Art, and the University of Pennsylvania. To these activities she added organizational work with the National Association of Colored Women and political activism of all sorts. She also wrote short stories, having published the ground-breaking collections *Violets and Other Tales* (1895) and *The Goodness of St. Rocque and Other Stories* (1899); newspaper columns; poetry; two plays; a diary; and two scholarly books. Dunbar-Nelson's personal life was equally full. In 1910 she married a fellow teacher at Howard High School, Arthur Callis, a man twelve years her junior, whom she had met at Cornell when he was an undergraduate. The relationship was short-lived, and very little is known about the long-concealed marriage. Her third marriage, to Robert Nelson, a journalist with whom she published *The Wilmington Advocate* from 1920 to 1922, lasted from 1916 until her death. Dunbar-Nelson was also involved in passionate relationships with women throughout the 1920s and before, which she recorded in her diary, since edited by Gloria Hull and published in 1984 (*Give Us Each Day*). Her primary literary contribution to the Harlem Renaissance was poetry, particularly "Violets," her signature piece, and her poems were published in the era's major journals and anthologies. A tireless campaigner for social justice, a feminist, a talented creative writer and scholar, and a hardworking teacher and editor, Alice Dunbar-Nelson left an inspiring legacy of accomplishments. She died of heart disease in 1935 at age sixty in Philadelphia.

I Sit and Sew

I sit and sew—a useless task it seems,
My hands grown tired, my head weighed down with dreams—
The panoply of war, the martial tread of men,*
Grim-faced, stern-eyed, gazing beyond the ken
Of lesser souls, whose eyes have not seen Death
Nor learned to hold their lives but as a breath—
But—I must sit and sew.

I sit and sew—my heart aches with desire—
That pageant terrible, that fiercely pouring fire
On wasted fields, and writhing grotesque things
Once men. My soul in pity flings
Appealing cries, yearning only to go
There in that holocaust of hell, those fields of woe—
But—I must sit and sew.—

The little useless seam, the idle patch;
Why dream I here beneath my homely thatch,
When there they lie in sodden mud and rain,
Pitifully calling me, the quick ones and the slain?
You need me, Christ! It is no roseate dream
That beckons me—this pretty futile seam,
It stifles me—God, must I sit and sew?

*A reference to World War I (1914–1918).

► *Negro Poets and Their Poems,* ed. Robert T. Kerlin, 1923; *Caroling Dusk,* ed. Countée Cullen, 1927.

The Lights at Carney's Point

O white little lights at Carney's Point,
    You shine so clear o'er the Delaware;
When the moon rides high in the silver sky,
    Then you gleam, white gems on the Delaware.
Diamond circlet on a full white throat,
    You laugh your rays on a questing boat;

Is it peace you dream in your flashing gleam,
  O'er the quiet flow of the Delaware?

And the lights grew dim at the water's brim,
  For the smoke of the mills shredded slow between;*
And the smoke was red, as is new bloodshed,
  And the lights went lurid 'neath the livid screen.

O red little lights at Carney's Point,
  You glower so grim o'er the Delaware;
When the moon hides low sombrous clouds below,
  Then you glow like coals o'er the Delaware.
Blood red rubies on a throat of fire,
  You flash through the dusk of a funeral pyre;
Are there hearth fires red whom you fear and dread
  O'er the turgid flow of the Delaware?

And the lights gleamed gold o'er the river cold,
  For the murk of the furnace shed a copper veil;
And the veil was grim at the great cloud's brim,
  And the lights went molten, now hot, now pale.

O gold little lights at Carney's Point,
  You gleam so proud o'er the Delaware;
When the moon grows wan in the eastering dawn,
  Then you sparkle gold points o'er the Delaware.
Aureate filigree on a Croesus brow,
  You hasten the dawn on a gray ship's prow.
Light you streams of gold in the grim ship's hold
  O'er the sullen flow of the Delaware?

And the lights went gray in the ash of day,
  For a quiet Aurora brought a halcyon balm;
And the sun laughed high in the infinite sky,
  And the lights were forgot in the sweet, sane calm.

*This poem describes the DuPont gunpowder mills, which operated on the Delaware River during World War I. A peace activist who lectured on behalf of the American Interracial Peace Committee from 1928 until the mid-1930s, Dunbar-Nelson here juxtaposes images of nature's serenity and beauty with the mill's infernal production.

► *Negro Poets and Their Poems*, ed. Robert T. Kerlin, 1923.

April Is on the Way

April is on the way!
I saw the scarlet flash of a blackbird's wing
As he sang in the cold, brown February trees;
And children said that they caught a glimpse
Of the sky on a bird's wing from the far South.
(Dear God, was that a stark figure outstretched in the bare branches
Etched brown against the amethyst sky?)

April is on the way!
The ice crashed in the brown mud-pool under my tread,
The warning earth clutched my bloody feet with great fecund fingers.
I saw a boy rolling a hoop up the road,
His little bare hands were red with cold,
But his brown hair blew backward in the southwest wind.
(Dear God! He screamed when he saw my awful woe-spent eyes.)

April is on the way!
I met a woman in the lane;
Her burden was heavy as it is always, but today her step was light,
And a smile drenched the tired look away from her eyes.
(Dear God, she had dreams of vengeance for her slain mate,
Perhaps the west wind has blown the mist of hate from her heart,
The dead man was cruel to her, you know that, God.)

April is on the way!
My feet spurn the ground now, instead of dragging on the bitter
      road.
I laugh in my throat as I see the grass greening beside the patches
      of snow.
(Dear God, those were wild fears. Can there be hate
When the southwest wind is blowing?)

April is on the way!
The crisp brown hedges stir with the bustle of bird wings.
There is business of building, and songs from brown thrush throats
As the bird-carpenters make homes against Valentine's Day.
(Dear God, could they build me a shelter in the hedge
From the icy winds that will come with the dark?)

April is on the way!
I sped through the town this morning.
The florist shops have put yellow flowers in the windows,
Daffodils and tulips and primroses, pale yellow flowers,
Like the tips of her fingers when she waved me that frightened
    farewell.
And the women in the market have stuck pussy willows
In long necked bottles on their stands.
(Willow trees are kind, dear God. They will not bear a body on
    their limbs.)

April is on the way!
The soul within me cried that all the husk of indifference to sorrow
Was but the crust of ice with which winter disguises life;
It will melt, and reality will burgeon forth like the crocuses in
    the glen.
(Dear God! Those thoughts were from long ago, when we read
    poetry
After the day's toil, and got religion together at the revival meeting.)

April is on the way!
The infinite miracle of unfolding life in the brown February fields.
(Dear God, the hounds are baying!)
Murder and wasted love, lust and weariness, deceit and
    vainglory—
What are they but the spent breath of the runner?
(God, you know he laid hairy red hands on the golden loveliness
Of her little daffodil body.)
Hate may destroy me, but from my brown limbs will bloom
The golden buds with which we once spelled love.
(Dear God! How their light eyes glow into black pin points of hate!)

April is on the way!
Wars are made in April, and they sing at Easter time of the
    Resurrection.
Therefore I laugh in their faces.
(Dear God, give her strength to join me before her golden petals
    are fouled in the slime!)
April is on the way!

► *Ebony and Topaz,* ed. Charles S. Johnson, 1927; *Readings from Negro Authors,* ed. Otelia Crom-
well et al., 1931.

The Proletariat Speaks

I love beautiful things:
Great trees, bending green winged branches to a velvet lawn,
Fountains sparkling in white marble basins,
Cool fragrance of lilacs and roses and honeysuckle
Or exotic blooms, filling the air with heart-contracting odors;
Spacious rooms, cool and gracious with statues and books,
Carven seats and tapestries, and old masters,
Whose patina shows the wealth of centuries.

And so I work
In a dusty office, whose grimed windows
Look out on an alley of unbelievable squalor,
Where mangy cats, in their degradation, spurn
Swarming bits of meat and bread;
Where odors, vile and breath-taking, rise in fetid waves
Filling my nostrils, scorching my humid, bitter cheeks.

I love beautiful things:
Carven tables laid with lily-hued linen
And fragile china and sparkling iridescent glass;
Pale silver, etched with heraldries,
Where tender bits of regal dainties tempt,
And soft-stepped service anticipates the unspoken wish.

And so I eat
In the food-laden air of a greasy kitchen,
At an oil-clothed table:
Plate piled high with food that turns my head away,
Lest a squeamish stomach reject too soon
The lumpy gobs it never needed.
Or in a smoky cafeteria, balancing a slippery tray
To a table crowded with elbows
Which lately the busboy wiped with a grimy rag.

I love beautiful things:
Soft linen sheets and silken coverlet,
Sweet cool of chamber opened wide to fragrant breeze;
Rose-shaded lamps and golden atomizers,
Spraying Parisian fragrance over my relaxed limbs,
Fresh from a white marble bath, and sweet cool spray.

And so I sleep
In a hot hall-room whose half-opened window,
Unscreened, refuses to budge another inch,
Admits no air, only insects, and hot choking gasps
That make me writhe, nun-like, in sackcloth sheets and lumps of
    straw.
And then I rise
To fight my way to a dubious tub,
Whose tiny, tepid stream threatens to make me late;
And hurrying out, dab my unrefreshed face
With bits of toiletry from the ten cent store.

► *The Crisis,* November 1929.

Of Old St. Augustine

Of old, St. Augustine* wrote wise
And curious lore, within his book.
I read and meditate, my eyes
See words of comforting, I look   .

Again, and thrill with radiant hope.
"They did not sin, those white-souled nuns of old,
Pent up in leaguered city, and despoiled
By knights, who battered at the peaceful fold,
And stole their bodies. Yet the fiends were foiled,
They could not harm their stainless, cloistered souls."

O wise St. Augustine, you give
Great joy to those whose earthly form
Is held in thrall. The soul may live
Unscathed—untouched—far from alarm,
True to its cloistered dream—unspoiled.

*St. Augustine was a Roman monk who came to England to convert the English to Christianity and became archbishop of Canterbury in AD 601.

▶ *Opportunity,* July 1925.

Violets (Sonnet)

I had not thought of violets of late,
The wild, shy kind that spring beneath your feet
In wistful April days, when lovers mate
And wander through the fields in raptures sweet.
And thought of violets meant florists' shops,
And bows and pins, and perfumed papers fine;
And garish lights, and mincing little fops,
And cabarets and songs, and deadening wine.
So far from sweet real things my thoughts had strayed,
I had forgot wide fields, and clear brown streams;
The perfect loveliness that God has made—
Wild violets shy and heaven-mounting dreams.
And now—unwittingly, you've made me dream
Of violets, and my soul's forgotten gleam.

▶ *The Crisis,* August 1919; *The Book of American Negro Poetry,* ed. James Weldon Johnson, 1922, 1931; *Negro Poets and Their Poems,* ed. Robert T. Kerlin, 1923; *Caroling Dusk,* ed. Countée Cullen, 1927; *Readings from Negro Authors,* ed. Otelia Cromwell et al., 1931.

Music

Music! Lilting, soft and languorous,
Crashing, splendid, thunderous,
Blare of trumpets, sob of violins,
Tinkle of lutes and mandolins;
Poetry of harps, rattle of castanets,
Heart-break of cellos, wood-winds in tender frets;
Orchestra, symphony, bird-song, flute;
Coronach* of contraltos, shrill strings a-mute.
Sakuntala† sobbing in the forest drear,
Melisande‡ moaning on crescendic fear;
Splendor and tumult of the organs roll,
Heraldic trumpets pierce the inner soul;
Symphonic syncopation that Dvorak wove,§
Valkyric crashes when the Norse gods strove;‖
Salome's triumph in grunt obscene,#
Tschaikowsky peering through forest green;
Verdi's high treble of saccharine sound,**
Celeste! Miserere! Lost lovers found.
Music! With you, touching my finger-tips!
Music! With you, soul on your parted lips!
Music—is you!

*A coronach is a song or lamentation for the dead.

†*Sakuntala* is a Sanskrit drama written in the sixth century.

‡A variation on the musical term *melisma*, an ornamental phrase of several notes sung to one sylla-
ble of musical text.

§Czech composer Antonin Dvorak.

‖Valkyries were beautiful attendants to the Norse god Odin in Teutonic myth.

#*Salome* is a late nineteenth-century play written by Oscar Wilde after a biblical story in which the
title character dances erotically for King Herod in order to get him to behead John the Baptist.

**Peter Ilyich Tschaikovsky was a nineteenth-century Russian composer; Guiseppe Verdi was a nine-
teenth-century Italian opera composer.

► *Opportunity*, July 1925.

You! Inez!

Orange gleams athwart a crimson soul
Lambent flames; purple passion lurks
In your dusk eyes.
Red mouth; flower soft,
Your soul leaps up and flashes
Star-like, white, flame-hot.
Curving arms, encircling a world of love.
You! Stirring the depths of passionate desire!

► Unpublished, February 1921.

Snow in October

Today I saw a thing of arresting poignant beauty:
A strong young tree, brave in its Autumn finery
Of scarlet and burnt umber and flame yellow,
Bending beneath a weight of early snow,
Which sheathed the north side of its slender trunk,
And spread a heavy white chilly afghan
Over its crested leaves.

Yet they thrust through, defiant, glowing,
Claiming the right to live another fortnight,
Clamoring that Indian Summer had not come,
Crying "Cheat! Cheat!" because Winter had stretched
Long chilly fingers into the brown, streaming hair
Of fleeing October.

The film of snow shrouded the proud redness of the tree,
As premature grief grays the strong head
Of a virile, red-haired man.

► *Caroling Dusk,* ed. Countée Cullen, 1927.

Jessie Redmon Fauset (1882–1961)

essie Fauset was one of the most important figures of the Harlem Renaissance; she was a brilliant woman who excelled at literary production and scholarly study. She is best known for her central role as literary editor of *The Crisis* from 1919 to 1926, when she discovered and helped promote Langston Hughes, Countée Cullen, Claude McKay, and other major writers of the period. So important was Fauset that she has become known as midwife of the Harlem Renaissance. In addition to her prowess as an editor, however, Fauset was herself a major writer in the movement she helped create. She was one of its most prolific writers, producing four novels: *There Is Confusion* (1924), *Plum Bun* (1928), *The Chinaberry Tree* (1931), and *Comedy, American Style* (1933). Fauset also wrote numerous short stories and essays and published many poems in *The Crisis;* the latter were also widely anthologized. Along with her friend Georgia Douglas Johnson, Jessie Fauset was a well-known woman poet of her day, and together they mentored other women writers in their homes, which they opened as literary salons. Born in New Jersey in 1882 to an African Methodist Episcopal minister, the Reverend Redmon Fauset, and his wife, Anna Seamon, Fauset was the seventh child in her family. Her mother died when Fauset was a child, and her father remarried. Raised in Philadelphia and educated at prestigious schools, she was the only black person in her classes in high school and college. She was discouraged from entering Bryn Mawr by its officials after her admission there because of her race, and she was the only African American student at Cornell University, from which she graduated Phi Beta Kappa in 1905, the first black woman to join that society and to graduate from Cornell. Denied a teaching post in Philadelphia, again because of racism, Fauset taught French and Latin at the M Street High School in Washington, D.C., from 1906 until 1918. In 1918 she enrolled in an MA program in French at the University of Pennsylvania, from which she graduated in 1919. She moved to New York and joined *The Crisis* staff that same year under the editorship of W.E.B. Du Bois. Along with her editing duties there, Fauset was the first literary editor (and later managing editor) of *The Brownies' Book,* a children's monthly begun by Du Bois. She attended the Second Pan-African Congress in 1921 and later studied at the Sorbonne, where she polished her French, which appears frequently in her poetry. When she quit *The Crisis* after a dispute with Du Bois in 1926, Fauset resumed teaching French in 1927 at De Witt Clinton High School in New York City, where she remained until 1944.

In 1929, when she was forty-five, she married Herbert Harris, an insurance broker. The couple moved to Montclair, New Jersey, in 1939. After Harris's death in 1958, she lived with her stepbrother in Philadelphia until her death in 1961. Jessie Fauset's contributions to the Harlem Renaissance cannot be overstated, although her creative writing is only now beginning to garner the critical respect it deserves.

The CRISIS

APRIL

15 cents

3. Laura Wheeler, "The Veil of Spring," cover of *The Crisis*, April 1924

Oriflamme

I can remember when I was a little, young girl, how my old mammy
would sit out of doors in the evenings and look up at the stars and
groan, and I would say, "Mammy, what makes you groan so?" And
she would say, "I am groaning to think of my poor children; they do
not know where I be and I don't know where they be. I look up at
the stars and they look up at the stars!"

—Sojourner Truth*

I think I see her sitting, bowed and black,
    Stricken and seared with slavery's mortal scars,
Reft of her children, lonely, anguished, yet
    Still looking at the stars.

Symbolic mother, we thy myriad sons,
    Pounding our stubborn hearts on Freedom's bars,
Clutching our birthright, fight with faces set,
    Still visioning the stars!

*Sojourner Truth was a former slave, abolitionist, and feminist active in the nineteenth century.
She was known for her eloquence, courage, and political activism.

► *The Crisis,* January 1920; *The Book of American Negro Poetry,* ed. James Weldon Johnson, 1922,
1931; *Negro Poets and Their Poems,* ed. Robert T. Kerlin, 1923.

Here's April!

I.

This town that yesterday was dark and mean,
    And dank and raw with Winter's freezing air,
Is Light itself today, and verdant Sheen
    Gold-tinted, and besprent with perfume rare;
Translated overnight to a parterre
    That makes me dream of Araby and Spain,
And all the healing places of the Earth,
    Where one lays by his woe, his bitter pain,—
    For peace and mirth.

II.
Old Winter that stayed by us black and drear,
 And laid his blighting seal on everything,
Is vanished.—Is it true he once was here?
 Mark how the ash-trees bud, and children sing,
And birds set up a faint, shy jargoning;
 And healing balm pours out from bole and leaf.
For Spring—sweet April's here in tree and grass!
 Oh foolish heart to fret so with your grief!
 This too shall pass!

► *The Crisis,* April 1924.

Stars in Alabama

In Alabama
Stars hang down so low,
So low, they purge the soul
With their infinity.
Beneath their holy glance
Essential good
Rises to mingle with them
In that skiey sea.

At noon
Within the sandy cotton-field
Beyond the clay, red road
Bordered with green,
A Negro lad and lass
Cling hand in hand,
And passion, hot-eyed, hot-lipped,
Lurks unseen.

But in the evening
When the skies lean down,
He's but a wistful boy,
A saintly maiden she,

For Alabama stars
Hang down so low,
So low, they purge the soul
With their infinity.

► *The Crisis,* January 1928.

Dilworth Road Revisited

The little road to Dilworth Town
    Still laughs and loiters by the brook,
And lovers love it in the Spring
    And haunt each blossomy nook.

Sad years ago my love and I
    Strolled all its sunny length one day,
To Dilworth's ivied church,—and then
    Sighing, we turned away.

Ah, Dilworth Road, can you still laugh
    When on another road's expanse,—
"The Ladies' Road," they call it,—lies
    My lover,—dead for France!*

*The reference is to a dead American soldier who fought with the U.S. Army on the side of France in World War I.

► *The Crisis,* August 1922.

Touché

Dear, when we sit in that high, placid room,
"Loving" and "doving" as all lovers do,
Laughing and leaning so close in the gloom,—

What is the change that creeps sharp over you?
Just as you raise your fine hand to my hair,
Bringing that glance of mixed wonder and rue?

"Black hair," you murmur, "so lustrous and rare,
Beautiful too, like a raven's smooth wing;
Surely no gold locks were ever more fair."

Why do you say every night that same thing?
Turning your mind to some old constant theme,
Half meditating and half murmuring?

Tell me, that girl of your young manhood's dream,
Her you loved first in that dim long ago—
Had *she* blue eyes? Did *her* hair goldly gleam?

Does *she* come back to you softly and slow,
Stepping wraith-wise from the depths of the past?
Quickened and fired by the warmth of our glow?

There, I've divined it! My wit holds you fast.
Nay, no excuses; 'tis little I care.
I knew a lad in my own girlhood's past,—
Blue eyes he had and such waving gold hair!

▶ *Caroling Dusk,* ed. Countée Cullen, 1927.

Words! Words!

How did it happen that we quarreled?
We two who loved each other so!
Only the moment before we were one,
Using the language that lovers know.
And then of a sudden a word, a phrase
That struck at the heart like a poniard's blow.*
And you went berserk, and I saw red,
And love lay between us, bleeding and dead!
Dead! When we'd loved each other so!

How *could* it happen that we quarreled!
Think of the things we used to say!

"What does it matter, dear, what you do?
Love such as ours has to last for aye!"
—"Try me! I long to endure your test!"
—"Love, we shall always love, come what may!"
What are the words the apostle saith?
"In the power of the tongue are Life and Death!"
Think of the things we used to say!

*A dagger.

► *Palms*, October 1926; *Caroling Dusk*, ed. Countée Cullen, 1927.

La Vie C'est la Vie

On summer afternoons I sit
Quiescent by you in the park,
And idly watch the sunbeams gild
And tint the ash-trees' bark.

Or else I watch the squirrels frisk
And chaffer in the grassy lane;
And all the while I mark your voice
Breaking with love and pain.

I know a woman who would give
Her chance of heaven to take my place;
To see the love-light in your eyes,
The love-glow on your face!

And there's a man whose lightest word
Can set my chilly blood afire;
Fulfillment of his least behest
Defines my life's desire.

But he will none of me. Nor I
Of you. Nor you of her. 'Tis said
The world is full of jests like these.—
I wish that I were dead.

La vie c'est la vie means "that's life."

► *The Crisis,* July 1922; *The Book of American Negro Poetry,* ed. James Weldon Johnson, 1922, 1931; *Caroling Dusk,* ed. Countée Cullen, 1927; *An Anthology of American Negro Literature,* ed. Victor Calverton, 1929.

Dead Fires

If this is peace, this dead and leaden thing,
Then better far the hateful fret, the sting,
Better the wound forever seeking balm
Than this gray calm!

Is this pain's surcease? Better far the ache,
The long-drawn dreary day, the night's white wake;
Better the choking sigh, the sobbing breath
Than passion's death!

► *The Book of American Negro Poetry,* ed. James Weldon Johnson, 1922, 1931; *Palms,* October 1926.

Rencontre

My heart, which beat so passionless,
  Leaped high last night when I saw you.
Within me surged the grief of years
  And whelmed me with its endless rue.
My heart which slept so still, so spent,
  Awoke last night—to break anew.

Rencontre means "encounter."

► *The Crisis,* January 1924; *Caroling Dusk,* ed. Countée Cullen, 1927.

The Return

I that had found the way so smooth
  With gilly-flowers that beck and nod,

Now find that same road wild and steep
　　With need for compass and for rod,
And yet with feet that bleed, I pant
　　On blindly—stumbling back to God!

► *The Crisis*, January 1919; *Palms*, October 1926; *Caroling Dusk*, ed. Countée Cullen, 1927.

Fragment

The breath of life imbued those few dim days!
Yet all we had was this,—
A flashing smile, a touch of hands, and once
A fleeting kiss.

Blank futile death inheres these years between!
Still, naught have you and I
But frozen tears, and stifled words, and once
A sharp caught cry!

► *Caroling Dusk*, ed. Countée Cullen, 1927.

Douce Souvenance

Again, as always, when the shadows fall,
　　In that sweet space between the dark and day,
I leave the present and its fretful claims
　　And seek the dim past where my memories stay.
I dream an old, forgotten, far-off dream,
　　And think old thoughts and live old scenes anew,
Till suddenly I reach the heart of Spring—
　　The Spring that brought me you!
I see again a little woody lane,
　　The moonlight rifting golden through the trees;
I hear the plaintive chirp of drowsy bird
　　Lulled dreamward by a tender, vagrant breeze;

I hold your hand, I look into your eyes,
   I touch your lips,—oh, peerless, matchless dower!
Oh, Memory thwarting Time and Space and Death!
   Oh, Little Perfect Hour!

Douce souvenance means "sweet remembrance."

► *The Crisis*, May 1920.

Oblivion

I hope when I am dead that I shall lie
   In some deserted grave—I cannot tell you why,
But I should like to sleep in some neglected spot
   Unknown to everyone, by everyone forgot.

There lying I should taste with my dead breath
   The utter lack of life, the fullest sense of death;
And I should never hear the note of jealousy or hate,
   The tribute paid by passers-by to tombs of state.

To me would never penetrate the prayers and tears
   That futilely bring torture to dead and dying ears;
There I should lie annihilate and my dead heart would bless
   Oblivion—the shroud and envelope of happiness.

► *The Book of American Negro Poetry*, ed. James Weldon Johnson, 1922, 1931.

Sarah Collins Fernandis (1863–1951)

Born in Baltimore, Maryland, on March 8, 1863, Sarah Collins became a teacher after graduating from Hampton Institute in Virginia in 1882 and attending the New York School of Social Work. For twenty years and more, she taught in various schools in the South as well as in her birthplace of Baltimore. After marrying John A. Fernandis in 1902, she and her husband devoted themselves to improving poor black neighborhoods in Baltimore and East Greenwich, Rhode Island, where they lived among some of the most poverty-stricken families of the country. Fernandis was bolstered by a deeply felt religious faith that sustained her in these endeavors and which informed her poetry. Many of her poems were published from 1891 to 1936 in the *Southern Workman,* a publication of Hampton Institute, where she studied and then taught. Although well outside the mainstream of the Harlem Renaissance, Fernandis published two collections of poetry in 1925: *Vision* and *Poems.* The four poems reprinted here from *Poems* reflect the reactions of an older conservative black woman to the currents of modernism swirling around her in the urban areas she attempted to rehabilitate.

In Protest

So they've sought a new sensation for this modern jazzing craze
    In the ruthless syncopation of those sweet old plaintive lays
That the souls of their forefathers, 'neath affliction's heavy rod,
    Coined from bitterness of sorrow as they reached for touch
    with God;

When they stole "away to Jesus" at the end of life's hard day
    And in loneliness of spirit "couldn't hear nobody pray";
Or, with faith at last triumphant, sang of "freedom" that would
    come,
    Of "Sweet Chariot," low swinging, sent to bear their spirits
    home;
Or of God who could deliver as in times of sacred lore;
    Of the chill of death's "deep river," crossed to Canaan's blissful
    shore!

O ye unthinking heritors of this rare and sacred trust—
    Of a race's soul's outpouring—jazz in pleasure if you must;
But give rein to modern fancy for the rhythmic thrills you crave,
    Leave, O leave untouched, unsullied, those dear songs your
    fathers gave!

► *Poems,* Sarah Collins Fernandis, 1925.

Her Voice

She stood where the spotlight focused
    And the hushed, expectant throng
Felt the unstudied grace of her form and face
    As they waited for her song.

She sang, and the distilled sweetness
    Of each lilting, liquid note
Bore our hearts along with the quaint old song
    That flowed from her dusky throat.

But my fancy tricked me strangely:
   I closed my weary eyes
And the lights became the shadow and flame
   Of Southern twilight skies;

And my head once more was pillowed
   On a softly sheltering breast
And a sweet low voice made my heart rejoice
   As it lulled me to childhood's rest.

► *Poems,* Sarah Collins Fernandis, 1925.

Little Ideals

Home tasks, we complain, give us little ideals—
The cleaning and budgeting, cooking of meals—
So taxing they weary, so trivial they pall—
They hold us, we feel, from life's loftier call;

We reach and we rub till all polished and clean
A room's hidden corners not like to be seen.
(So in larger affairs we are apt to be true
And clean in the things we are called on to do.)

We stretch slender purse-strings till each debt is paid
And qualms of a scrupulous conscience allayed.
(And the Christ-standard reach for a man to his brother—
"Owe no man anything but to love one another.")

We cook frugal meals with the calories right
And keep bodies fit for stern labor's grim fight.
(Well seasoned with love they make souls true and strong
To win in the battle of right against wrong.)

Ah, little ideals, little chores in the home!
Our dreams lead us forth wider pathways to roam,

We fail, we succeed, gather wealth or grow poor
But the ideal divine came within that loved door!

► *Poems*, Sarah Collins Fernandis, 1925.

The Meeting

They called an outdoor meeting and all the country folk
From near and far were gathered—one from the city spoke.
From "firstly," reaching onward he lengthened his harangue,
His raucous voice the echoes sent back in answering clang.

But straying went my senses from the bombastic words,
Intrigued by murmuring tree-tops and minstrelsy of birds;
And rhythmic, noiseless motion of drifting clouds o'erhead
Till, ere they turned from wandering, the "lastly" had been said.

Silent beside my neighbors, I went my homeward way,
Hearing their loud discussions, having no words to say,
Only a nameless feeling, like worship or a prayer,
Too sacred for expression, too intimate to share.

► *Poems*, Sarah Collins Fernandis, 1925.

Sarah Lee Brown Fleming (1876–1963)

Born Sarah Lee Brown in Charleston, South Carolina, on January 10, 1876, this remarkable woman was raised in Brooklyn, New York, where she ultimately became the first black teacher in the Brooklyn school system despite her father's admonition that she set her sights on domestic work as the most viable occupation available to her. She would go on to overturn other barriers after marrying Richard Stedman Fleming in 1902, the first black dentist in the state of Connecticut, where they lived in New Haven. The couple had two children, a girl and a boy, early in their marriage, and Fleming would become the first black woman to be named Connecticut Mother of the Year, but she excelled at community activism while maintaining a robust creative life as a songwriter, playwright, poet, and novelist. Although her creative writing is flawed, Fleming was one of the few black women to publish a novel and a collection of poetry at a time when little was being produced by African Americans: *Hope's Highway* (1918), an antislavery novel, and *Clouds and Sunshine* (1920), a small collection of poems from which the following pieces are taken. Fleming led a remarkable life, and although her poetry never made it into journals of the Harlem Renaissance, she exemplifies many of the movement's tenets in her determination to combine political, intellectual, and creative work as a way to move the race forward. The two poems reprinted here are a throwback to the dialect poetry of Paul Laurence Dunbar, but they subtly probe musical and cultural aspects of the black vernacular that would be brought to a high art form by Zora Neale Hurston, Langston Hughes, and others.

Put Away That Ukelele and Bring Out the Old Banjo

I.
Don't you hear old Orpheus* calling to you, Alexander Poe?
He says just quit that ukelele and play on the old banjo,†
Those Honolulu jingles, like the dog, has had its day,
Go put the faithful banjo down, put the ukelele away.

Chorus:
Way down upon the,‡—I'm coming, yes, I hear that music, oh,
Put away that ukelele, man, and play on the old banjo.

II.
Put away that ukelele, bring me down the old banjo,
Sing again for me the tunes I love, Swanee River and Old Black Joe,
Then play for me those melodies my mother used to hum,
That between each syncopating note, the banjo went "Tum, tum."

Chorus:
Way down upon the,—I'm coming, yes, I hear that music, oh,
Put away that ukelele, man, and play on the old banjo.

*Orpheus is a poet and musician of Greek mythology.

†The ukelele was a popular instrument in the 1920s with white college students at Yale University
in New Haven, where Fleming lived, and elsewhere. It came to symbolize the jazz age, along with
hip flasks and raccoon coats. The banjo, in contrast, was an instrument of the rural South and was
associated with black men of musical talent.

‡"Way down upon the Swanee River, far far away" is a line from the popular song "Old Folks at
Home" by Stephen Foster.

► *Clouds and Sunshine,* Sarah Lee Brown Fleming, 1920.

Night Song (Negro Lullaby)

I.
Honey, take yo' res', on yo' Mammy's breas',
See dat light a-fadin' 'mong de pine trees in de wes'.
Yes, de day is gone, night is comin' on,

Darksome night mus' come to us before another dawn.

Chorus
Whippo-will is callin', callin' to his mate,
Mockin'-bird is callin' too,
Pine trees is a-sighin', babies is a-cryin',
As the darksome night is passin' through.
　Go to sleep, ma little honey, go to sleep,
　Shut yo' weary eyelids an' don' you weep,
　　Sleep and take yo' res',
　　On yo' Mammy's breas',
　Night can never harm you here.

II.
Honey, don' you see, dat it's got to be,
Day an' night, yes, day an' night, until yo' spirit's free,
Den you'll quit ma breas', fer to go an' res'
Wid Anodder, who can pro-tec' you from harm de bes'!

► *Clouds and Sunshine*, Sarah Lee Brown Fleming, 1920.

Alice E. Furlong (?–?)

There is no biographical information available on this poet. A founding member of the Saturday Evening Quill Club in Boston, a group of black writers, Alice E. Furlong published a substantial number of poems in the April 1929 issue of *The Saturday Evening Quill,* but nothing else by her appears in other journals or in anthologies. Her poetry describes a broken heart and suggests the poet felt she did not have long to live, but we have nothing on which to speculate as to what the origins of these themes might be.

The Sea's Warning

Dear, eager child, upon my shining shore,
With questing, outstretched hands,
Seek not the secret of the breaker's roar,
But stay you safe upon the sands.

► *The Saturday Evening Quill,* April 1929.

Destruction

I saw a gem of gleaming red,
With pulsing, shimmering sheen.
This shall be mine, I proudly said,
Who wears this, is a queen.
With avid hand I clasped it tight,
Guarding it as I felt I must.
But, when I held it to the light,
Desire had crushed my gem to dust!

► *The Saturday Evening Quill,* April 1929.

Possession

A perfect crimson rose unfolds for me;
My starving heart with ecstacy is torn;
Eager, I reach to pluck it from Life's tree—
My bleeding fingers grasp a piercing thorn.

► *The Saturday Evening Quill,* April 1929.

Suicide

Poor, eager heart, so willing all to give!
Soon shall you know

How short a time such ardent love can live
And all bestow.

► *The Saturday Evening Quill,* April 1929.

Unfulfillment

A thrill, a softly spoken word, a kiss;
A perfect, golden hour of Love's own bliss;
An anguished moan, a broken cry of pain;
And weary years of yearning—just for this!

► *The Saturday Evening Quill,* April 1929.

When Love Is Laid Away

That sudden, short, sharp stab of bitter pain,
When love is laid away forevermore!
Ah, who can say he'll never feel pain
When Love is laid away forevermore?
Whose love sleeps quietest through sun and rain,
Through whose sad door shall Love come nevermore—
Will he dare say he'll never feel again
When Love is laid away forevermore?

► *The Saturday Evening Quill,* April 1929.

Laurel Leaves

Emblem that one heart has reached the ending
Of Life's journey, perilous and steep.
Symbol that a victor lies here, spending
These last hours in deep, majestic sleep.

How can this be called a badge of sorrow?
Who will weep, when burdens are laid down?
Rather say, "A king goes forth tomorrow
Who has proved his right to wear the crown."

► *The Saturday Evening Quill,* April 1929.

Riches and Poverty

Some have, but they may never hold, alas.
Which would you be?
Someone who a resounding title has,
Without security?
Or would you rather go your way alone,
In happiness;
And, having nothing you may call your own,
Still all possess?

► *The Saturday Evening Quill,* April 1929.

Awaiting

I shall be gone, my Love, before you find me,
So long, so long the day till dreams come true;
But I shall leave a blazoned trail behind me,
Clearly defined, to point the way for you.
And when the earthly things that now enthrall you
Unbind their clinging tendrils, one by one,
Then from some far off, lonely peak I'll call you
So you may climb to rest—when strife is done.

► *The Saturday Evening Quill,* April 1929.

Edythe Mae Gordon (1896 – ?)

Born Edith Chapman in 1896 in Washington, D.C., it appears that Gordon was raised by her grandmother, mother, and maternal aunt, who lived together and whose last name was Bicks. Nothing is known about her father. She attended the M Street School in D.C. (later Dunbar High School), when Jessie Fauset taught French there, and graduated in 1916, the same year she married Eugene Gordon, a student at Howard University who graduated in 1917. By 1919, the Gordons were living in Boston, where Eugene became a journalist and worked for the *Boston Post* from 1919 to 1940. Edythe continued her education by enrolling in 1926 at Boston University, where she attended classes as an undergraduate until 1934, when she earned a BS in religious education and social services. She earned her master's degree there in the School of Social Services in 1935, having completed her thesis, "The Status of the Negro Woman in the United States from 1619 to 1865." Gordon's husband, who by the 1930s had joined the Communist Party, was president of the Saturday Evening Quill Club of Boston, a group of African American writers that included Helene Johnson and Dorothy West, and he was the editor of its magazine, *The Saturday Evening Quill*, from 1928 to 1930. Edythe published short stories and poetry in this magazine and later published two poems in a 1938 anthology, *Negro Voices*, edited by Beatrice Murphy. The Gordons separated in 1932 and divorced some time around 1942. At this point, Edythe Mae Gordon disappears from the historical record despite the research efforts of her biographer Lorraine Elena Roses, who has reprinted Gordon's work. Gordon's short stories are dark portraits of unhappy marriages in urban black environments and foreshadow the urban realism of fiction writer Ann Petry in the 1940s. Her poetry, however, is typical of the lyrical nature poetry of other women from the Harlem Renaissance. Its poignancy lies in the sensuality and optimism of the speakers, whose obvious love for the object of their affection contrasts markedly with the Gordons' impending separation and divorce just a few years after this poetry was published.

April Night

The moon illuminates the April sky
With a white, crystalline, filtering light.
A shrill, piercing wind whistles high
Above the rustling pines, in flight,
And the cool, dripping rain gleams,
Splashing the desolate night with dreams.

► *The Saturday Evening Quill,* June 1930.

Let Your Rays

Let your rays
Beam upon me,
O sun!
Illuminate my soul.
Whirl your waves of heat
Against my breast,
And melt my frozen heart.

► *The Saturday Evening Quill,* June 1930.

Worship

A bird carolling
Among the trees—
And dewdrops glittering
On a rod—
A sunbeam quivering
In the breeze—
Rosebuds opening their
Beauty to God.

► *The Saturday Evening Quill,* June 1930.

Young Love

Let my hair hang
Upon my shoulders.
Weave a wreath of jasmine
Into its strands.
Kiss each blossom, and promise
You'll love me always.
Then I'll bind my hair
Tight about my head
To hold your love secure.

► *The Saturday Evening Quill*, April 1929.

Tribute

Your graceful bronze limbs
Are like palm leaves
Moving rhythmically
In the wind.

You'd wear your nudity
With charming candor:
The artificial and false
You abhor.

Your body is beautiful
And strong,
Your sensibilities
Fragile,
Your nature artistic.
My dormant soul is stimulated
By your smile.

► *The Saturday Evening Quill*, April 1929.

Elysium

Beloved, tonight
You and I walk hand in hand,
Over hard, barren ground
In the cool, nebulous darkness.
The dusty, trodden road
Rambles along, dingy and grey
From rains and rotting leaves.
The trees murmur in the breeze
Like the sound of distant violins.
Let us return,
You and I,
To the land of dreams
That once was yours and mine.
Let us return
And quench our thirst
At wells of old forgotten memories.

► *The Saturday Evening Quill*, June 1930.

I Understand

I did not understand:
I only knew
That ere he turned to go
His eyes strayed to the Madonna,
There on my chamber wall.
She smiled on the Infant Jesus
Cradled in her arms.
Sorrow wells in this breast
No child has e'er caressed.
From my window, I see
Naked trees, stripped of their leaves.
Now he is gone,
I understand.

► *The Saturday Evening Quill*, April 1929.

Buried Deep

When I am cold and buried deep away,
And have no zest to live or to return,
Come to my grave and flower-strew the clay,
And dance and sing, but never weep or mourn.

► *Negro Voices,* ed. Beatrice M. Murphy, 1938.

Angelina Weld Grimké (1880–1958)

Angelina Weld Grimké was born in Boston on February 27, 1880, the only child of an emancipated slave and Harvard Law School graduate, Archibald Henry Grimké, and a white woman, Sarah Stanley. Archibald, who became a lawyer, activist, and diplomat, was the son of Henry Grimké, himself the son of a South Carolina slaveholder, and Nancy Weston, a slave on the Grimké plantation. Henry's sisters were the famous abolitionists Sarah Moore Grimké and Angelina Grimké Weld, after whom Angelina was named. When her parents separated in 1883, Grimké lived with her mother for four years and then returned to her father, a U.S. consul and attorney, to whom she was devoted until his death in 1930. Grimké was educated at elite schools where she was frequently the only African American student; she attended the Fairmount School in Boston, the Carleton Academy in Minnesota, the Cushing Academy in Massachusetts, and the Boston Normal School of Gymnastics. After her graduation there in 1902, she taught high school in Washington, D.C., at the Armstrong Manual Training School and, in 1916, at the Dunbar High School, where she stayed until her retirement in 1933. Despite the absence of her mother (who died in 1898, when Grimké was eighteen), Grimké's creative writing frequently centered on motherhood and contained loving mother figures. Grimké herself, however, vowed early on, when she was only twenty-three, not to marry or have children. This decision appears to have resulted from Grimké's determination not to bring black children into such a racist society as the early twentieth-century United States. As well, she suffered at a young age from an unhappy love affair, perhaps with a woman, that ended with Grimké in despair. It is known that she formed a close romantic attachment to African American actress and playwright Mary Burrill in the mid-1890s when they were schoolmates, but it is not clear that Burrill was the person with whom she was involved. Grimké's biographer, Gloria Hull, relates that her unpublished poetry contains many explicitly lesbian allusions but that she was without an intimate relationship beyond girlhood. Grimké's fame rests on a slender, though distinguished, selection of poems written in the 1920s and published in *Opportunity* and every major anthology of her day. Countée Cullen's *Caroling Dusk* (1927) included more of Grimké's poems than those of any other female poet in the collection. Her poetry is lyrical, imagistic, passionate, delicate, and frequently woman-centered; Grimké is known for her meditations on nature and her love poetry to women. She is also known for her anti-lynching play,

Rachel (1916), which was credited by Alain Locke as the first successful drama written by an African American and interpreted by African American actors. Grimké's fiction also centered on lynching. These writings grew out of Grimké's political activism, which began in 1899, when she was only nineteen, and continued through her support of the Dyer Anti-Lynching Bill of 1922. She wrote a novella, *Jettisoned*, which was praised by *Opportunity* editor Charles S. Johnson when he read it in 1925, but she could find no publisher. She also assembled a collection of poems at this time entitled *Dusk Dreams*, but it, too, failed to materialize. Although encouraged by Georgia Douglas Johnson, who also lived in Washington, D.C., Grimké could not sustain her writing career beyond the 1920s. After a railway accident in 1911 that severely injured her back, she struggled with her health, finally retiring from teaching in 1933, largely as a result of poor health and having nursed her father through a long illness of his own. Shortly after his death in 1930, she moved permanently to New York City, where she lived reclusively but in relative financial comfort until her death nearly thirty years later in 1958.

Laura Wheeler, cover of *The Crisis*, April 1926

At April

Toss your gay heads, brown girl trees;
Toss your gay lovely heads;
Shake your downy russet curls
All about your brown faces;
Stretch your brown slim bodies;
Stretch your brown slim arms;
Stretch your brown slim toes.
Who knows better than we,
With the dark, dark bodies,
What it means
When April comes a-laughing and a-weeping
Once again
At our hearts?

► *Opportunity,* March 1925.

The Black Finger

I have just seen a most beautiful thing:
Slim and still,
Against a gold, gold sky,
A straight, black cypress
Sensitive
Exquisite
A black finger
Pointing upwards.
Why, beautiful still finger, are you black?
And why are you pointing upwards?

► *Opportunity,* November 1923, April 1927; *The New Negro,* ed. Alain Locke, 1925.

A Winter Twilight

A silence slipping around like death,
Yet chased by a whisper, a sigh, a breath;
One group of trees, lean, naked and cold,
Inking their crests 'gainst a sky green-gold;
One path that knows where the cornflowers were;
Lonely, apart, unyielding, one fir;
And over it softly leaning down,
One star that I loved ere the fields went brown.

▶ *Negro Poets and Their Poems*, ed. Robert T. Kerlin, 1923; *Caroling Dusk*, ed. Countée Cullen, 1927.

Tenebris

There is a tree, by day,
That, at night,
Has a shadow,
A hand huge and black,
With fingers long and black.
   All through the dark,
Against the white man's house,
   In the little wind,
The black hand plucks and plucks
   At the bricks.
The bricks are the color of blood and very small.
   Is it a black hand,
   Or is it a shadow?

Tenebris means "darkness."

▶ *Caroling Dusk*, ed. Countée Cullen, 1927.

At the Spring Dawn

I watched the dawn come,
   Watched the spring dawn come.

And the red sun shouldered his way up
   Through the grey, through the blue,
Through the lilac mists.
The quiet of it! The goodness of it!
   And one bird awoke, sang, whirred,
A blur of moving black against the sun,
   Sang again—afar off.
And I stretched my arms to the redness of the sun,
   Stretched to my fingertips,
      And I laughed.
Ah! It is good to be alive, good to love,
   At the dawn,
      At the spring dawn.

► *Negro Poets and Their Poems*, ed. Robert T. Kerlin, 1923.

Little Grey Dreams

Little grey dreams,
I sit at the ocean's edge,
   At the grey ocean's edge,
   With you in my lap.

I launch you, one by one,
   And one by one,
      Little grey dreams,
Under the grey, grey clouds,
Out on the grey, grey sea,
You go sailing away,
From my empty lap,
      Little grey dreams.

      Sailing! sailing!
Into the black,
At the horizon's edge.

► *Opportunity*, January 1924.

Dawn

Grey trees, grey skies, and not a star;
    Grey mist, grey hush;
And then, frail, exquisite, afar,
    A hermit-thrush.

► *Negro Poets and Their Poems,* ed. Robert T. Kerlin, 1923; *Readings from Negro Authors,* ed. Otelia Cromwell et al., 1931.

Dusk

Twin stars through my purpling pane,
    The shriveling husk
Of a yellowing moon on the wane—
    And the dusk.

► *Opportunity,* April 1924; *Caroling Dusk,* ed. Countée Cullen, 1927.

For the Candle Light

The sky was blue, so blue, that day,
    And each daisy white, so white;
Oh! I knew that no more could rains fall gray,
    And night again be night.

I *knew!* I *knew!* Well, if night is night,
    And the gray skies grayly cry,
I have in a book, for the candle light,
    A daisy, dead and dry.

► *Opportunity,* September 1925; *Caroling Dusk,* ed. Countée Cullen, 1927; *Anthology of American Negro Literature,* ed. V. F. Calverton, 1929.

A Mona Lisa

1.

I should like to creep
Through the long brown grasses
   That are your lashes;
I should like to poise
   On the very brink
Of the leaf-brown pools
   That are your shadowed eyes;
I should like to cleave
   Without sound,
Their glimmering waters,
   Their unrippled waters;
I should like to sink down
   And down
      And down . . .
         And deeply drown.

2.

Would I be more than a bubble breaking?
   Or an ever-widening circle
   Ceasing at the marge?
Would my white bones
   Be the only white bones
Wavering back and forth, back and forth
   In their depths?

Mona Lisa is a famous portrait by da Vinci of a young woman with an enigmatic smile.

► *Caroling Dusk,* ed. Countée Cullen, 1927.

El Beso

Twilight—and you,
Quiet—the stars;
Snare of the shine of your teeth,
Your provocative laughter,
The gloom of your hair;

Lure of you, eye and lip;
Yearning, yearning,
Languor, surrender;
   Your mouth,
And madness, madness,
Tremulous, breathless, flaming,
The space of a sigh;
Then awakening—remembrance,
Pain, regret—your sobbing;
And again, quiet—the stars,
Twilight—and you.

El beso means "the kiss."
► *Negro Poets and Their Poems,* ed. Robert T. Kerlin, 1923.

I Weep

—I weep—
Not as the young do, noisily,
Not as the aged, rustily,
   But quietly.
Drop by drop, the great tears
Splash upon my hands,
And save you saw them shine,
   You would not know
      I wept.

► *Opportunity,* July 1924; *Caroling Dusk,* ed. Countée Cullen, 1927.

The Want of You

A hint of gold where the moon will be;
Through the flocking clouds just a star or two;
Leaf sounds, soft and wet and hushed;
And oh! the crying want of you.

► *Negro Poets and Their Poems,* ed. Robert T. Kerlin, 1923.

The Eyes of My Regret

Always at dusk, the same tearless experience,
The same dragging of feet up the same well-worn path
To the same well-worn rock;
The same crimson or gold dropping away of the sun,
The same tints—rose, saffron, violet, lavender, grey,
Meeting, mingling, mixing mistily;
Before me the same blue-black cedar rising jaggedly to a point;
Over it, the same slow unlidding of twin stars,
Two eyes unfathomable, soul-searing,
Watching, watching—watching me;
The same two eyes that draw me forth, against my will dusk after
    dusk;
The same two eyes that keep me sitting late into the night, chin on
    knees,
Keep me there lonely, rigid, tearless, numbly miserable,
    —The eyes of my Regret.

► *Caroling Dusk,* ed. Countée Cullen, 1927.

To Keep the Memory of Charlotte Forten Grimké

Still are there wonders of the dark and day;
The muted shrilling of shy things at night,
So small beneath the stars and moon;
The peace, dream-frail, but perfect while the light
Lies softly on the leaves at noon.
These are, and these will be
Until eternity;
But she who loved them well has gone away.

Each dawn, while yet the east is veil'd grey,
The birds about her window wake and sing;
And far away, each day, some lark
I know is singing where the grasses swing;
Some robin calls and calls at dark.
These are, and these will be

Until eternity;
But she who loved them well has gone away.

The wild flowers that she loved down green ways stray;
Her roses lift their wistful buds at dawn,
But not for eyes that loved them best;
Only her little pansies are all gone,
Some lying softly on her breast.
And flowers will bud and be
Until eternity;
But she who loved them well has gone away.

Where has she gone? And who is there to say?
But this we know: her gentle spirit moves
And is where beauty never wanes,
Perchance by other streams, 'mid other groves;
And to us here, ah! she remains
A lovely memory
Until eternity;
She came, she loved, and then she went away.

Charlotte Forten Grimké was an African American poet, diarist, journalist, teacher, and activist of the nineteenth century. She married a Princeton theologian, Rev. Francis Grimké, brother of Angelina Weld Grimké's father. The Grimké brothers had a white father and a slave mother.

► *Negro Poets and Their Poems*, ed. Robert T. Kerlin, 1923; *The Crisis*, November 1931.

When the Green Lies over the Earth

When the green lies over the earth, my dear,
A mantle of witching grace,
When the smile and the tear of the young child year
Dimple across its face,
And then flee, when the wind all day is sweet
With the breath of growing things,
When the wooing bird lights on restless feet
And chirrups and trills and sings
    To his lady-love
    In the green above,

Then oh! my dear, when the youth's in the year,
Yours is the face that I long to have near,
   Yours is the face, my dear.

But the green is hiding your curls, my dear,
Your curls so shining and sweet;
And the gold-hearted daisies this many a year
Have bloomed and bloomed at your feet,
And the little birds just above your head
With their voices hushed, my dear,
For you have sung and have prayed and have pled
   This many, many a year.

   And the blossoms fall,
   On the garden wall,
And drift like snow on the green below.
   But the sharp thorn grows
   On the budding rose,
And my heart no more leaps at the sunset glow.
For oh! my dear, when the youth's in the year,
Yours is the face that I long to have near,
Yours is the face, my dear.

► *Caroling Dusk,* ed. Countée Cullen, 1927.

Greenness

Tell me is there anything lovelier,
Anything more quieting
Than the green of little blades of grass
And the green of little leaves?

Is not each leaf a cool green hand,
Is not each blade of grass a mothering green finger,
Hushing the heart that beats and beats and beats?

► *Caroling Dusk,* ed. Countée Cullen, 1927.

Grass Fingers

Touch me, touch me,
Little cool grass fingers,
Elusive, delicate grass fingers.
With your shy brushings,
Touch my face—
My naked arms—
My thighs—
My feet.
Is there nothing that is kind?
You need not fear me.
Soon I shall be too far beneath you
For you to reach me, even,
With your tiny, timorous toes.

► *Caroling Dusk,* ed. Countée Cullen, 1927; *Readings from Negro Authors,* ed. Otelia Cromwell et al., 1931.

Death

When the lights blur out for thee and me,
    And the black comes in with a sweep,
I wonder—will it mean life again,
    Or sleep?

► *Opportunity,* March 1925.

Under the Days

The days fall upon me;
One by one, they fall,
Like leaves . . .
They are black;
They are gray;
They are white;

They are shot through with gold and fire.
They fall,
They fall
Ceaselessly.
They cover me;
They crush;
They smother.
Who will ever find me
Under the days?

► Unpublished.

Gladys May Casely Hayford (1904–1950)
(a k a Aquah Laluah)

Frequently publishing under the name Aquah Laluah, Gladys May Casely Hayford was an African woman born on May 11, 1904, to West African parents in Axim, the Gold Coast (Ghana). Her mother, Adelaide Smith Casely Hayford, was a well-known educator who visited the United States, participated in social welfare and peace activities, and founded the Girls' Vocational and Industrial School in Freetown, Sierra Leone. Her father was a prominent Gold Coast lawyer and leader in the Pan-African movement; indeed, Marcus Garvey, founder of the United Negro Improvement Association and a proponent of the Back to Africa Movement, was initially inspired by J. E. Casely Hayford's *Ethiopia Unbound* (1912). Gladys was their only child. She was educated in England and Wales, attending college at Colwyn Bay when she was only fifteen. Frail in health and born slightly lame in one leg, Hayford was drawn to a rather bohemian existence during her youth. A talented musician, visual artist, and writer, she resisted her mother's wishes that Gladys take over the Freetown school where her mother taught African folklore and literature, although she returned there in 1926 to teach. Hayford secured an invitation from Columbia University to become a student after sending some of her poetry and received an invitation from Radcliffe as well upon the 1927 publication of three of her poems in *The Atlantic Monthly.* She never made it to either institution, however, since she lacked the money to complete her journey to New York and got waylaid by an African jazz troupe in Berlin when she fell in love with one of the musicians. Nevertheless, she continued to be published in the United States by *The Messenger, The Crisis,* and *Opportunity* and is included in Countée Cullen's *Caroling Dusk* (1927). Twice hospitalized for emotional breakdowns in Europe, Hayford returned to Africa for good in late 1932 at the behest of her mother, who wanted Gladys to resume teaching in her school. In 1936, she married a Freetown man from whom she became estranged and then left Freetown for Accra in 1939, giving birth to a son that year. Returning a few years later with her son to Freetown, Hayford opened a café for Allied soldiers during World War II, raised her son, took care of her mother, and finally died of cholera at the age of forty-six in 1950. Hayford's poetry is marked by pride in her African heritage and loving portraits of African babies and women. In an era when African American writers were trying to recapture their African roots, Hayford could write about Africa from experience, and she did so with vivid imagery, musicality, strong identification with women, and political sophistication.

A Poem

Let my song burst forth on a major note,
Check the minor lilt in the Negro's throat.

But how can the Negroes play their harps,
With sorrow for intervals, pain for sharps?

With a knife in the wound, and tears on the face
Should the song be quavered in treble or bass?

Though the tempo is kept by the shining stars,
Notation is writ on prejudice bars.

When God gives no sign when we reach the refrain
Have we the courage to start again?

With conflicting fugues and odd times to keep,
It's a wonder we laugh as well as weep.

It is a most marvelous wonderful thing
That in spite of all this, the Negro can sing.

► *The Messenger,* March 1926; *Opportunity,* July 1929.

Poem

Why do the bards of black folk
Sing grief brushed over with gladness?
Because God sculptured the soul of the race
In a moment of wistful sadness.

Why do the bards of black folk
Sing joy that follows all sorrow?
God's tool when He sculptured the soul of the race
Was "The Hope of the Unborn Morrow."

► *The Crisis,* October 1927.

Creation

A flush, a curve, a wind that blows—
A breath of life, 'twas called a rose.

A little sorrow and joy in part,
A breath of love, 'twas called a heart.

A heart, a rose, God took those two,
He wove them together; He called them you.

► *The Messenger,* May 1926.

Baby Cobina

Brown Baby Cobina with his large black velvet eyes,
His little coos of ecstasies, his gurgling of surprise,
With brass bells on his ankles, that laugh where'er he goes;
It's so rare for bells to tinkle, above brown dimpled toes.

Brown Baby Cobina is so precious that we fear
Something might come and steal him, when we grownups are
    not near;
So we tied bells on his ankles, and kissed on them this charm—
"Bell, guard our Baby Cobina from all devils and all harm."

► *Caroling Dusk,* ed. Countée Cullen, 1927.

Lullaby

Close your sleepy eyes, or the pale moonlight will steal you,
Else in the mystic silence, the moon will turn you white.
Then you won't see the sunshine, nor smell the open roses,
Nor love your Mammy anymore, whose skin is dark as night.
You will only love the shadows, and the foam upon the billows,
The shadow of the vulture's wings, the call of mystery.
The hooting of the night owl, and the howling of the jackal,

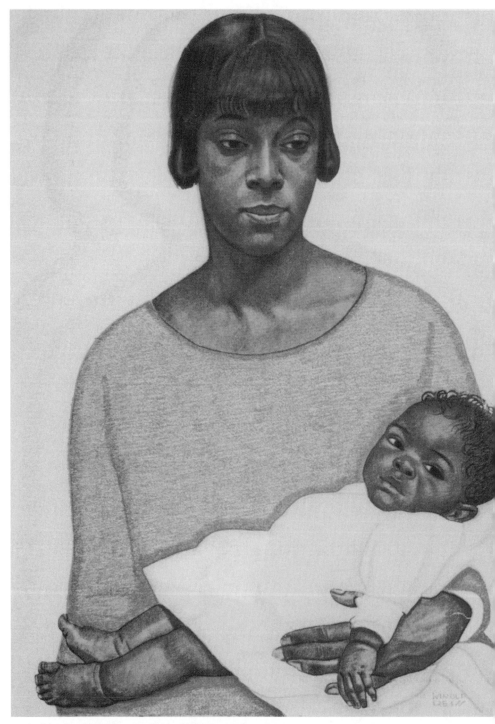

5. Winold Reiss, "The Brown Madonna," *The New Negro*, 1925

The sighing of the evil winds, the call of mystery.
Wherever moonlight stretches her arms across the heavens,
You will follow, always follow, till you become instead,
A shade in human draperies, with palm fronds for your pillow,
In place of Mammy's bibini, asleep on his wee bed.

► *The Crisis*, March 1929.

Nativity

Within a Native hut, ere stirred the dawn,
Unto the pure one was an Infant born
Wrapped in blue lappah that His mother dyed.
Laid on His father's home-tanned deer-skin hide
The babe still slept,—by all things glorified.
Spirits of black bards burst their bonds and sang,
"Peace upon earth" until the heavens rang.
All the black babies who from earth had fled,
Peeped through the clouds—then gathered round His head,
Telling of things a baby needs to do,
When first he opens his eyes on wonders new;
Telling Him that to sleep was sweeter rest,
All comfort came from His black mother's breast.
Their gifts were of Love caught from the springing sod,
Whilst tears and laughter were the gifts of God.
Then all the wise men of the past stood forth
Filling the air East, West and South and North;
And told Him of the joys that wisdom brings
To mortals in their earthly wanderings.
The children of the past shook down each bough,
Wreathed Frangepani blossoms for His brow;
They put pink lilies in His mother's hand,
And heaped for both the first fruits of the land;
His father cut some palm fronds that the air
Be coaxed to zephyrs, while He rested there.
Birds trilled their hallelujahs, and the dew
Trembled with laughter till the Babe laughed too.

All the black women brought their love so wise,
And kissed their motherhood into His mother's eyes.

► *Opportunity*, January 1927; *The Atlantic Monthly*, January–June 1927; *Caroling Dusk*, ed. Countée Cullen, 1927.

Mammy

It's funny how I keep on wanting Mammy,
Just wanting Mammy, the whole day through;
When you come to think of it—it's quite uncanny,
The sort of things a Mammy does for you.
She cleans a fellow up and leaves no patches,
Just by sheer faith, in what a chap can do;
And how can you be dirty for a minute?
When she thinks you're the honest timber, through and through;
And she feels no storm on earth can set you creaking,
And no worms can penetrate your grain and hide;
And if rumor has an evil way of speaking
Of things you do—she'll up and say, they lied;
And if Life reveals the truth when big storms thunder,
Her frail body comes betwixt you and the night,
Though you feel her very heart being torn asunder
She'll face the world unflinching, say you're right.
Do you think you're worth the heartbreak and the heartache
Or worth your salt—and manhood's distance run?
Is that why she's such a guardian angel to ye?
Don't you fool yourself—it's 'cause you're just her son.

► *The Messenger*, March 1926.

The Palm Wine Seller

Akosua selling palm wine
In the broiling heat;

Akosua selling palm wine
Down our street.

Frothing calabashes
Filled unto the brim;
Boatmen quaffing palm wine
In toil's interim.

Tossing off their palm wine,
Boatmen deem her fair;
Through the haze of palm wine,
Note her jet-black hair.

Roundness of her bosom,
Brilliance of her eyes,
Lips that form a cupid's bow,
Whereon love's dew lies.

Velvet gleam of shoulder,
Arch of bare black feet,
Soft caressing hands,
These her charms complete.

Thus illusioned boatmen
Dwell on 'Kosua's charms,
Blind to fallen bosom,
Knotted thin black arms.

Lips creased in by wrinkles,
Eyes dimmed with the years,
Feet whose arch was altered,
Treading vales of tears.

Hair whose roots life's madness
Knotted and turned wild.
On her heart a load of care,
On her back, a child.

Akosua selling palm wine
In the broiling heat;
Akosua selling palm wine
Down our street.

► *Opportunity,* February 1930.

Rainy Season Love Song

Out of the tense awed darkness, my Frangepani comes;
Whilst the blades of Heaven flash round her, and the roll of
     thunder drums,
My young heart leaps and dances, with exquisite joy and pain,
As, storms within and storms without, I meet my love in the rain.

"The rain is in love with you darling; it's kissing you everywhere,
Rain pattering over your small brown feet, rain in your curly hair;
Rain in the vale that your twin breasts make, as in delicate mounds
     they rise;
I hope there is rain in your heart, Frangepani, as rain half fills
     your eyes."

Into my hands she cometh, and the lightning of my desire
Flashes and leaps about her, more subtle than Heaven's fire;
"The lightning's in love with you darling; it is loving you so much
That its warm electricity in you pulses wherever I may touch.
When I kiss your lips and your eyes, and your hands like twin
     flowers apart,
I know there is lightning, Frangepani, deep in the depths of your
     heart."

The thunder rumbles about us, and I feel its triumphant note
As your warm arms steal around me, and I kiss your dusky throat;
"The thunder's in love with you darling; it hides its power in your
     breast,
And I feel it stealing o'er me as I lie in your arms at rest.

I sometimes wonder, beloved, when I drink from life's proffered
  bowl,
Whether there's thunder hidden in the innermost parts of
  your soul."

Out of my arms she stealeth, and I am left alone with the night,
Void of all sounds save peace, the first faint glimmer of light.
Into some quiet, hushed stillness my Frangepani goes.
Is there peace within like the peace without? Only the darkness
  knows.

► *Opportunity,* September 1927; *Caroling Dusk,* ed. Countée Cullen, 1927.

The Serving Girl

The calabash wherein she served my food
Was smooth and polished as sandalwood;
Fish, as white as the foam of the sea,
Peppered, and golden fried for me.
She brought palm wine that carelessly slips
From the sleeping palm tree's honeyed lips.
But who can guess, or even surmise,
The countless things she served with her eyes?

► *Caroling Dusk,* ed. Countée Cullen, 1927; *The Atlantic Monthly,* January–June 1927.

Alvira Hazzard (1899–1953)

Alvira Hazzard was born in North Brookfield, Massachusetts, in 1899; her parents were John and Rosella Hazzard and she was the oldest of six children. A graduate of Worcester Normal School in Massachusetts, Hazzard taught for a time in Boston, where she lived, and then earned her living as a clerk at Boston City Hospital. Not much is known about Hazzard except that she was a member of the Saturday Evening Quill Club in Boston, a group of black writers, many of whom were women. She published two plays in *The Saturday Evening Quill* along with a short story and the small group of poems reprinted here. Hazzard remained unmarried and died at a relatively young age in 1953 of lymphatic leukemia, a fate her poetry seems to anticipate.

Predestination

I want to live.
Dark pitfalls all about me
Close their black depths where'er my wanderings lead;
My feet are guided by an unseen force
O'er paths I would avoid for strangely treacherous ways.

I want to see.
Stark drama all about me
Finds no respondent note within the chaos of my soul;
My eyes are drawn by some magnetic power
To a mirage of weird ethereal pictures.

► *The Saturday Evening Quill*, April 1929.

To My Grandmother

Past beauty on a withering stem
With hands like wilting petals
Folded in languid repose.

Today, vivacity and mischief
Are memories in your dimming eyes
Challenging the future.
Throughout those years to come,
I shall seek often
In the pregnant meadows of my soul
For renewed courage and unerring zeal,
The seedlings of your example.

► *The Saturday Evening Quill*, April 1929.

Beyond

Down a steep pathway
Stygian black
Past fettered shapes whose gnashing teeth
Flash feeble sparks of fire.
Yet, I do not fear to tread the way alone
Fleeing a world of ceaseless, aimless din;
My way is charted.

But mark the fate of yonder dove,
Who, with a mating call,
Plunges in dizzy ecstasy
Past me,
To its doom.

► *The Saturday Evening Quill*, April 1929.

The Penitent

A cowering figure
Clutching a cross
Enters Heaven
By the back way.

► *The Saturday Evening Quill*, June 1928.

Virginia Houston (?–?)

There is no biographical information about this poet except the brief head-note that appears in Beatrice M. Murphy's *Negro Voices* (1938): "Virginia Houston lives in Cleveland, Ohio, where she has worked with a social agency and is now connected with the social service end of the City Police Force. Her poems have been widely published and highly praised." It is unusual for a writer to appear in the pages of *The Crisis* and *Opportunity*, which Houston did with some regularity from 1929 to 1931, without having more known about her. She resurfaces in Murphy's 1938 anthology but then disappears. Houston's poetry is unusually critical of the black figures she describes in "Dark Cleveland" and "Troubadour." Interesting for its candor in this respect and for its technical sophistication, Houston's sensibility suggests a keen intelligence wedded to a sensitive reflective lens.

Query

In what coinage, America
   Will you repay your darker children
   For lost illusions,
   Embittered youth,
   Redeem the blood of our fathers?
With what coin, O my country?

► *Opportunity,* September 1930; *Negro Voices,* ed. Beatrice M. Murphy, 1938.

Troubadour

I do not like you.
You strut about your ghetto streets
Revering no one, despising yourself;
Your yellow skin, and reddened eyes
Are dull within your yellow face,
And your body is soft.

An unremembered, sorrowful man,
Scarred body and black face
Yearning toward a starry sky,
Sat before a cabin door
And gave his soul to make the songs
You distort to a silly dancing rhythm.
You deny your heritage, put him to shame,
With your narrow chest and pimpled skin.

You are mongrel,
Like your songs and your uke.*
There is nothing of beauty in you,
And I do not like you.

*Uke is short for ukelele.

► *The Crisis,* July 1930.

Dark Cleveland

Being Five Verses in Lieu of Vitriol,
with a sixth added for good measure.

I.

For a Gossip

Incredible that silly you
Of stunted mind and muddied soul,
Could so defile with evil words,
Things of beauty, inestimable worth,
Friendships, love, one's very thoughts.

II.

For an Intellectual

At bridge, at tea, at dinner too,
You ask with supercilious air,
"Have you read this, do you know that?"
So tiring that I sigh and wish
You buried under half *my* wit!

III.

For a Business Man

By day, a pillar of the "race"
Madly pursuing a filthy ore,
By night, a tortured prodigal,
Prostrate before the sullied Venus.

IV.

For a Schoolteacher

Just beyond your dusty window,
Vendor of the useless arts,
Life and beauty and sorrow and love
Taunt your age-old cowardice
Seeking escape in lifeless books.

V.
For a Snob
How is it possible you can be
Sure of superiority,
Since various mirrors exist?

VI.
For One Approaching Senility
It is centuries since a great man
Wrote words of deep profundity
Concerning old age and the fullness thereof;
Read them, poor deflated Priapus;*
Cicero was a wise man;†
I recommend him to you.

*Priapus was a god of classical Greek mythology with legendary procreative power.

†Cicero was a Roman statesman, orator, and writer.

► *The Crisis*, January 1931.

Class Room

Behind him a picture.
Blue-gray skies,
Phantom clouds
Chasing a topsy-turvy ship
Across an indigo sea . . .

And on those joyous sails
A mirrored image of a bald head,
Shattering my dream
Of faraway, mysterious lands,
Gold-red sunsets,
Silver-white nights,
Of seas shattering against
A sun-splashed deck.

The whisper of the sea in my ears
And the whistle of the wind in the sails

Are replaced by the wheezy murmur
Of an anti-Freudian.

► *The Crisis*, March 1929.

Ecstasy

Even here, dwelling in chaos,
I find your charm is all-pervasive
And I remember only the ecstasy
Of soft lips covering mine,
Dragging my soul through my mouth,
The joy of strong young arms
Clinging, holding me ever closer,
The exquisite agony of holding you
In unfulfilled embrace.

► *The Crisis*, February 1929.

Fugit Amor

I am sorry, Beloved,
That our hands were seared
By the star we reached for,
That our fingers ache
Because a golden moon turned ice,
And that our eyes, blinded
By the too strong light of our love,
Dare not look upon our hearts
Grown ponderous with emptiness.

We, who flaunted in Fortune's grim face
Our boast that we had no need of wisdom.

Fugit amor means "love flees."

► *The Crisis*, September 1929; *Negro Voices*, ed. Beatrice M. Murphy, 1938.

Interim

I am so tired
Waiting for my heart to break,
Waiting for tears to heal my soul,
For a blessed hand to melt away
The agony within me.

Eons since you went from me
Into an alien world. And still
Stranger to beauty are all my days,
My nights dark making of libations
Where once the myrtle grew!

I could carry the weight of winter,
The glory of autumn nights and days,
But I cannot bear the spring.
And I am ill, unto death, my Beloved!
Sick with longing, sick with weeping,
Waiting for my heart to break.

► *The Crisis,* May 1930; *Negro Voices,* ed. Beatrice M. Murphy, 1938.

Recapitulation

I have made a garden with infinite care,
And, finished now, I stand surveying my work.
And I know that shortly, briefly,
These seeds will quicken and bloom
And fade and wither and come again
In other springs, and ever be
Poignant reminders of you.

And yet, I buried you over and again
In the soft rich earth beneath each tiny seed . . .

► *Negro Voices,* ed. Beatrice M. Murphy, 1938.

Dorothy Vena Johnson (1898–1970)

Born to James and Namie Vena in 1898, Dorothy Vena added the surname Johnson when she married a lawyer on an unknown date. A lifelong resident of California, she received her AB degree at the University of Southern California in an unknown year and attended Teacher's College at UCLA. Johnson was a junior high teacher of creative writing in Los Angeles for forty years. Perhaps because she was on the West Coast, Johnson did not publish during the main years of the Harlem Renaissance and appears only at the period's tail end in Beatrice M. Murphy's *Negro Voices* (1938). Later, her poetry was also published by Arna Bontemps in a children's poetry anthology, *Golden Slippers* (1941), and in Beatrice Murphy's *Ebony Rhythm* (1948). The three poems reprinted here from the 1938 anthology reflect the period's strong protest against lynching, which reached its zenith at the turn of the century but continued well into the twentieth century.

Crystal Shreds

Have you seen the rain
Dripping
Like a silver pendant
Out of God's crown?
I have!

Does it fall unguarded by celestial muses?
Or does God weep,
And so weeping,
Release absolution
In crystal shreds
Of ethereal dew
To cleanse our souls?

► *Negro Voices,* ed. Beatrice M. Murphy, 1938.

Jerked to God

He gave His Son
In this world of strife,
That we might have
Eternal Life.

He made a tree
To shade, to adorn—
Perfectly patterned,
Without a thorn.

A life, a tree,
A rope, a rod.
Headlines: Humans
Jerked to God.

► *Negro Voices,* ed. Beatrice M. Murphy, 1938.

Ode to Justice

(Dedicated to the Scottsboro Boys)*

Lady Justice is often blind
To honor, duty, and fair play
And seems to be devoid of mind,
Reason and virtue; and some say
She seems to be both deaf and dumb,
Like barren earth when all the snow
Leaves its warm brown soul quite numb.
For buds, like Justice, will not grow
Where faith and duty lie asleep
And where you find the soul within
Is warped and stained, and buried deep
In tainted earth and vicious sin.

The soul of Justice cannot thrive
On barren soil and stay alive.

*The Scottsboro Boys were a group of nine black teenagers who in 1931 were falsely accused of rap-
ing two white female hoboes on a train and sentenced to death in Scottsboro, Alabama. The NAACP
and the Communist Party both took up their cause and the case went through several appeals while
the accused remained in jail until finally they were freed.

► *Negro Voices,* ed. Beatrice M. Murphy, 1938.

Georgia Douglas Johnson (1877–1966)

Georgia Douglas Camp Johnson was the most prolific woman poet of the Harlem Renaissance and, along with Jessie Fauset, one of its most important female members. Her poetry was published in every major anthology and journal of the movement, and she published three well-received collections between 1918 and 1928. She was also a gifted playwright and short story writer. Johnson's house on S Street in Washington, D.C., became a central gathering place for the most noted African American writers of the 1920s and 1930s. Despite the fact that Johnson rarely made it to Harlem and never to Paris, she was a key artist and organizer of the New Negro Movement. It appears that Johnson falsified her birth date; the recorded date of 1886 in most biographical material is not the date on her birth certificate, September 10, 1877. Her parents were Laura Douglas and George Camp, both of mixed-race descent. They separated when Johnson was a young girl, and Laura Douglas resumed her maiden name. Johnson dropped her paternal family name and adopted that of her mother as her middle name when she married Henry Lincoln Johnson on September 28, 1903. The feminism implicit in this gesture is a hallmark of her verse and life. Born and raised in Atlanta, Johnson studied at Atlanta University's Normal School, from which she graduated in 1893. She also studied at the Oberlin Conservatory of Music in Ohio, the Cleveland College of Music, and Howard University. She taught music at a high school in Atlanta for ten years, later becoming an assistant principal. When she met and married her attorney husband, Lincoln Johnson, she resigned her position, and the couple moved to Washington, D.C., in 1910 with their two sons. Lincoln Johnson was appointed to the prestigious post of Recorder of Deeds by Republican president Howard Taft in 1912, a position held by a black man since Frederick Douglass's appointment in the nineteenth century. Georgia Douglas Johnson would remain a lifelong Republican. Johnson's husband died of a stroke in 1925, forcing her to seek employment to support and educate her two sons. Working at government clerical jobs, mostly in the Department of Labor, Johnson sent one son to Bowdoin College and Howard Law School and the other to Dartmouth and Howard Medical School. Despite the enormous distraction of full-time employment, it was at this time that Johnson began to play an important role in the Harlem Renaissance. Her Saturday night gatherings became an important site of contact for Harlem Renaissance writers from 1920 to 1936. By this time she was able to publish a third collection of verse,

An Autumn Love Cycle (1928), with a foreword by Alain Locke. This joined *The Heart of a Woman and Other Poems* (1918) and *Bronze: A Collection of Verse* (1922), with forewords by William Stanley Braithwaite and W.E.B. Du Bois, respectively. (She later self-published one more poetry collection, *Share My World*, in 1962.) Johnson never succeeded in getting the writing fellowships for which she repeatedly applied, which would have released her from the burden of earning a living. Amazingly resilient in the face of repeated rejection by award committees and publishers, she continued to write her entire life, leaving behind an enormous catalogue, which she deposited with Atlanta University. Many of the seventeen books listed in the catalogue, along with countless poems and other writings, were lost when Johnson's home was cleaned out by sanitation workers after her death. Johnson did, however, receive recognition from her peers, and she was given an honorary PhD in literature from Atlanta University the year before she died.

Calling Dreams

The right to make my dreams come true,
I ask, nay, I demand of life;
Nor shall fate's deadly contraband
Impede my steps, nor countermand;
Too long my heart against the ground
Has beat the dusty years around;
And now at length I rise! I wake!
And stride into the morning break!

► *The Crisis*, January 1920.

The Ordeal

Ho: my brother,
Pass me not by so scornfully;
I'm doing this living of being black,
Perhaps I bear your own life-pack,
And heavy, heavy is the load
That bends my body to the road.

But I have kept a smile for fate;
I neither cry, nor cringe, nor hate;
Intrepidly, I strive to bear
This handicap: The planets wear
The Maker's imprint, and with mine
I swing into their rhythmic line;
I ask—only for destiny,
Mine, not thine.

► *The New Negro*, ed. Alain Locke, 1925.

Wishes

I'm tired of pacing the petty round of the ring of the thing I
    know—
I want to stand on the daylight's edge and see where the sunsets go.

I want to sail on a swallow's tail and peep through the sky's blue
    glass.
I want to see if the dreams in me shall perish or come to pass.

I want to look through the moon's pale crook and gaze on the
    moon-man's face.
I want to keep all the tears I weep and sail to some unknown place.

► *The Crisis*, April 1927.

Armageddon

In the silence and the dark
I fought with dragons:
I was battered, beaten, sore,

But rose again.
On my knees I fought, still rising,
Dull with pain!

In the dark I fought with dragons—
Foolish tears! Cease your flowing!
Can't you see the dawn appears?

► *The Crisis*, March 1925.

The Suppliant

Long have I beat with timid hands upon life's leaden door,
Praying the patient, futile prayer my fathers prayed before,

Yet I remain without the close, unheeded and unheard,
And never to my listening ear is borne the awaited word.

Soft o'er the threshold of the years there comes this counsel cool:
The strong demand, contend, prevail; the beggar is a fool!

► *Caroling Dusk,* ed. Countée Cullen, 1927.

Your World

Your world is as big as you make it.
I know, for I used to abide
In the narrowest nest in a corner,
My wings pressing close to my side.

But I sighted the distant horizon
Where the skyline encircled the sea
And I throbbed with a burning desire
To travel this immensity.

I battered the cordons around me
And cradled my wings on the breeze,
Then soared to the uttermost reaches
With rapture, with power, with ease!

► *Bronze,* Georgia Douglas Johnson, 1922.

The Heart of a Woman

The heart of a woman goes forth with the dawn,
As a lone bird, soft winging, so restlessly on;
Afar o'er life's turrets and vales does it roam
In the wake of those echoes the heart calls home.

The heart of a woman falls back with the night,
And enters some alien cage in its plight,

And tries to forget it has dreamed of the stars
While it breaks, breaks, breaks on the sheltering bars.

► *The Heart of a Woman*, Georgia Douglas Johnson, 1918; *The Book of American Negro Poetry*, ed. James Weldon Johnson, 1922, 1931; *Caroling Dusk*, ed. Countée Cullen, 1927; *Readings from Negro Authors*, ed. Otelia Cromwell et al., 1931.

Prejudice

These fell miasmic rings of mist with ghoulish menace bound,
Like noose-horizons tightening my little world around.
They still the soaring will to wing, to dance, to speed away,
And fling the soul insurgent back into its shell of clay.
Beneath incrusted silences, a seething Etna lies,*
The fire of whose furnaces may sleep, but never dies!

*Mount Etna is an active volcano in Sicily.
► *Bronze*, Georgia Douglas Johnson, 1922.

The Octoroon

One drop of midnight in the dawn of life's pulsating stream
Marks her an alien from her kind, a shade amid its gleam;
Forevermore her step she bends insular, strange, apart—
And none can read the riddle of her wildly warring heart.

The stormy current of her blood beats like a mighty sea
Against the man-wrought iron bars of her captivity.
For refuge, succor, peace and rest, she seeks that humble fold
Whose every breath is kindliness, whose hearts are purest gold.

Octoroon is a Louisiana Creole term for a woman with one-eighth African American heritage.
► *Bronze*, Georgia Douglas Johnson, 1922; *Negro Poets and Their Poems*, ed. Robert T. Kerlin, 1923.

Your Voice Keeps Ringing Down the Day

Your voice keeps ringing down the day
In accents soft and mild
With which you have beguiled
And wooed me as a child.
Your presence bounds me every way
And thrills me in its fold
With phantom hands that hold
Like cherished chains of gold.

► *The Messenger,* July 1924.

Motherhood

Don't knock on my door, little child,
I cannot let you in;
You know not what a world this is
Of cruelty and sin.
Wait in the still eternity
Until I come to you.
The world is cruel, cruel, child,
I cannot let you through.

Don't knock at my heart, little one,
I cannot bear the pain
Of turning deaf ears to your call,
Time and time again.
You do not know the monster men
Inhabiting the earth.
Be still, be still, my precious child,
I cannot give you birth.

► *The Crisis,* October 1922; *Bronze,* Georgia Douglas Johnson, 1922.

Smothered Fires

A woman with a burning flame
　　Deep covered through the years
With ashes—ah! she hid it deep,
　　And smothered it with tears.

Sometimes a baleful light would rise
　　From out the dusky bed,
And then the woman hushed it quick
　　To slumber on, as dead.

At last the weary war was done,*
　　The tapers were alight,
And with a sigh of victory
　　She breathed a soft—goodnight!

*A reference to World War I (1914–1918).

► *The Heart of a Woman*, 1918; *Negro Poets and Their Poems*, ed. Robert T. Kerlin, 1923; *The Book of American Negro Poetry*, ed. James Weldon Johnson, 1922, 1931.

Old Black Men

They have dreamed as young men dream
　　Of glory, love and power;
They have hoped as youth will hope
　　Of life's sun-minted hour.

They have seen as others saw
　　Their bubbles burst in air,
And they have learned to live it down
　　As though they did not care.

► *Opportunity*, November 1925; *Caroling Dusk*, ed. Countée Cullen, 1927.

The Hegira

Oh, black man, why do you northward
  roam and leave all the farmlands
    bare?
Is your house not warm, tightly thatched
  from storm, and a larder replete your
    share?
And have you not schools fit with books and
  with tools, the steps of your young to
    guide?
Then—what do you seek in the North cold
  and bleak, 'mid the whirl of its teeming
    tide?

I have toiled in your cornfields and parched in the sun,
  I have bowed beneath your load of care;
I have patiently garnered your bright golden grain
  in seasons of storm and fair;
I have lifted a smile to your glowering gloom
  while my wounded heart, quivering, bled;
Trailing mute in your wake as your rosy dawns break,
  I have curtained the mound of my dead.

While my children are taught in the schools you have wrought,
  they are blind to the sheen of the sky;
For the brand of your hand casts a pall o'er the land
  that enshadows the gleam of the eye.
My sons deftly sapped of the brawnhood of man,
  self-rejected and impotent stand;
My daughters unhaloed, unhonored, undone,
  feed the lust of a dominant land.

Unstrange is the pathway to Calvary's Hill,
  —oft I wend in my dumb agony
Up its perilous height, in the pale morning light,
  to dissever my own from the tree.

I would not remember, yet cannot forget,
    how to hearts beating true to your own,
You've tortured, and wounded, and filtered their blood,
    'til a budding *Hegira* has blown.

And, so I'm away where the skyline of day
    lifts the arch of its rainbow on high—
From the land of my birth, where the low mounds of earth
    lift their impotent arms to the sky.
For the soul of me yearns with a passion that burns
    for the reach of the ultimate star
In the land of the North, where the leaven of worth
    flings the infinite portals ajar!

The Hegira was the flight of Muhammad from Mecca to Medina to escape persecution in AD 622; it is regarded as the beginning of the Muslim era; it also refers to any flight or journey to a more desirable place. In this case, the poet is referring to the Great Migration of African Americans from the South to the North in the years just preceding and extending into World War I as they fled a boll weevil epidemic that decimated the cotton fields, as well as poverty, racism, and the terrorism of lynching.

► *The Crisis,* March 1917.

The True American

America, here is your son, born of your iron heel;
Black blood and red and white contend along this frame of steel.
The thorns deep in his brow are set and yet he does not cower;
He goes with neither fears nor tears to crucifixion hour.
Nor yet does hatred blur his view of mankind's frail parade;
From his commanding triple coign, all prejudices fade.
The ebbing nations coalesce in him and flow as one;
The bright shining rainbow sweeping back to God at set of sun!
Mark well the surety of tread, the new song high in air,
The new note in the nation's throat, as permanent as prayer.
America, regard your son, The Cosmopolitan,
The pattern of posterity, The True American.

► *The Crisis,* April 1927.

Common Dust

And who shall separate the dust
That later we shall be;
Whose keen discerning eye will scan
And solve the mystery?

The high, the low, the rich, the poor,
The black, the white, the red,
And all the chromatique between,
Of whom shall it be said:

Here lies the dust of Africa;
Here are the sons of Rome;
Here lies the one unlabelled,
The world at large his home!

Can one then separate the dust?
Will mankind lie apart,
When life has settled back again
The same as from the start?

► *Bronze,* Georgia Douglas Johnson, 1922.

The Riddle

White men's children spread over the earth—
A rainbow suspending the drawn swords of birth,
Uniting and blending the races in one,
The World-Man, Cosmopolite, Everyman's Son!

He channels the stream of the red blood and blue,
Behold him! A Triton—the peer of the two;
Unriddle this riddle of "outside in"—
White men's children in black men's skin.

► *Opportunity,* August 1925; *The New Negro,* ed. Alain Locke, 1925.

A Sonnet in Memory of John Brown

We lift a son to you across the day
Which bears through travailing, the seed you spread
In terror's morning, flung with fingers red
In blood of tyrants, who debarred the way
To Freedom's dawning. Hearken to the lay
Chanted by dusky millions, soft and mellow-keyed
In minor measure, Martyr of the Freed,
A song of memory across the Day!

Truth cannot perish, though the earth erase
The royal emblems, leaving not a trace;
And time still burgeoneth the fertile seed
Though he is crucified who wrought the deed;
O, Alleghenies, fold him to your breast
Until the Judgment! Sentinel his rest!

John Brown was a white abolitionist who led an uprising of slaves at Harpers Ferry, West Virginia, where he was captured, found guilty of treason, and hanged in 1859.

► *The Crisis,* August 1922.

To a Young Wife

I was a fool to dream that you
Might cross the bridge of years
From your soft springtime to my side
Where autumn shade appears.

I am sedate while you are wild,
Elusive like a sprite;
You dance into the sunny morn
While I approach the night.

I was a fool—the dream is done;
I know it cannot be.

Return and live those burning years . . .
And then, come back to me!

► *The Crisis*, May 1931.

Requiem

I weep these tears upon my bier
    Another may not shed,
For there is none save I alone
    Who knows that I am dead.

► *Ebony and Topaz*, ed. Charles S. Johnson, 1927.

Escape

Shadows, shadows,
Hug me round
So that I shall not be found
By sorrow;
She pursues me
Everywhere,
I can't lose her
Anywhere.

Fold me in your black
Abyss;
She will never look
In this,—
Shadows, shadows,
Hug me round
In your solitude
Profound.

► *The Crisis*, May 1925; *The New Negro*, ed. Alain Locke, 1925.

Lethe

I do not ask for love,—ah! no,
   Nor friendship's happiness;
These were relinquished long ago,
   I search for something less.

I seek a little, tranquil bark
   In which to drift at ease
Awhile, and then quite silently
   To sink in quiet seas.

► *Opportunity,* July 1926; *Caroling Dusk,* ed. Countée Cullen, 1927.

Song of the Sinner

Just a bit of ashes
Grey, grey ashes, spent—
God! how fierce the ashes burned
Down to this content.

Just a bit of ashes,
Not a single spark
Lives in this residuum
Crumbling cold and dark.

Just a bit of ashes—
To the judgment day,
I go with my memories—
Pray, sweet Virgins, pray!

► *Palms,* October 1926.

Afterglow

Through you, I entered heaven and hell,
    Knew rapture and despair;
I vaulted o'er the plains of earth
    And scaled each shining stair;
Drank deep the waters of content
    And drained the cup of gall;
Was regal and was impotent,
    Was suzerain and thrall.

Now by reflection's placid pool,
    At evening's tranquil hour,
I smile across the backward way
    And pledge anew my vow:
For every glancing, golden gleam,
    I offer, gladly, pain;
And I would give a thousand worlds,
    To live it all again.

► *The Crisis,* March 1920.

My Little Dreams

I'm folding up my little dreams
    Within my heart tonight,
And praying I may soon forget
    The torture of their sight.

For time's deft fingers scroll my brow
    With fell relentless art—
I'm folding up my little dreams
    Tonight, within my heart.

► *Caroling Dusk,* ed. Countée Cullen, 1927.

I Want to Die While You Love Me

I want to die while you love me,
  While yet you hold me fair,
While laughter lies upon my lips
  And lights are in my hair.

I want to die while you love me,
  And bear to that still bed
Your kisses turbulent, unspent,
  To warm me when I'm dead.

I want to die while you love me,
  Oh, who would care to live
Til love has nothing more to ask
  And nothing more to give?

I want to die while you love me,
  And never, never see
The glory of this perfect day
  Grow dim or cease to be!

This was the poet's signature piece and was read at her funeral.

► *Caroling Dusk,* ed. Countée Cullen, 1927; *An Autumn Love Cycle,* Georgia Douglas Johnson, 1928; *The Anthology of American Negro Literature,* ed. V. F. Calverton, 1929; *The Book of American Negro Poetry,* ed. James Weldon Johnson, 1931.

Helen Aurelia Johnson (?–?)

No biographical information is available for this poet. Her single published poem, "Roaring Third," appears in Beatrice M. Murphy's *Negro Voices* (1938) and is interesting for its blank verse, vivid imagery, and realism. It points forward to the urban realism that would become the hallmark of African American writing after the Harlem Renaissance.

Roaring Third

Dark life is moist
with hidden waters
down this rough-brick street,
and maggots
teem no faster than these dark folk
in late summer sundown
when an early moon,
wrapped in sky-wide bandanna
grins a yellow haggish grin.
Here trees
point green leaf-thumbs downward
and crooked roofs
hug tightly stuffy garrets.

Downstairs
a dead red light
seeps dully round the shoulders
of a tall black woman
in the doorway
and stretches weak rays to the street
strewn with pink and white confetti—
slips of Policy
and Clearing-houses.*
Now
the daily numbers of the winnings
hang on thick lips
of dusky men
who bunch around a broken-shouldered house
with broken teeth of window panes,
who wait with hot-breathed anguish
or ardor (as the god of luck decrees).

Pass by
these rough-necked houses,
tumbled-down garages,
scarred by drivers
wild with coins quickly gained

from fortune's fingers.
Pass by,
and know
that a thousand tragedies and comedies
arise and die
within these dingy theatres,
and that a thousand hearts beat quick life
on this street of night
where both police and street-lamps
fail to penetrate,
but where the lamp of life glows strongly
on and on despite high adverse winds.

Look down—
a half of watermelon
lies along the gutter,
rotting, reeking with sweet-sickness
attracting myriads of green-eyed flies;
and everywhere
there is the strange, tense feeling
that people watch with countless eyes—
They peer from half-drawn shades
or boldly ogle from their porches,
but still they stare and gaze and listen,
seeming fearful of the fight of life itself.
And everywhere
to break the stillness strong as vinegar,
a myriad children
roll their tires and balls down the broken walks
or ride their bicycles
as silently as dreams now back and forth,
avoiding shattered whisky bottles
that lie about like idle drunkards
in shadowed streets.

What life,
what hot thoughts must thrive here?
There is no comic kitchen-talk

when one seeks God
with puzzled eyes and muted thoughts—
a quiet God
above the cigar-smoke,
loud winey talk of hard-cash gamblers.
There is no kitchen-talk
when one works hard all day,
"stays on the place"
for little money,
then on Sundays,
goes to hear God's word
through flapping lips of store-front preachers.
"And where and when is heaven?"
washerwomen, porters, cooks cry out.
And now a passing train
roars out its scorn
and spits out pungent coal-smoke far and wide—
It says with rumbling wheels,
"Oh, no, there is no God, no God!" . . .
and so on into distance . . .
"No God! No God!"
"What low-pinned minds are these,
what mole-like creatures!
Are there no wings that soar?"
one asks.

While mockingly
at end of street,
the happy fumes of barbeque
alone
are twisting bluely to the sky,
and seem to say,
"You see, *we* rise—
we rise!"

Roaring Third refers to Third Avenue in Harlem.

*Policy slips and clearing-houses are references to gambling.

► *Negro Voices*, ed. Beatrice M. Murphy, 1938.

Helene Johnson (1906–1995)

Born Helen Johnson in Boston on July 7, 1906, Helene Johnson was an only child whose mother, Ella Benson Johnson, worked as a domestic in Cambridge, Massachusetts; her father, George Johnson, was unknown to her; both were from the South. She was told that her father was of Greek origin and that he lived in Chicago, but she never met him. Raised in part by her maternal aunts in Oak Bluffs of Martha's Vineyard, an African American resort community, her childhood was spent in Boston with them, her mother, and her cousin, fiction writer Dorothy West, with whom she traveled to New York in 1927. It was one of these aunts who gave her the name Helene. After graduating from Boston Girls' Latin School, Johnson attended Boston University before traveling to Harlem at age nineteen with West; there she studied journalism at Columbia University. The cousins became good friends of Zora Neale Hurston. Johnson had already gained critical attention with the publication of her prizewinning poems in *Opportunity* beginning in 1925, and she was a member of the Saturday Evening Quill Club in Boston. Her work also appeared in William Stanley Braithwaite's *Anthology of Magazine Verse for 1926* and in the only issue of *Fire!!* (November 1926) as well as in *The Messenger* and a special issue of *Palms* edited by Countée Cullen. A rising young star of the Harlem Renaissance movement, Johnson reached the zenith of her fame in May 1927 when her poem "Bottled," a work with innovative use of street vernacular and unorthodox rhythms, appeared in *Vanity Fair*. These were all impressive achievements for a young African American woman experimenting with erotic themes and urban slang, a new form mastered by Langston Hughes but avoided, for a variety of reasons, by women poets. Her best vernacular poetry is represented here by "Bottled," "Poem," and "Regalia." Eight of Johnson's poems appeared in Countée Cullen's influential anthology, *Caroling Dusk* (1927). Her work was also published in James Weldon Johnson's *The Book of American Negro Poetry* in the 1931 edition. Because Helene Johnson's poetry appears in every major periodical and anthology of the Harlem Renaissance from 1925 through her final 1935 publication in *Challenge,* edited by her cousin Dorothy West, and because much of her poetry is both innovative and thematically relevant beyond her time, she is one of the movement's most important poets despite her short time in the public eye. Dividing her time between New York and Boston after 1929, Johnson married William Warner Hubbell III, a shipyard worker, in 1933 and had a daughter in 1940. She was later divorced and settled in Greenwich

Village for the remainder of her life. According to her obituary in the *New York Times,* Helene Johnson continued to write a poem a day for the rest of her life, but she stopped publishing after 1935. She addressed this silence in an interview published in 1992: "It's very difficult for a poor person to be that fastened. They have to eat. In order to eat, you have to be fastened, and tightly." Helene Johnson died in Manhattan on July 6, 1995, the day before she would have turned eighty-nine.

Bottled

Upstairs on the third floor
Of the 135th Street library
In Harlem, I saw a little
Bottle of sand, brown sand,
Just like the kids make pies
Out of down at the beach.
But the label said: "This
Sand was taken from the Sahara desert."
Imagine that! The Sahara desert!
Some bozo's been all the way to Africa to get some sand.

And yesterday on Seventh Avenue
I saw a darky dressed fit to kill
In yellow gloves and swallowtail coat
And swirling a cane. And everyone
Was laughing at him. Me too,
At first, till I saw his face
When he stopped to hear a
Organ grinder grind out some jazz.
Boy! You should a seen that darky's face!
It just shone. Gee, he was happy!
And he began to dance. No
Charleston or Black Bottom for him.
No sir. He danced just as dignified
And slow. No, not slow either.
Dignified and *proud!* You couldn't
Call it slow, not with all the
Cuttin' up he did. You would a died to see him.

The crowd kept yellin' but he didn't hear,
Just kept on dancin' and twirlin' that cane
And yellin' out loud every once in a while.
I know the crowd thought he was coo-coo.
But say, I was where I could see his face,
And somehow, I could see him dancin' in a jungle,
A real honest-to-cripe jungle, and he wouldn't leave on them

Trick clothes—those yaller shoes and yaller gloves
And swallowtail coat. He wouldn't have on nothing.
And he wouldn't be carrying no cane.
He'd be carrying a spear with a sharp fine point
Like the bayonets we had "over there."*
And the end of it would be dipped in some kind of
Hoo-doo poison. And he'd be dancin' black and naked and
    gleaming.
And he'd have rings in his ears and on his nose
And bracelets and necklaces of elephants' teeth.
Gee, I bet he'd be beautiful then all right.
No one would laugh at him then, I bet.
Say! That man that took that sand from the Sahara desert
And put it in a little bottle on a shelf in the library,
That's what they done to this shine, ain't it? Bottled him.
Trick shoes, trick coat, trick cane, trick everything—all glass—
But inside—
Gee, that poor shine!

*A reference to black troops in World War I fighting against the German army in France.

► *Vanity Fair,* May 1927; *Caroling Dusk,* ed. Countée Cullen, 1927.

Poem

Little brown boy,
Slim, dark, big-eyed,
Crooning love songs to your banjo
Down at the Lafayette—*
Gee, boy, I love the way you hold your head,
High sort of and a bit to one side,
Like a prince, a jazz prince. And I love
Your eyes flashing, and your hands,
And your patent-leathered feet,
And your shoulders jerking the jig-wa.
And I love your teeth flashing,
And the way your hair shines in the spotlight
Like it was the real stuff.

6. Aaron Douglas, "To Midnight Nan at Leroy's," *Opportunity*, January 1926

Gee, brown boy, I loves you all over.
I'm glad I'm a jig.[†] I'm glad I can
Understand your dancin' and your
Singin', and feel all the happiness
And joy and don't-care in you.
Gee, boy, when you sing, I can close my eyes
And hear tom-toms just as plain.
Listen to me, will you, what do I know
About tom-toms? But I like the word, sort of,
Don't you? It belongs to us.
Gee, boy, I love the way you hold your head,
And the way you sing and dance,
And everything.
Say, I think you're wonderful. You're
Alright with me,
You are.

*The Lafayette Theater in Harlem.

†Slang for black person.

► *Caroling Dusk,* ed. Countée Cullen, 1927; *The Book of American Negro Poetry,* ed. James Weldon
Johnson, 1931.

Regalia

Stokin' stoves,
Emptin' garbage,
Fillin' ash cans,
Fixin' drain pipes,
Washin' stairs,
Answerin' a million calls,
Answerin' a million bells,
All day, half the night —
The yassuhs, the nosuhs,
The grins, the nods, the bowin' —
It sure wasn't no picnic
Bein' a janitor in a big apartment house in Harlem.
But, say, it was better than bein' back down home

Scrapin' to the buchra.* And he made good money, too,
With tips, now and then, for extra. His wife didn't have
To go out to do day's work† any more, and Sammy, his only child,
Went to school and learned readin' and writin'. And he,
Big Sam, had been able to join the local lodge.‡
He would have rather gone without his vittles§
Than not pay his lodge dues,
Than not march in the lodge parade,
Than not wear his uniform of blue and gold and orange,
And high white plumes and yellow braid and gold epaulets,
And snow-white gloves and shining black shoes and tassels,
And silk ribbons and feathers and big bright buttons and
Color, color, color.
God, how he loved it! He loved it better than food and drink,—
Better than Love itself.
Every night after work, after
The stove stokin',
The garbage slingin',
The ashcan fillin',
The stair washin',
The yassuhs and nosuhs and the grins and nods and bowin',
He'd go downstairs to his basement flat and put it on.
And stand in front of his crazy old mirror and make funny
Gestures and military signs and talk to himself and click
His heels together and curse and swear like a major or a
General. And always he'd be the leader, the head, and
The others, the make-believe others, would say yassuh and nosuh,
And grin and nod and bow. Gold and yellow and blue—
God, how he loved it!

That old Rev. Giddings was a fool, telling him it was a sin
To dress up and have music and march when somebody died.
"God don't like that," he said. "God, He wants mourning
And wailing and dark clothes. He don't want all that worldly
Music and color for his dead children. He don't want all that
Regalia. It hurts Him, Brother, it hurts Him. It's vanity,
That's all. You don't know, Brother, that blue and gold
You wear—the flames of Hell; that red—the blood of His

Crucified Son, those plumes and feathers—they mocked Christ
With them once. God don't like that regalia, son. God don't
Like it. I got to stay in the lodge or I'd lose my flock.
You know that, Brother. But dress in black when I die, Brother,
And beat your breast. I don't want no regalia."
But Sam couldn't understand. He loved it so, that uniform.
What had it to do with God?
Nights when the lodge went on parade. Nights when there was
A funeral and they had to march in a long, beautiful procession.
His wife was proud of him, and so was Sammy, his son,
Who wanted to be a general in the army.
If only there might be a funeral . . .

And then one night Rev. Giddings died
And Sam had a chance to wear his uniform—
His uniform of blue and gold and orange—
And high white plumes and yellow braid and gold epaulets,
And snow-white gloves and shining black shoes and tassels,
And silk ribbons and feathers and big bright buttons,
And color, color, color.
But it was different. Reverend Giddings must have conjured him.‖
He was scared. His plumes bent him over and the color before
Him was like Hell fire. And there was Rev. Giddings
Smiling at him. "God don't like all that regalia, Brother,
God don't like it." The blue and gold flames leaped up
And burned him. Red swarmed before him, banners,
Ribbons. He saw strips of blood, streams of blood flowing
About him—"The blood of His Crucified Son." And the music,
The drums, the bugles—The little red devils dancing before
His eyes—The flames lapping up the blood—Red, blue, gold.
God, how he hated it!
He snatched off his plumes, tore off his colors, beat his breast.

It was hard to make him out in all that flood of color.
He seemed so little and tired and bent and dark and humble.
He looked so funny, beating his breast that way.
In fact, he looked more like the little colored janitor
Who stoked stoves,

And emptied garbage,
And piled ashcans,
And scrubbed stairs
In a big apartment house in Harlem,
Than anything else.

*Down home refers to the subject's former home in the South; buchra is slang for a white employer in the South.

†Day's work is domestic work for a white employer.

‡Lodges were popular private clubs for men in the 1920s and 1930s, with elaborate rules, rituals, and uniforms.

§Vittles is slang for food.

‖Conjured him; i.e., a spell was cast on him.

► *The Saturday Evening Quill,* April 1929.

Plea of a Plebeian

I'd like to be a lady. Gee—
A lady with a pedigree—
With haughty airs and careless grace,
Nobility writ on my face.
    The peasant class is very well,
    But I like something awfully swell.

I strongly wish my blood were blue.
Think of the things that I could do.
Think of the places I could go
If I were Lady So-and-So.
    And in my elegant salon
    I could make charming liaisons.

A gallant in both word and deed
Would bear me on his handsome steed
To some romantic palisade
For an historic escapade.
    The middle class has quite a pull,
    But they are so respectable.

I could be either fat or slight
(A lady bows to appetite).
And I could wear my last year's hat,
Or the chapeau prior to that
   And still inspire gallantry,
   Were I a dame of pedigree.

A plebeian is a common person.
► *Opportunity,* May 1934.

I Am Not Proud

I am not proud that I am bold
Or proud that I am black.
Color was given me as a gauge
And boldness came with that.

► *The Saturday Evening Quill,* April 1929.

My Race

Ah, my race,
Hungry race,
Throbbing and young—
Ah, my race,
Wonder race,
Sobbing with song—
Ah, my race,
Laughing race,
Careless in mirth—
Ah, my veiled
Unformed race,
Fumbling in birth.

► *Opportunity,* July 1925.

The Road

Ah, little road, all whirry in the breeze,
A leaping clay hill lost among the trees,
The bleeding note of rapture streaming thrush
Caught in a drowsy hush
And stretched out in a single singing line of dusky song.
Ah, little road, brown as my race is brown,
Your trodden beauty like our trodden pride,
Dust of the dust, they must not bruise you down.
Rise to one brimming golden, spilling cry!

► *Opportunity,* July 1926; *Caroling Dusk,* ed. Countée Cullen, 1927; *Readings for Negro Authors,* ed. Otelia Cromwell et al., 1931; *The Book of American Negro Poetry,* ed. James Weldon Johnson, 1931.

Sonnet to a Negro in Harlem

You are disdainful and magnificent—
Your perfect body and your pompous gait,
Your dark eyes flashing solemnly with hate,
Small wonder that you are incompetent
To imitate those whom you so despise—
Your shoulders towering high above the throng,
Your head thrown back in rich, barbaric song,
Palm trees and mangoes stretched before your eyes.
Let others toil and sweat for labor's sake
And wring from grasping hands their meed of gold.
Why urge ahead your supercilious feet?
Scorn will efface each footprint that you make.
I love your laughter, arrogant and bold.
You are too splendid for this city street!

► *Caroling Dusk,* ed. Countée Cullen, 1927; *Ebony and Topaz,* ed. Charles S. Johnson, 1927; *The Book of American Negro Poetry,* ed. James Weldon Johnson, 1931.

Magalu (Magula)

Summer comes.
The ziczac hovers
'Round the greedy-mouthed crocodile.
A vulture bears away a foolish jackal.
The flamingo is a dash of pink
Against dark green mangroves,
Her slender legs rivaling her slim neck.
The laughing lake gurgles delicious music in its throat
And lulls to sleep the lazy lizard,
A nebulous being on a sun-scorched rock.
In such a place,
In this pulsing, riotous gasp of color,
I met Magalu, dark as a tree at night,
Eager-lipped, listening to a man with a white collar
And a small black book with a cross on it.
Oh Magalu, come! Take my hand and I will read you poetry,
Chromatic words,
Seraphic symphonies,
Fill up your throat with laughter and your heart with song.
Do not let him lure you from your laughing waters,
Lulling lakes, lissome winds.
Would you sell the colors of your sunset and the fragrance
Of your flowers, and the passionate wonder of your forest
For a creed that will not let you dance?

► *Palms*, October 1926; *Caroling Dusk*, ed. Countée Cullen, 1927.

A Southern Road

Yolk-colored tongue
Parched beneath a burning sky,
A lazy little tune
Hummed up the crest of some
Soft sloping hill.
One streaming line of beauty
Flowing by a forest

Pregnant with tears.
A hidden nest for beauty
Idly flung by God
In one lonely lingering hour
Before the Sabbath.
A blue-fruited black gum,
Like a tall predella,*
Bears a dangling figure,—
Sacrificial dower to the raff,
Swinging alone,
A solemn, tortured shadow in the air.

*The base of an altarpiece.

► *Fire!!* November 1926.

Fiat Lux

Her eyes had caught a bit of loveliness—
A flower blooming in the prison yard.
She ran to it and pressed it to her lips,
This Godsend of a land beyond the walls;
She drank its divine beauty with her kiss—
A guard wrested the flower from her hand,
With awful art, her humble back laid bare—
Soft skin, and darker than a dreamless night;
He tossed aside the burden of her hair.
"I'll teach you to pick flowers in this yard.
They ain't for niggers." He began to flog.
Her pale palmed hands grasped the thin air in quest.
Until, like two antalgic words, they fell,
And whispered something to her bleeding breast.
And she forgot the misery of her back.
Somehow she knew that God, HER God was there—
That what was pain was but her striped flesh.
Her soul, inviolate, was havened in prayer.
On a cross of bigotry she was crucified
Because she was not white. And like her Father

On the holy rood, whispered, "Forgive."
And in her eyes there shone a Candlemas light.

He flung the whip into the flower bed,
He did not even note that she was dead.

Fiat lux means "let there be light."

► *The Messenger,* July 1926; *Opportunity,* December 1928.

What Do I Care for Morning

What do I care for morning,
For a shivering aspen tree,
For sunflowers and sumac
Opening greedily?
What do I care for morning,
For the glare of the rising sun,
For a sparrow's noisy prating,
For another day begun?
Give me the beauty of evening,
The cool consummation of night,
And the moon like a love-sick lady,
Listless and wan and white.
Give me a little valley,
Huddled beside a hill,
Like a monk in a monastery,
Safe and contented and still.
Give me the white road glistening,
A strand of the pale moon's hair,
And the tall hemlocks towering,
Dark as the moon is fair.
Oh what do I care for morning,
Naked and newly born—
Night is here, yielding and tender—
What do I care for dawn!

► *Caroling Dusk,* ed. Countée Cullen, 1927.

Night

The moon flung down the bower of her hair,
A sacred cloister while she knelt at prayer.
She crossed pale bosom, breathed a sad amen—
Then bound her hair about her head again.

► *Opportunity,* January 1926.

Trees at Night

Slim sentinels
Stretching lacy arms
About a slumberous moon;
Black quivering
Silhouettes,
Tremulous,
Stenciled on the petal
Of a bluebell;
Ink splattered
On a robin's breast;
The jagged rent
Of mountains
Reflected in a
Stilly sleeping lake;
Fragile pinnacles
Of fairy castles;
Torn webs of shadows;
And printed 'gainst the sky—
The trembling beauty
Of an urgent pine.

► *Opportunity,* May 1925.

Metamorphism

Is this the sea?
This calm emotionless bosom,
Serene as the heart of a converted Magdalene—
Or this?
This lisping, lulling murmur of soft waters
Kissing a white beached shore with tremulous lips;
Blue rivulets of sky gurgling deliciously
O'er pale smooth stones—
This too?
This sudden birth of unrestrained splendor,
Tugging with turbulent force at Neptune's leash;
This passionate abandon,
This strange tempestuous soliloquy of Nature,
All these—the sea?

► *Opportunity,* March 1926; *Readings from Negro Authors,* ed. Otelia Cromwell et al., 1931.

Fulfillment

To climb a hill that hungers for the sky,
  To dig my hands wrist deep in pregnant earth,
To watch a young bird, veering, learn to fly,
  To give a still, stark poem shining birth.

To hear the rain drool, dimpling, down the drain
  And splash with a wet giggle in the street,
To ramble in the twilight after supper,
  And to count the pretty faces that you meet.

To ride to town on trolleys, crowded, teeming
  With joy and hurry and laughter and push and sweat—
Squeezed next a patent-leathered Negro dreaming
  Of a wrinkled river and a minnow net.

To buy a paper from a breathless boy,
  And read of kings and queens in foreign lands,
Hyperbole of romance and adventure,
  All for a penny the color of my hand.

To lean against a strong tree's bosom, sentient
  And hushed before the silent prayer it breathes,
To melt the still snow with my seething body
  And kiss the warm earth tremulous underneath.

Ah, life, to let your stabbing beauty pierce me
  And wound me like we did the studded Christ,
To grapple with you, loving you too fiercely,
  And to die bleeding—consummate with Life.

► *Opportunity,* June 1926; *Caroling Dusk,* ed. Countée Cullen, 1927.

Sonnet [1]

Be not averse to Beauty or to Love.
Entreat them in your daily prayer and song.
Make them your truth and know the peace thereof,
And they will nourish you, sweetly, and long.
Ah, let your swaddled psychic strength unfold,
Grow in awareness, delicate and keen.
But keep the tingleness of life and mold
Your way in Beauty, vigorous and clean.
Believe in things; all living is belief.
The doubting heart when hungry must be fed;
And freely, for the meal is fine, tho brief,
Beauty's the wine, and Love the loaf of bread.
They are the sacrament of Life I think,
So eat your warm white bread and drink and drink.

► *Opportunity,* December 1931.

Love in Midsummer

Ah love
Is like a throbbing wind,
A lullaby all crooning,
Ah love
Is like a summer sea's soft breast.
Ah love's
A sobbing violin
That naive night is tuning,
Ah love
Is down from off the white moon's nest.

▶ *The Messenger,* October 1926.

Futility

It is silly—
This waiting for love
In a parlor.
When love is singing up and down the alley
Without a collar.

▶ *Opportunity,* August 1926.

Sonnet [2]

Your dark head lies complacent on my breast.
Your lovely mouth is satiate. I fear
You know me far too well. Your childlike rest
Reflects my placid constancy too clear.
Of late even my thoughts are not my own.
You hum the tune I'm humming in my mind.
You know me thoroughly, flesh to the bone.

Therefore, think me not utterly so blind
That I heed not that you have been untrue,
That soon you will forsake me, leave me bare,
Will pity me for ever trusting you,
The while you learn that other arms are fair.
But what avails it to foretell the end?
Wisdom may caution, but it will not mend.

► *Opportunity,* March 1932.

Summer Matures

Summer matures. Brilliant Scorpion
Appears. The pelican's thick pouch
Hangs heavily with perch and slugs.
The brilliant-bellied newt flashes
Its crimson crest in the white water.
In the lush meadow, by the river,
The yellow-freckled toad laughs
With a toothless gurgle at the white-necked stork
Standing asleep on one red reedy leg.
And here Pan dreams of slim stalks clean for piping,
And of a nightingale gone mad with freedom.
Come. I shall weave a bed of reeds
And willow limbs and pale night flowers.
I shall strip the roses of their petals,
And the white down from the swan's neck.
Come. Night is here. The air is drunk
With wild grape and sweet clover.
And by the sacred fount of Aganippe,*
Euterpe†sings of love. Ah, the woodland creatures,
The doves in pairs, the wild sow and her shoats,
The stag searching the forest for a mate,
Know more of love than you, my callous Phaon.‡
The young moon is a curved white scimitar
Pierced through the swooning night.
Sweet Phaon. With Sappho, sleep like the stars at dawn.

This night was born for love, my Phaon.
Come.

*A fountain in Greek mythology sacred to the muses and believed to inspire those who drank its
water.

†The muse of music and lyric poetry in Greek mythology.

‡An aged boatman who was given youth by Aphrodite in Greek mythology. According to legend, the
Greek lesbian poet Sappho took Phaon as a lover on the island of Lesbos, populated solely by les-
bians, when he rowed there from shore.

► *Opportunity*, July 1927; *Caroling Dusk*, ed. Countée Cullen, 1927.

Vers de Société

And if I was mistaken—
If your fealty is glossed,
If all your vows were taken
With every finger crossed—

Later I shall be wary,
But later I shall be old.
There is no time to tarry
Since only the young are bold.

Love's an omelette, rum sprinkled,
Set on fire and served while hot,
Puffed to a heavenly fragrance,
Light as a pollen dot.

Be careful it does not fall, dear.
Make haste and have your meal.
Only the dotard* is prudent.
Only the dead are leal.†

Vers de société means "humorous light verse."

*A feeble-minded old man.

†True, loyal.

► *Opportunity*, July 1930.

[Why do they prate of youth so much?]

Why do they prate of youth so much?
'Tis too near to the root.
A budding, yes, but I prefer
The ripening of the fruit.

► *The Saturday Evening Quill,* April 1929.

Monotone

My life is but a single attitude,
An endless preface,
An old day-by-day.
My soul is a slack gesture of content—
Plump eiderdown piled high upon the bed.
My mind is like a scene in pastels that
A careful child paints on a china plate;
Precisely pretty, if impersonal;—
But half conceived, yet not inadequate.

► *Opportunity,* September 1932.

Invocation

Let me be buried in the rain
In a deep, dripping wood,
Under the warm wet breast of Earth
Where once a gnarled tree stood.
And paint a picture on my tomb
With dirt and a piece of bough
Of a girl and a boy beneath a round ripe moon
Eating of love with an eager spoon
And vowing an eager vow.
And do not keep my plot mowed smooth
And clean as a spinster's bed,

But let the weed, the flower, the tree,
Riotous, rampant, wild and free,
Grow high above my head!

► *The Saturday Evening Quill,* April 1929; *The Book of American Negro Poetry,* ed. James Weldon
Johnson, 1931.

Gertrude Parthenia McBrown (1902–1989)

Not much is known about Gertrude McBrown, including the names of her parents, whether she married or had children, and where or how she died. She was born in Charleston, South Carolina, and educated at Emerson College of Drama in Boston, from which she graduated in 1922, as well as Boston University, from which she received a Master's of Education in 1926. Some time during the 1920s, McBrown moved to Washington, D.C., where she became a director of children's theater and published a good deal of children's and adult poetry in *The Saturday Evening Quill,* among other journals, as well as publishing a collection for children in 1935, *The Picture Poetry Book.* She was a founding member of Boston's Saturday Evening Quill Club. She was also a playwright. Although McBrown at some point moved to New York and studied in Europe and Africa, nothing more is known about her circumstances beyond the fact that she directed drama at the Carnegie Hall Studio and wrote a weekly column for a local paper in Queens. Although McBrown is known for her children's poetry, many of her poems are aimed at adults, including those reprinted here.

. Lois M. Jones, "Fire-Flies," *The Saturday Evening Quill,* April 1929

Lost

A bit of me flew up to the sky,
And sailed with the clouds passing by.

I lost my voice in the song of a bird,
In all things beautiful heard. . . .

I gave my ears to the roar of the sea,
And crowned my head with the green of a tree.

I hid my eyes in the morning dew,
And wrapped my soul in the sunset hue.

I gave myself to the harmony true;
Beauteous nature, I'm lost, lost in you.

► *The Saturday Evening Quill*, June 1930.

Fire-Flies

When the tired day
Smiles with the happy night,
A thousand fireflies
Flicker lanterns bright.
Happy at their play,
Flashing yellow lights,
A thousand fireflies
Shine with stars at night.

► *The Saturday Evening Quill*, April 1929.

Purple Dawn

You led me over the ancient bridge,
   And I leaned on you
   More than you knew.

Now beneath the shimmering moon,
   I'll clasp your hand
   Until I understand.

Somnus* has bound the eyes of day,
And muffled her noisy throat
That I might sit in the glow
And think, and feel, and know.

Beneath the shimmering moon—
   A symphony of silence . . .
   Ah, God! What a night.

*The ancient Roman god of sleep.

► *The Saturday Evening Quill*, June 1928; *Readings from Negro Authors*, ed. Otelia Cromwell
et al., 1931.

Full Moon

Awake, love, see the glory of the night,
   The glory of the night!
Let's walk the silver carpet
Under heaven's lantern bright.

Still is the air,
Silent are the trees;
Even the stars have closed their peeping eyes
And left us to the night.
   The glory of the night!

Alone on the silver carpet.
Alone, love . . . alone . . .

Awake, love, awake! . . . the lark!

► *The Saturday Evening Quill*, April 1929.

Flights

I've a dream
Spun from your silken hair,
And jewelled
With the starlight of your eyes.

I've a dream
Swaying with the rhythm of your form,
And sparkling
With the melody of your song.

I've a dream
Woven out of the soul of you
Into the soul of me.
And now,—I see the moon!

► *The Saturday Evening Quill*, April 1929.

Unseen

A dark old woman with weary feet
Struggled up the city street.

Weak and worn, but with heavenly look,
She clasped in her hand the Holy Book.

No one saw that the light in her eyes
Were angels' smiles from paradise.

No one helped her on her way,—
They were hurrying on to pray.

No one saw her drink the gall;
No one saw her gasp and fall.

She had climbed the mighty hill;
But no one knew her lips were still.

▶ *The Saturday Evening Quill,* June 1930.

Jehovah's Gesture

All night long
Yielding bodies
Swayed
To the syncopated tunes
Of the jazzers.

Jazz-hounds everyone they were
As they poured their souls
Into the instruments of choice.

The fierce wind howled without,
Then, speaking in angry tones,
Shattered the window panes
And blew out the lights.
Zeus hurled his thunderbolts
And zigzagged the lightning through the dark.

The dancers' feet stood still;
The jazz-hounds were mute.

Angry winds,
Serpentine lightning,
Rolling thunder . . .
A crash!

A hurricane of souls . . .
The hand of God . . . in the dark.

▶ *The Saturday Evening Quill,* April 1929.

Two Worshipers

Away from the busy crowd
A penitent woman stole one day,
And hurried into a church to pray.

Away from the noisy throng
A tall red man stole one day,
And climbed Mount Henry to pray.

She knelt before the holy cross;
He communed with the sacred tree.
Both bowed to worship;
Both felt the need of Thee.

► *The Saturday Evening Quill,* April 1929.

Love Not Fame

I would not, Lord, be kingly great,
Nor sit on a throne most high;
I'd rather walk with lowly men,
And talk with passersby.

I would not, Lord, be over proud,
Nor crave the halls of fame;
I'd rather feel the love of friends
Than claim a hero's name.

► *The Saturday Evening Quill,* June 1930.

Sunset Calm

A crimson blush bids me look on high
As the scarlet dimples deepen in the dark'ning sky.

How fast the blending colors come and go . . .
O infinite miracle I dare not know!
Fold me in your veil of rest. . . .

Now all is calm . . . I'm blest.

► *The Saturday Evening Quill*, April 1929.

Myra Estelle Morris (?–?)

No biographical information is available on this poet. Her only published poems are in Beatrice M. Murphy's *Negro Voices* (1938). Two of the three in that volume are reprinted here because they are so innovative in form and contemporary in their feminist subject matter. "Man and Maid" concerns domestic abuse while "Women in Politics" concerns the ironies of a woman being lectured to by men and the lack of political progress despite women getting the vote in 1920. The poems are conversational, witty, and daring in their unconventional use of punctuation and language.

Man and Maid

Dear human beings:
For forty long years
I've tried to learn
What puzzled philosophers
For four hundred years;
The thing that Solomon
Four thousand years ago
Didn't know—
To wit:
The way of a man
With a maid.
Now just last night
While we cozily sat
Around the fire
Digesting our food
And thanking God
'Way off in His heaven
That all's well with our world;
From out of the night
Came a woman's scream
That chilled our spines;
And someone yelled:
They're fighting!
We dropped our papers
And forgot our peace
And madly rushed
To the little white house
Next door to us.
We grabbed his wife
And held them tight
But they continued to fight
In spite of us
With words.
The man was driven
From the door
Never to return

Again.
We cleared the house
Of broken vases
Of smashed chairs
And pieces of dishes;
We even bandaged
As best we could
The maid's hurt feelings
With condemnations
And offered refuge
In our house for the night.
But that very same night
The man returned
To his wife and bed;
Forgotten the fight
And what was said.
All that the woman
Had solemnly vowed
She'd never again do
She did.
Such is the way
Of a man with a maid
Which passes all understanding.

► *Negro Voices*, ed. Beatrice M. Murphy, 1938.

Women in Politics

Dear human beings:
Sunday I heard a lecture
Or maybe 'twas a panel discussion—
I don't know.
But anyway
The talk was about
Women in Politics.
It was slated for 3 P.M.
But didn't get started till 4:45,

But never mind that.
I sat in the back row
In a corner near the window
Which furnished an excellent view
Of the new fall hats!
Twice I was scared to death
When the man in charge
Called for points of view
From folks in the audience
And looked at me
And no one else.
I stared and stared,
But he stared right back.
I tried as hard as I knew how
To look intelligent—
Yet his eyes seemed to say:
You ought to know;
Which I knew I should.
I grinned in a sickly way
And looked to the man at his side
For mortal assistance.
The second man said something—
I don't know what—
But I swore then and there
That the very next day
I would subscribe
To a good magazine
That would keep me informed
About such things
As women in politics
(Which I did).
I came away from that lecture
Or panel discussion,
Whichever it was,
With jumbled ideas
That politics are no better
Since women entered
For they haven't had time

To make a change
As it took men 170 years
To do
What they expect women
To undo in twenty-two
And that women are not inferior
To men or men superior
To women or vice versa
But that both are equal
In mentality
And that it's not so much
What women have done
In politics
But what they are going to do
In politics
That makes them great.

► *Negro Voices*, ed. Beatrice M. Murphy, 1938.

Beatrice M. Murphy (1908–1992)
(a k a Beatrice Campbell Murphy)

Born in Monessen, Pennsylvania, in 1908 to Benjamin and Maude Murphy, this poet was an important editor of black poetry anthologies of the late 1930s and 1940s: *Negro Voices: An Anthology of Contemporary Verse* (1938) and *Ebony Rhythm: An Anthology of Contemporary Negro Verse* (1948). She also edited *Today's Negro Voices: An Anthology by Young Negro Poets* (1970). These anthologies have preserved African American poetry that, for the most part, did not make it into major journals and that appeared when few such collections were on the scene. Murphy was a poet herself and published two collections: *Love Is a Terrible Thing* (1945) and *The Rocks Cry Out* (1969). Having graduated from Dunbar High School in Washington, D.C., in 1928, Murphy carved out a distinguished career in that city, writing a column for the *Washington Tribune* and becoming an editor of the features and children's pages, as well as writing for various other newspapers and magazines across the nation. She was also a stenographer in the Office of Price Administration and a secretary at Catholic University. Finally, Murphy founded the Negro Bibliographic and Resource Center. Not enough is known about this important poet, editor, and journalist who did so much to preserve African American voices at mid-century. She was evidently married in the 1930s and had a son, but we do not know her husband's name nor the dates of her marriage and son's birth. There is a lot of pain at the center of Murphy's poetry, but we do not know enough about her to define its sources.

The Parting

'Tis not the parting
That means so much.
Ah! No!—
It is the frequent
After meetings
That carry
The deeper sting.

When your eyes meet mine
(Those eyes once full of love)
In a chilling stare—
When your lips say
A curt "good day"
(Those lips that once clung to mine)—
When your arms
(That held me once in such a tight embrace)
Are raised now
Only to tip your hat
Or for formal handshakes—
When we meet again
At the old trysting places
Among the old
Familiar scenes
And cannot recall
Even by a glance
The sweet memories
That flock about us
As bees about honey—

Ah! These! These
Hold the deeper sting!

► *The Crisis*, May 1928.

Waste

She didn't want his love;
Yet she came to him
Willingly—eagerly
And gave him all she had.

He didn't want her love;
Yet he took from her
Tenderly—avidly;
And each in his heart was glad

To have comforted the other.

➤ *Negro Voices,* ed. Beatrice M. Murphy, 1938.

Hatred

My hatred for you is a beautiful thing
Made up of songs you would not let me sing;
It's tended in anguish and grows in pain.
Your taunts were its sunshine; your scorn its rain.
When you gleefully hurled at me jibes and jeers,
I watered this plant with my falling tears.
Rooted in bitterness and pruned with care,
It grew very fast; and oh, how fair!

My hatred for you is a healthy thing.
It thrives in winter as well as in spring.
Sweet as the opening flowers of May;
Perfect and lovely in every way;
Strong as the love that once was your due,
Nurtured with pride is my hatred for you!

➤ *Negro Voices,* ed. Beatrice M. Murphy, 1938.

Release

My house is filled with simple fools
Who—now that you are gone—
Bring wreaths to crown the head that they
In life heaped curses on.

They know you killed my soul within;
Of love and joy bereft me;
Just one kind thing you did for me—
Last night you died and left me.

And yet they fill my house today.
They've come to "mourn" with me;
And I—while they shed Judas tears—
Rejoice because I'm free!

► *Negro Voices*, ed. Beatrice M. Murphy, 1938.

Pauli Murray (1910–1985)

A stunningly accomplished and fiercely political writer, Pauli Murray pioneered several pathways for African American women over the course of her life. She was one of the first black women to earn a law degree, the first black deputy attorney general for California, the first black woman priest ordained by the Episcopal Church, the first black woman to be a resident writer at the MacDowell Colony, and a founding member of the National Organization for Women. Having taught at Yale University and the University of Ghana Law School, she was awarded an endowed chair of law at Brandeis University in 1973. On top of this impressive career, Murray is a well-respected and well-known writer who published three autobiographical books with prominent publishers, *Proud Shoes: The Story of An American Family* (1956); *Song in a Weary Throat: An American Pilgrimage* (1978); *Pauli Murray: The Autobiography of a Black Activist, Feminist, Lawyer, Priest, and Poet* (1989), and a collection of poetry, *Dark Testament and Other Poems* (1970). Born in Baltimore in 1910, and raised by her maternal grandparents in Durham, North Carolina, she went on to get a BA in English from New York's Hunter College in 1933 and then three law degrees from Howard University in Washington, D.C., the University of California at Berkeley, and Yale University. While a law student at Howard during World War II, Murray reported on the first lunch counter sit-ins, conducted by Howard undergraduates, in downtown D.C. for *The Crisis*. As is evident from her poetry, she was a political activist who took seriously her role as a black writer in ending segregation and other forms of racism. Although her participation in the Harlem Renaissance came in its declining years, the youthful Murray expressed some of its most politically challenging themes as the Great Depression radicalized members of her generation.

8. Richard Bruce Nugent, "Drawing for Mulattoes, No. 4," *Ebony and Topaz*, 1927

Mulatto's Dilemma

I curse the summer sun
That burned me thus to fateful recognition.
Should such a thought strike terror to my frame
More than another? I am the strongest of this lot
And fit to do the work of two. Were I but paler
By a single tone they would not see me tremble;
Or if in shackles here, they'd buy my strength
And let another starve—but being free,
(If being dark is freedom),—they stare
At me; they note the curl below my hat;
They trace the darker line below my chin.

Oh God! My face has slipped them but my soul
Cries with the fear of brownness before a bar
Where brown's already judged by sight. Can I
Endure the killing weight of time it takes them
To be sure?

      If I could lay my quivering brain
Before them, they'd see a brain is but a brain
And know that brown men think and feel, are hurt
And broken even as they.

      Oh, for the pride
Of blackness! To stand unmasked before them,
Nor moved by inquisition. Accepted or refused—
Not crucified.

A mulatto is an African American of mixed race with a lighter complexion. It is a term no longer in use.

► *Opportunity,* June 1938.

The Newer Cry

I am weary, O God, of dark lamentations,
Of angry voices and sullen faces,

Of empty hands stretched heavenward
Pleading for mercy and justice.

We are not dumb driven beasts—
We are men!
Our hands have been taught
To work and to fight.

We have known bondage,
We have known hunger and need,
We have known pain and humiliation;
But man is slave only to himself,
And pain is but the door to deeper Understanding.

Let us laugh—not in deceit,
Not in childish pleasure—but out of gladness,—
Joy in our youth, pride in our strength.

Let us view all men with calm untroubled eyes,
But never grow smug in our own self-righteousness;
Let us give pity where pity is due, but scorn it
From our inferiors.
Let us grow strong, but never in our strength
Forget the weaker brother.

Let us fight—but only when we must fight!

Let us work—for therein lies our salvation;
Let us conquer the soil—for therein lies our sustenance;
Let us conquer the soul—for therein lies our power;
Let us march!—in steady unbroken beat—
For therein lies our progress.

Let us never cease to laugh, to live, to love and to grow.

► *Opportunity,* February 1934.

Youth

I.

I sing of Youth, imperious, inglorious;
Dissatisfied, unslaked, untaught, unkempt Youth.
Youth who admits neither God nor country,
Youth proud and eager—proud of its broken heads,
Eager to martyr itself for any and all Causes.

II.

Youth, bloody with flags; hot with protests;
Youth who would wage war, decrying War;
Armed with pistols, razors, knives,
Armed with gin-bottles and machine guns,
Armed with tin cans and broom handles,
Armed with rotten eggs and tomatoes,
Armed with red banners, placards and worthless diplomas.

Youth perched on soap-boxes, platforms and ladders,
Preaching to any who will stop to listen;
Giving out hand-bills, pamphlets and tickets—
"The true information, the one authentic
Story of this case or that case,—
The trouble with the world is—you'll find it right here!
Read it, Comrade, and join the Movement!"

III.

Youth who boasts of its strong personality,
Youth who is certain of its individuality,—
Yet dares not walk alone, stand alone, think alone;
But cries, "Follow the Leader! Follow the Leader!
Follow the Leader to Washington! To London! To Berlin!
We've got to see the President! The Premier! The Chancellor!
We'll get what the Administration has failed to get!
We've so much to offer—such Faith and such Vision,—
Damn the historians! Damn the experienced!
We've nothing to lose!"

IV.
Fighting, bleeding, falling, dying,—
Dying for the Movement—
"Down with the Capitalists! The bourgeois! The lynchers!
Down with Politics! Ethics! Religion!
Down with everything but the Youth Movement!—
Never mind what it means,—on with the Movement!"

V.
Youth apathetic, youth energetic,
Breeding children before they are striplings,
Destroying Life before they've begun Life.

Peace conferences ending in bedlam and riot,
Race meetings boiling the pot of Race Hatred—
Communist, Socialist, Negro and Jew—
Sore spots of Nations.

VI.
On they go, this Youth the world over,
Headed for Chaos with wrangling and snarling,
Bursting all bonds, junking all ideals,
Shouting in chorus, "We protest! We demand!"

Having one weapon, they wield it unsparingly—
Youth—hot-headedness, energy, passion.
"Make way, you slackers, money-hounds, Party guns!*
We are your Leaders, trust or outlaw us,—
We are the Youth of the World's New Deal!!"†

* Major leaders of national political parties.

† The New Deal was President Franklin D. Roosevelt's political platform for ending the Great Depression of the 1930s and for ameliorating its most damaging effects on working people.

► *Opportunity,* July 1934.

Effie Lee Newsome (1885–1979)
(a k a Mary Effie Lee)

Born Mary Effie Lee on January 19, 1885, in Philadelphia, Effie Lee New-some was one of two daughters born to Benjamin Franklin and Mary Elizabeth Ashe Lee. Her sister, Consuelo, was also a poet, and both were illustrators for children's magazines. Their childhood was spent in Texas and then Ohio, where their father was a bishop. Newsome attended Wilberforce University (1901–1904), where her father became a president, Oberlin College (1904–1905), the Philadelphia Academy of Fine Arts (1907–1908), and the University of Pennsylvania (1911–1914). She married the Rev. Henry Nesby Newsome in 1920 and moved with him to Birmingham, Alabama. Despite her vast amount of verse aimed at children, it is not known whether Newsome's marriage resulted in children of her own. She later returned to Wilberforce, Ohio, where she worked as a librarian in an elementary school and then at Wilberforce University. Newsome is best known for her children's literature. She edited "The Little Page," which was aimed at children, for *The Crisis,* contributing both poems and drawings, and she edited children's columns for *Opportunity.* Newsome published one volume of children's poetry, *Gladiola Gardens* (1940). She also wrote articles, poems, and reviews for adults, many of which appeared in *The Crisis* from 1917 to 1934, and several of these poems for adults are reprinted here.

The Bronze Legacy (To a Brown Boy)

'Tis a noble gift to be brown, all brown,
    Like the strongest things that make up this earth,
Like the mountains grave and grand,
    Even like the trunks of trees—
Even oaks, to be like these!
    God builds His strength in bronze.

To be brown like thrush and lark!
    Like the subtle wren so dark!
Nay, the king of beasts wears brown;
    Eagles are of this same hue.
I thank God, then, I am brown.
    Brown has mighty things to do.

► *The Crisis*, October 1922.

Morning Light (The Dew-Drier)

1.
Brother to the firefly—
For as the firefly lights the night,
So lights he the morning—
Bathed in the dank dews as he goes forth
Through heavy menace and mystery
Of half-waking tropic dawn,
Behold a little black boy,
A naked black boy,
Sweeping aside with his slight frame
Night's pregnant tears,
And making a morning path to the light
For the tropic traveler!*

2.
Bathed in the blood of battle,
Treading toward a new morning,

May not his race—
Its body long bared to the world's disdain,
Its face schooled to smile for a light to come—
May not his race, even as the Dew-Boy leads,
Bear onward the world to a time
When tolerance, forbearance,
Such as reigned in the heart of One
Whose heart was gold,
Shall shape the earth for that fresh dawning
After the dews of blood?

*Newsome here describes the colonial practice of sending African children out into the jungle ahead of white travelers to beat a path through tall jungle grasses, thereby sometimes flushing predatory animals hiding in them.

► *Caroling Dusk,* ed. Countée Cullen, 1927.

The Baker's Boy

The baker's boy delivers loaves
All up and down our street.
His car is white, his clothes are white,
White to his very feet.
I wonder if he stays that way.

I don't see how he does all day.
I'd like to watch him going home
When all the loaves are out.
His clothes must look quite different then,
At least I have no doubt.

► *Caroling Dusk,* ed. Countée Cullen, 1927.

The Bird in the Cage

I am not better than my brother over the way,
But he has a bird in the cage and I have not.

It beats its little fretted green wings
Against the wires of its prison all day long.
Backward and forward it leaps,
While summer air is tender and the shadows of leaves
Rock on the ground,
And the earth is cool and heated in spots,
And the air from rich herbage rises teeming,
And gold of suns spills all around,

And birds within the maples
And birds upon the oaks fly and sing and flutter.
And there is that little green prisoner,
Tossing its body forward and up,
Backward and forth mechanically!
I listen for its hungry little song,
Which comes unsatisfying,
Like drops of dew dispelled by drought.
O, rosebud doomed to ripen in a bud vase!
O, bird of song within that binding cage!
Nay, I am not better than my brother over the way,
Only he has a bird in a cage and I have not.

► *The Crisis*, February 1927.

Wild Roses

What! Roses growing in a meadow
Where all the cattle browse?
I'd think they'd fear the very shadow
Of daddy's big rough cows.

► *The Crisis*, June 1925; *Caroling Dusk*, ed. Countée Cullen, 1927.

Exodus

Rank fennel and broom
Grow wanly beside
The cottage and room
We once occupied,
But sold for the snows!

The dahoon berry weeps in blood,
I know,
Watched by the crow—
I've seen both grow
In those weird wastes of Dixie!

► *The Crisis*, January 1925.

Negro Street Serenade

(In the South)
The quavering zigzag of the fiddler's notes;
The thumping "tum-tum" of the banjo and guitar;
The gauzy quiver, flutter of the fiddle;
The measured muffled thud of that guitar!
And then a voice breaks forth—
Loose, careless, mellow—
A wealth of voice that rolls, soars,
Rolls and falls,
A reveling, rich voice,
Deeper than the banjo's;
With more of melody than fiddles' trebles,
Yet with that subtle minor trembling through
Which shakes the viol's slender vibrance
As the winds might—
And all of this out in a half-hushed autumn dusk!
The autumn air itself is tense, suspended,
And into this that most spontaneous song!
Which ripples on and floats and floats

Midst "thum" of banjo
And rhythmic background of that constant taut guitar,
And travels with the wavers of the fiddle,
To float and rise and rest with moon and star!

► *The Crisis*, July 1926.

Sun Disk

Grand old Egypt dead, what words shall thank thee
For the tenuous touch that carved the portion,
And wrought apart the place unchanging
That marks the dark man's challenge
From the ancient world of art?

That winged sun has wended through the ages,
And known its shape on silk and blinding page;
Been inset with the gems of burning jewels
By artisans who swung again the disk
On wings outspread, which sweep e'en centuries by!

Signet of Ra that the swart Pharaohs singled,
Sons of the sun,
When time and the russet mummy are lost in abyss,
And symbols and sun disk shall no longer bind death
By mystical strands to the cycles of earth,

That wisdom supernal which made wise the Pharaohs,
Will judge generations more knowing than they,
Which bury themselves deep in His Life Eternal,
That fain would fold races in Infinity.

► *The Crisis*, June 1923.

Memory

I have seen the robins
Molding their nests with their bosoms—
Now I live in the town.

Yet street nor swirl of traffic
Can dim this vision fresh,
Which shines in memory
As the spruce lives, verdant,
And glows with the freshness of cress—
I have seen brisk robins
Molding their nests with their bosoms.

I have heard the orioles
Singing their gurgling songs.
Streets of the town,
My hungry heart stares past you
To the greens and greens of the spring,
And I pity the city-bred throng
That feels not the birds in its heart a-nesting,
To whom the spring brings no breath
Of building birds in maples and poplars and oaks,
And the budding orchards
That rain down the blooms and the dew.

▶ *The Crisis*, January 1931.

My Roads

Sometimes at night
They're ashen white
Like highways built of bones.
Shadows of trees shred into these
Gray, dimly darkish tones.

The road that bore my horses off
Was just the path of time.

But the wan white pike
Makes me miss the tread
Of the jolly hoofs
In the times now dead.
And memory plies my pikes today.
And even this will ride away.

► *The Crisis,* May 1931.

Spring Rains

Spring rains, you weep the wistfulness
Of dead years,
And unearth the spring-purged smell of
Wilted leaves
That are as memories
Moldering.

You are blue as the violet,
Sad as the dove,
Dimly, dimly you sing on the roof.
Your murmuring puts my eyes to sleep.
But my heart remains awake
And my nostrils are full of the roses
That shall come
After this gray smoldering.

► *The Crisis,* May 1933.

Red Indians of Dawn

Red Indians of dawn, come chase
Across the eastern sky
But save, I pray, that calm "pale face,"
My Lady Moon, so shy.

► *The Crisis,* June 1925.

Passage

My grandmother has a strange little door
That opens upon the lawn
With panels across—
I've counted them, four—
And it's just as gray as the dawn.
When Patience* and I are there in the spring
We pass through this way to go violet-ting.
When Patience and I are out there in fall
We rush through this door
To hear the crows call.
In bright summertime beneath the blue skies
We often steal through to find butterflies.
It has an old knocker we just love to try.
We hammer it hard each time we go by.

*The poet's companion.
► *The Crisis*, April 1930.

Sassafras Tea

The sass'fras tea is red and clear
In my white china cup,
So pretty I keep peeping in
Before I drink it up.

I stir it with a silver spoon,
And sometimes I just hold
A little tea inside the spoon,
Like it was lined with gold.

It makes me hungry just to smell
The nice hot sass'fras tea,
And that's one thing I really like
That they say's good for me.

► *Caroling Dusk,* ed. Countée Cullen, 1927.

The Rich Beggar

In jasper and onyx and gold
His city I soon shall behold.
    O Paradise!
Though on earth naught to me has been told
Of jasper, in onyx and gold,
Yet in spite of what earth may have doled,
    I've Paradise!

► *The Crisis,* April 1922.

Lucia Mae Pitts (1904–1973)

L ucia Mae Pitts participated in two important aspects of African American history: she worked at Booker T. Washington's Tuskegee Institute in Alabama as a secretary; and she was a member of the Women's Army Corps in World War II, serving in the first group of black WACs assigned overseas. These two activities bracket the Harlem Renaissance and frame our understanding of Pitts's significance as a historical figure and poet. She was born in Chattanooga, Tennessee, to Janie Jones and Jarriett Pitts, one of five children, but spent much of her early life in Chicago, where she edited a poetry page for a magazine and wrote for the *Chicago Defender,* a black newspaper. Later, Pitts lived for a while in New York City when the Renaissance was in full swing and moved to Washington, D.C., another center of artistic activity, in 1933. It is unclear when Pitts began to write poetry, and her published work during the Harlem Renaissance is confined to three poems in the journals *Challenge* and *Opportunity,* along with several included by Beatrice M. Murphy in both *Negro Voices* (1938) and *Ebony Rhythm* (1948). She was well enough thought of as a poet to warrant a visit from Langston Hughes during the 1940s while she was stationed at the army post for African American soldiers, Fort Huachuca, Arizona. After the war, Pitts began a personnel service in Los Angeles and then worked for the U.S. Department of Public Housing there until the time of her death. She never married.

Challenge

Love, I adore your timid tenderness . . .
I love your soul-filled eyes, your naïve way,
Your dark-hued head, your softly sweet caress,
The voiceless, lilting things you sometimes say.
But I am clay, my sweet, to earth hard-bound;
I cry for passion's breath hot on my cheek.
Demands I make may frighten and confound,
For these are what I need and what I seek:
A burning love that deepest depths can plumb;
A love that adds and heightens inborn fire—
That leaves the breathless body tired and numb
When it has catered warmly to desire.

You are so sweet—so sweet! I love you much . . .
But I am raging flame. Dare you to touch . . . !

► *Challenge*, May 1935; *Negro Voices*, ed. Beatrice M. Murphy, 1938.

Requiem

If I should hear tonight that you were dead,
forsaking me and all this earthly place,
I do not think that I would bow my head
and weep wild tears into a square of lace.
I think I'd only silently arise
and step outside, then walk and walk and walk
until I found some hill that touched the skies,
long leagues away from any madd'ning talk.
High up, where stars swarm bright, I'd disembark
my sorrow on the cool, receptive ground.
And in that quiet place, warmed by the spark
of memory, I think strength could be found
to bear my loss dry-eyed, and see the days
go by much as before—though with less praise. . . .

► *Negro Voices*, ed. Beatrice M. Murphy, 1938.

This Is My Vow

This I have made my sacred vow:
The god of bitterness shall never be my god.
Whatever is, or was, or is to be,
When I go down to death, to greet the sod,
I'll go with a taste in my mouth
Of the wine of very heaven.
The bitter cup the jaded Life need never give,
For I shall never drink it—never while I live.

The sweeter draught I take for mine.
The cup of life, when first we sip, has little taste
But may, upon our whims as years go by,
Be filled with sweetest wine or bitter waste.
I have known pain and misery
But that I swear I will forget,
Remembering only hours that made the happy years:
I will not spoil my piquant wine with bitter tears.

I shall pluck moments from the days
As I would pluck the loveliest flowers from their bed.
These I will keep for my remembering—
Forgetting fingers that the thorns have bled.
Love and beauty, these will I hold,
And dancing hours, with music in my ears.
This is my vow: When I go down at last to death,
Who leans near me will catch the sweetness of my breath.

► *Negro Voices*, ed. Beatrice M. Murphy, 1938.

Esther Popel (1896–1958)

This poet published her poetry in *Opportunity, The Crisis,* and in her collec-
tion, *A Forest Pool* (1934), under the name Esther Popel. It is unknown
when she married William A. Shaw, who died in 1946; she had one child with
him, a daughter. Popel's connection with the Harlem Renaissance came while
she lived in Washington, D.C., after residing in Baltimore for a short time as a
teacher. She was born and raised in Harrisburg, Pennsylvania, by parents
whose families had resided there for quite some time. She graduated from
Dickinson College in Carlisle, Pennsylvania, in 1919 with a BA degree, training
in several languages, and membership in Phi Beta Kappa. Once she was in
D.C., Popel met regularly with Harlem Renaissance writers at Georgia Douglas
Johnson's house, published frequently in *Opportunity,* and taught foreign lan-
guages to junior high school students. The mother of a daughter, Popel also
lectured to women's clubs on the subject of race relations. Popel's poetry
spans the range of her era's interest in both lyrical nature meditations and
condemnation of lynching.

Ditch-Digger

"Poor devil!"—This they call you
As they stand, these lesser men
Who could not bear the strain
Of sweating toil and its monotony,
Watching the rhythmic swing
Of your strong arms and
Mighty, earth-daubed hands
That grip and guide
Your pick-axe up and down—
And down—and up—and down—
And up—and down—and
Up—and down—
To fashion from resistant earth
And rock—a cesspool!

► *The Crisis*, April 1931.

Flag Salute

(Note: In a classroom in a Negro school a pupil gave as his news
topic during the opening exercises of the morning a report of the
Princess Anne lynching of October 18, 1933. A brief discussion of the
facts of the case followed, after which the student in charge gave this
direction: pupils rise, and give the flag salute! They did so without
hesitation!)

"I pledge allegiance to the flag"—
They dragged him naked
Through the muddy streets,
A feeble-minded black boy!
And the charge? Supposed assault
Upon an aged woman!
"Of the United States of America"—
One mile they dragged him
Like a sack of meal,

A rope around his neck,
A bloody ear
Left dangling by the patriotic hand
Of Nordic youth! (A boy of seventeen!)
"And to the Republic for which it stands"—
And then they hanged his body to a tree,
Below the window of the county judge
Whose pleadings for that battered human flesh
Were stifled by the brutish, raucous howls
Of men, and boys, and women with their babes,
Brought out to see the bloody spectacle
Of murder in the style of '33!
(Three thousand strong, they were!)
"One Nation, Indivisible"—
To make the tale complete
They built a fire—
What matters that the stuff they burned
Was flesh—and bone—and hair—
And reeking gasoline!
"With Liberty—and Justice"—
They cut the rope in bits
And passed them out,
For souvenirs, among the men and boys!
The teeth no doubt, on golden chains
Will hang
About the favored necks of sweethearts, wives,
And daughters, mothers, sisters, babies, too!
"For ALL!"

► *The Crisis*, August 1934.

Blasphemy—American Style

(A Kentucky mob, at a recent lynching, helped their victim say the "Lord's Prayer" when he seemed to have forgotten the words, after which they hanged him and burned his body.)

Look, God,
We've got a nigger here
To burn;

A goddam nigger,
And we're goin' to plunge
His cringin' soul
To Hell!

Now watch him
Squirm and wriggle
While we swing him
From this tree!

And listen, God,
You'll laugh at this
I know—

He wants to pray
Before we stage
This show!

He's scared
And can't remember
What to say—

Imagine, God,
A nigger tryin'
To pray!

Lean over, God,
And listen while we tell
This fool

The words
He couldn't even
Spell!

"Our Father
Who art in Heaven,"
(Say it again!)

"Thy will be done
On earth . . . (Laugh, God!)
Amen!"

To Hell with him!
Come on, men,
Swing him high!

A prayin' nigger,
Golly—
Watch him die!

► *Opportunity,* December 1934.

Credo

I think
That God must be
A Music-Master
Who directs the play,
And we the players in His Orchestra,
Make harmonies or discords
As He wills———
He crooks His little finger
And the chords
Come swelling from the instruments we hold
Within our eager hands.
He nods His head
And majesty sublime comes crashing forth,

Or, with a simple drop of His baton,
Makes silent all the quivering, dancing strings
We play upon———
Mere puppets?
Yes, but who would not be proud
To be a player in a Symphony
So mighty?
And to be directed by
The Hand of such an Artist!

► *Opportunity,* January 1925.

Bagatelle

A cloud to God is such a little thing:
A puff of dust by careless angels stirred
And left curled up beneath the celestial chair
On which He sits to watch this puppet show,
This toy of His creation—call it World
Or what you will—go on 'till He is tired
Of all its futile dawdlings; then beneath
His chair, where dust enshrouds it, lets it lie
Forgotten while the greater pageantry
Of Sky and Time and Space delights His eye!
   *   *   *   *   *   *   *   *
To God a cloud is such a little thing!

► *Opportunity,* November 1931.

Theft

The moon
Was an old, old woman tonight,
Hurrying home;
Calling pitifully to her children,
The stars,

Begging them to go home with her,
For she was afraid,
But they would not.
They only laughed
While she crept along
Huddling against the dark blue wall of the Night.
Stooping low,
Her old black hood wrapped close to her ears,
And only the pale curve of her yellow cheek,
With a tear in the hollow of it,
Showing through.
And the wind laughed too,
For he was teasing the old woman,
Pelting her with snowballs,
Filling her old eyes with the flakes of them,
Making her cold.
She stumbled along, shivering,
And once she fell,
And the snow buried her;
And all her jewels
Slid from the old bag
Under her arm
And fell to earth,
And the tall trees seized them,
And hung them about their necks,
And filled their bony arms with them—
All their nakedness was covered by her jewels—
And they would not give them back to her.
The old moon-woman moaned piteously,
Hurrying home;
And the wild Wind laughed at her
And her children laughed too,
And the tall trees taunted her
With their glittering plunder.

▶ *Opportunity*, April 1925; *Readings from Negro Authors*, ed. Otelia Cromwell et al., 1931.

Night Comes Walking

Night comes walking out our way
In a velvet gown.
Soft she steps to music gay,
As only lovely ladies may,
While hidden cricket pipers play
In Ardwick Towne!

And in her hair, wind-tossed and free,
A million stars are tucked away—
The glint of silver carelessly
Encrusting polished ebony—
A true coquette and bold is she,
This lady gay!

The gleam of laughter in her eyes
While low she bends o'er growing things,
Is caught by roguish fireflies
Who flit about her, fall and rise,
Like stars gone crazy in the skies,
On magic wings!

Night treads softly out our way
In her sable gown,
Holds her breath while babies pray,
Chuckles, seeing Love at play;
Then with Dawn she slips away,
In Ardwick Towne!

► *Opportunity,* August 1929.

Reach Down, Sweet Grass

(For H.K.P.)

Reach down,
Oh long grass fingers,
Touch her hair
And stroke—but softly—her tired eyes!
Make soft
The pillow there
Beneath her weary head,
And maybe, then,
She will not care
That she is dead!

And when
The wild things cry
Their mating songs,
And pregnant Time makes ready to bring forth
Her issue,
Gentle grass
Caress her still,
And loose the earth a bit
So she may hear
The birthing sounds
Of lovely Spring
This year.

Then Beauty
Such as you have never known
Before, dear grass,
Will come to you, I swear,
For being kind to her
Where, quietly,
Alone, yet not alone,
She rests—
In silence—there!

Sweet grass
Reach down
And let her know—
When it is time, this year—
That Spring
Is here—
Because
She loved it so!

► *Opportunity,* April 1934.

Little Grey Leaves

Little grey leaves
Hanging so listlessly,
Wrinkled,
Like chattering old women,
Huddling together, a-tremble,
In the chill loneness of the Night—
Tell me—
Are you afraid
To let go of Life?

► *Opportunity,* September 1925; *Readings from Negro Authors,* ed. Otelia Cromwell et al., 1931.

October Prayer

Change me, oh God,
Into a tree in autumn
And let my dying
Be a blaze of glory!

Drape me in a
Crimson, leafy gown,
And deck my soul
In dancing flakes of gold!

And then when Death
Comes by, and with his hands
Strips off my rustling garment,
Let me stand

Before him, proud and naked,
Unashamed, uncaring,
All the strength in me revealed
Against the sky!

Oh, God
Make me an autumn tree
If I must die!

▶ *Opportunity,* October 1933.

Grace Vera Postles (1906 –?)

Born in Philadelphia to David W. Postles and a mother whose name is not known, Postles was educated at Boston's Emerson College, from which she graduated with a degree in oratory in 1929. In Boston, Postles served as secretary of the Saturday Evening Quill Club while she was an undergraduate at Emerson and published all of her poetry in the club's journal, *The Saturday Evening Quill* (1928–1930). Her poetry is imagistic in form and content, sensitive, passionate, and reflective. It appears that Postles remained single and made her living teaching drama and English at institutes and colleges in South Carolina during the 1930s. It is unknown what happened to her after that or when she died.

The Prisoner

All I ask is a violin
On which to pour
Pent feelings.

I would paint a picture
Of melody
With the strings
Of a violin.

▶ *The Saturday Evening Quill*, June 1928.

In Winter

The sky is blue,
The clouds are white and heavy
The air is pungent, and
Winds are strong, in winter.
The hills are covered with ice,
The nights are tranquil,
The mornings shiver, in winter.

▶ *The Saturday Evening Quill*, April 1929.

The Blue Ridge Mts.

A delicate blue
Silken veil
Is draped over
Abrupt elevations.

▶ *The Saturday Evening Quill*, June 1928.

Moonlight

The soft silvery rays
Of the beautiful moon
Light the tops
Of some tall aspens.

► *The Saturday Evening Quill,* June 1928.

Sans Words

Hand in hand
We walked
Thru the orchard,
You and I.

Only the gentle rain
Of apple blossoms
Was heard,
Until a balmy breeze
Broke the silence.

Sans means "without."

► *The Saturday Evening Quill,* June 1928.

The Scar

Lord,
Playing with fire,
I was burned.
I was burned, Lord,
But I didn't mind the pain,
Lord;
I didn't mind the pain.
If only pain came with a burn

It wouldn't be so bad,
Lord,
It wouldn't be so bad.
For pain goes,
Lord,
Pain goes.
But the scar . . .
Lord,
The scar stays.

Playing with fire,
I was burned—
I was burned, Lord.
But I didn't mind the pain . . .
But the scar—
Lord,
The scar. . . .

► *The Saturday Evening Quill*, June 1930.

A Lighted Candle

You move with a slight tremulous motion
As you plead earnestly for a chance;
You sway and dance so frantically,
But you grow weak and dim,
And as the shades of darkness fall,
Your life becomes extinct.

The little thoughts we cherish,
And strive in our hearts to kindle,
Are often smothered by a stronger flame
And passed into oblivion.

► *The Saturday Evening Quill*, April 1929.

Golden Sorrow

The heart that's
Sealed with joy
Will melt in sorrow ere long;
The heart that beats with gladness
Must throb with affliction
And expel the commingling elements
Into the cup of golden sorrow.

We drink the bitter tonic
And live another life.

► *The Saturday Evening Quill,* April 1929.

Ida Rowland (1904–?)

A distinguished educator with impressive academic credentials, Ida Row-
land was born in Texas, educated in Oklahoma, Nebraska, and Quebec,
and she taught in Arkansas. Rowland's heartland background is reflected in
her poetry collection, *Lisping Leaves* (1939), especially in the poem "Lines to
a Friend," which features migrating birds, coyotes, and a rolling plain. The vol-
ume's autumnal theme appropriately reflects the waning of her era's artistic
movement. Rowland was not the only Harlem Renaissance artist from the
Great Plains, as Anita Scott Coleman (Texas), Langston Hughes (Kansas), and
Aaron Douglas (Nebraska) also emerged from the region, but it was a lonely
outpost in some ways, and she published only the single volume with no rep-
resentation in the period's journals or anthologies. Rowland was one of the
few black women of her generation to earn a PhD, a degree in social science
from Laval University in Quebec in 1948. She had earned a BA and MA in soci-
ology from the University of Nebraska–Omaha in 1936 and 1939, respectively.
Rowland married, on an unknown date, the son of an exiled Haitian diplomat,
A. D. Bellegarde, who taught at Langston University in Oklahoma; she was evi-
dently childless and became a professor at the University of Arkansas–Pine
Bluff (formerly Arkansas AM&N). After her retirement, she established a com-
pany which published books about African Americans for young people. It is
not known if or when she has died.

Our Heritage

Shall we say now, as we have before,
There is no welcome, no open door?
That all the world has shut us out,
And hopelessness and strife lay all about?
O lazy cowards! It shall not be,
For an open door we all should see.
We shall face the future and demand of life
Our heritage, and no deadening strife.

We have a right to a life that is full,
    A life that is useful and happy and gay,
And out of the chaos of vibrant things
    We should have faith to carve our way,
And cling to the faith of struggling men,
    Though deep sorrow may come our way.

► *Lisping Leaves*, Ida Rowland, 1939.

Lines to a Friend

I cannot offer the wind from the sea
    Or the salty tang of the breeze,
But only the lisping wind that comes at dawn
    And calls from the trees.

I do not barter palm trees in a western gale,
    Graceful white trunks bending to leeward,
Or frosty waves against blackened rocks,
    Or sea gulls flying seaward.

I give only the white birch tree
    With her lofty head in the sky,
Wild geese flying northward,
    And the South wind's sigh.

I do not bring the tropical moon,
    Or the nightingale's song when dusk is falling
But only a western moon over a rolling plain
    And the coyote's calling.

Nor can I offer the gardenia's chalky whiteness
    Against a clinging night,
But only the fragrance of roses across a dew-drenched lawn
    And a lost love's plight.

► *Lisping Leaves*, Ida Rowland, 1939.

Autumn Evening

I love the wild, stormy beauty
Of a lake in autumn,
Like crumpled silver in the stinging winds—
Wild winds pregnant with slanting rain.

I love the silver dust of rising mist
Against the green and gray of dim shore lines,
The lonely call of some lost fowl,
And the croaking frogs in the falling dusk.

► *Lisping Leaves*, Ida Rowland, 1939.

Wind among Leaves

You are the boom of a mighty ocean,
Foaming waves dashing hard
Against blackened rocks.

You are the lonely cry of a sea-gull
Afar at sea
Winging its uncertain way
Across the green expanse.

You are the hue and cry of a busy thoroughfare—
The hustle and bustle of prosperity regained.

You are the timid whimper of a little fawn,
Or the cry of a new-born babe.

You are my heart-beat
O rush of wind among leaves!

► *Lisping Leaves*, Ida Rowland, 1939.

Autumn

I knew you were coming,
For I heard you in the lisping leaves,
And I saw your fingers in the sky.

But so quietly did you come
I hardly knew you were there.
I heard your skirts trailing in the withered grass,
And put out my hand to feel you pass,
But felt only the stir in the dying leaves.

► *Lisping Leaves*, Ida Rowland, 1939.

Anne Spencer (1882–1975)

The only child of Joel Cephus and Sarah Louise Scales Bannister, Annie Bethel Bannister was born on February 6, 1882, on a Virginia plantation, where her mother was the daughter of a former slave and a white member of the slave-owning aristocracy. Anne's father was also of mixed descent, African American and Seminole. She spent her early childhood in Martinsville, Virginia, where her father owned a saloon, until her mother divorced him and took her daughter to North Carolina, then to Bramwell, West Virginia, in 1887. There her mother served as cook for a mining camp and placed Anne in the middle-class home of an African American barber and his wife to protect her from the camp's rough atmosphere. Bramwell was virtually an all-white town, and although Anne lived in the segregated section reserved for blacks, she was able to cross the color barrier through her friendship with a white girl. She received no formal schooling until the age of eleven because her mother did not want her to attend the school for blacks, at which the miners' children were also educated. In 1893, Anne was enrolled in the Virginia Seminary, a boarding school for African Americans in Lynchburg, Virginia, from which she graduated in 1899. While in school, Anne met Edward Spencer, another student, and in 1901 they married and settled in Lynchburg for the rest of their lives. They had three children. The first black postal worker in Lynchburg, Edward took the unusual step of hiring housekeepers to take over the domestic chores so that Anne could write and tend her beloved garden. In the early 1920s, Anne's mother came to live with the Spencers and took responsibility for the household work. Anne became a librarian at the Lynchburg branch of Dunbar High School in 1924, remaining in the position for twenty years, until her retirement in 1945. Although Spencer published only thirty poems in her lifetime, she became one of the most respected poets of the Harlem Renaissance, and her work was frequently anthologized. Her poetry appeared in *Opportunity, The Crisis,* and all the major anthologies of her day. Known for her nature poetry and feminist themes, Spencer was one of the few women poets to be included in anthologies of the Harlem Renaissance after it was over, so highly regarded was her verse. She did not start publishing until she was forty, when James Weldon Johnson read her poetry during a visit to the Spencer home when he was in Lynchburg organizing a branch of the NAACP. He became her mentor from 1920, when he arranged for her first poem, "Before the Feast at Shushan," to be published in *The Crisis,* until his tragic death in a car accident in 1938. Johnson was one of several prominent intellectuals and artists who visited the Spencers at 1313 Pierce Street (where their son Chauncey continued to live after their deaths) over several decades; others included Langston Hughes, Georgia Douglas Johnson, W.E.B. Du Bois, Claude McKay, and the singer Paul Robeson. Anne Spencer fought as a political activist against racism in Lynchburg while continuing to write poetry and prose in the cottage her husband built for her as a study. Most of her writing is unpublished. Her final piece was a long poem about John Brown, which she did not finish. After her husband's death in 1964, Anne Spencer became reclusive, although she continued to write until her own death at the age of ninety-three. Anne Spencer's poetry is elusive, subtle, convoluted, but it consistently paints nature as a palliative for the jarring effects of racism and sexism in human society.

White Things

Most things are colorful things—the sky, earth, and sea.
Black men are most men; but the white are free!
White things are rare things; so rare, so rare
They stole from out a silvered world—somewhere.
Finding earth-plains fair plains, save greenly grassed,
They strewed white feathers of cowardice, as they passed,
    The golden stars with lances fine,
    The hills all red and darkened pine,
They blanched with their wand of power;
And turned the blood in a ruby rose
To a poor white poppy-flower.

They pyred a race of black, black men,
And burned them to ashes white; then,
Laughing, a young one claimed a skull,
For the skull of a black is white, not dull,
    But a glistening awful thing;
    Made, it seems, for this ghoul to swing
In the face of God with all his might,
And swear by the hell that sired him:
    "Man-maker, make white!"

► *The Crisis*, March 1923.

Letter to My Sister (Sybil Warns Her Sister)

It is dangerous for a woman to defy the gods;
To taunt them with the tongue's thin tip,
Or strut in the weakness of mere humanity,
Or draw a line daring them to cross;
The gods who own the searing lightning,
The drowning waters, tormenting fears,
The anger of red sins. . . .

Oh, but worse still if you mince along timidly—
Dodge this way or that, or kneel, or pray,
Be kind, or sweat agony drops,
Or lay your quick body over your feeble young;
If you have beauty or none, if celibate,
Or vowed—the gods are juggernaut,
Passing over . . . over . . .

This you may do:
Lock your heart, then, quietly,
And, lest they peer within,
Light no lamp when dark comes down
Raise no shade for sun;
Breathless must your breath come through
If you'd die and dare deny
The gods their god-like fun.

► *Ebony and Topaz,* ed. Charles S. Johnson, 1927.

Lady, Lady

Lady, Lady, I saw your face,
Dark as night withholding a star . . .
The chisel fell, or it might have been
You had borne so long the yoke of men.

Lady, Lady, I saw your hands,
Twisted, awry, like crumpled roots,
Bleached poor white in a sudsy tub,
Wrinkled and drawn from your rub-a-dub.

Lady, Lady, I saw your heart,
And altared there in its darksome place
Were the tongues of flames the ancients knew,
Where the good God sits to spangle through.

► *Survey Graphic,* March 1925; *The New Negro,* ed. Alain Locke, 1925.

Innocence

She tripped and fell against a star,
A lady we all have known;
Just what the villagers lusted for
To claim her one of their own;
Fallen but once, the lower felt she,
So turned her face and died,—
With never a hounding fool to see
'Twas a star-lance in her side!

► *Caroling Dusk,* ed. Countée Cullen, 1927.

Before the Feast at Shushan

Garden of Shushan!
After Eden, all terrace, pool, and flower recollect thee:
Ye weavers in saffron and haze and Tyrian purple,
Tell yet what range in color wakes the eye;
Sorcerer, release the dreams born here when
Drowsy, shifting palm-shade enspells the brain;
And sound! ye with harp and flute ne'er essay
Before these star-noted birds escaped from paradise awhile to
Stir all dark, and dear, and passionate desire, till mine
Arms go out to be mocked by the softly kissing body of the wind—
Slave, send Vashti to her King!

The fiery wattles of the sun startle into flame
The marbled towns of Shushan:
So at each day's wane, two peers—the one in
Heaven, the other on earth—welcome with their
Splendor the peerless beauty of the Queen.

Cushioned at the Queen's feet and upon her knee
Finding glory for mine head,—still, nearly shamed
Am I, the King, to bend and kiss with sharp
Breath the olive-pink of sandaled toes between;

Or lift me high to the magnet of a gaze, dusky,
Like the pool when but the moon-ray strikes to its depth;
Or closer press to crush a grape 'gainst lips redder
Than the grape, a rose in the night of her hair;
Then—Sharon's Rose in my arms.

And I am hard to force the petals wide;
And you are fast to suffer and be sad.
Is any prophet come to teach a new thing
Now in a more apt time?
Have him 'maze how you say love is sacrament;
How, says Vashti, love is both bread and wine;
How to altar may not come to break and drink,
Hulky flesh nor fleshly spirit!

I, thy lord, like not manna for meat as a Judahn;
I, thy master, drink, and red wine, plenty, and when
I thirst. Eat meat, and full, when I hunger.
I, thy King, teach you and leave you, when I list.
No woman in all Persia sets out strange action
To confuse Persia's lord—
Love is but desire and thy purpose fulfillment;
I, thy King, so say!

► *The Crisis*, February 1920; *The Book of American Negro Poetry,* ed. James Weldon Johnson,
1922, 1931.

The Sévignés

Down in Natchitoches* there is a statue in a public square,
A slave replica—not of Uncle Tom, praise God,
But of Uncle Remus . . . a big plinth holding a little man bowing
    humbly to a master-mistress.†
This shameless thing set up to the intricate involvement of human
    slavery,
Go, see it, read it, with whatever heart you have left.
No penance, callous beyond belief,

For these women who had so lately fled from the slavery of Europe
to the great wilds of America.‡

The Marquise de Sévigné was a seventeenth-century French aristocrat whose letters reveal insensi-
tivity to the poor.

*Natchitoches, Louisiana.

†Uncle Remus is the major fictional character of a nostalgic, stereotyped portrayal of a slave story-
teller by white novelist Joel Chandler Harris at the turn of the century.

‡A reference to poor French immigrants fleeing an aristocracy in France for America.

► Unpublished.

Rime for the Christmas Baby

(At 48 Webster Place, Orange)
Dear Bess,
   He'll have rings and linen things,
   And others made of silk;
   There'll be toys like other boys'
   And cream upon his milk;
   True, some sort of merit in a mart
   Where goods are sold for money,
   But packed with comfort is the heart
   That shares with you what's funny;
   So, please, kiss him when he's very bad
   And laugh with him in gladness,—
   Life is too long a way to go,
   And age will bring him sadness . . .
   Pray you for unceasing springs,
   Swelling deep in pard'n,
   That into twin lives may grow
   Time's unfading garden.

► *Opportunity,* December 1927.

Black Man O' Mine

Black man o' mine,
If the world were your lover,
It could not give you what I give to you,
Or the ocean would yield and you could discover
Its ages of treasure to hold and to view;
Could it fill half the measure of my heart's portion . . .
Black man o' mine.

Black man o' mine,
As I hush and caress you, close to my heart,
All your loving is just your needing what's true;
Then with your passing dark comes my darkest part,
For living without your loving is only rue.
Black man o' mine, if the world were your lover
It could not give what I give to you.

► Unpublished.

At the Carnival

Gay little Girl-of-the-Diving-Tank,
I desire a name for you,
Nice, as a right glove fits;
For you—who amid the malodorous
Mechanics of this unlovely thing,
Are darling of spirit and form.
I know you—a glance, and what you are
Sits-by-the-fire in my heart.
My Limousine-Lady knows you, or
Why does the slant-envy of her eye mark
Your straight air and radiant inclusive smile?
Guilt pins a fig-leaf; Innocence is its own adorning.
The bull-necked man knows you—this first time
His itching flesh sees form divine and vibrant health,
And thinks not of his avocation.

I came incuriously—
Set on no diversion save that my mind
Might safely nurse its brood of misdeeds
In the presence of a blind crowd.
The color of life was gray.
Everywhere the setting seemed right
For my mood!
Here the sausage and garlic booth
Sent unholy incense skyward;
There a quivering female-thing
Gestured assignations, and lied
To call it dancing;
There, too, were games of chance
With chances for none;
But oh! the Girl-of-the-Tank, at last!
Gleaming Girl, how intimately pure and free
The gaze you send the crowd,
As though you know the dearth of beauty
In its sordid life.
We need you—my Limousine-Lady,
The bull-necked man, and I.
Seeing you here brave and water-clean,
Leaven for the heavy ones of earth,
I am swift to feel that what makes
The plodder glad is good; and
Whatever is good is God.
The wonder is that you are here;
I have seen the queer in queer places,
But never before a heaven-fed
Naiad of the Carnival-Tank!
Little Diver, Destiny for you,
Like as for me, is shod in silence;
Years may seep into your soul
The bacilli of the usual and the expedient;
I implore Neptune to claim his child today!

► *The Book of American Negro Poetry,* ed. James Weldon Johnson, 1922, 1931; *Negro Poets and Their Poems,* ed. Robert T. Kerlin, 1923; *Caroling Dusk,* ed. Countée Cullen, 1927.

Lines to a Nasturtium (A Lover Muses)

Flame-flower, Day-torch, Mauna Loa,
I saw a daring bee, today, pause and soar
    Into your flaming heart;
Then did I hear crisp crinkled laughter
As the furies after tore him apart?
    A bird, next, small and humming,
Looked into your startled depths and fled. . . .
Surely, some dread sight, and defter
    Than human eyes as mine can see,
Set the stricken air waves drumming
    In his flight.

Day-torch, Flame-flower, cool-hot Beauty,
I cannot see, I cannot hear your fluty
Voice lure your loving swain,
But I know one other to whom you are in beauty
Born in vain:
Hair like the setting sun,
Her eyes a rising star,
Motions gracious as reeds by Babylon, bar
All your competing;
Hands like, how like, brown lilies sweet,
Cloth of gold were fair enough to touch her feet. . . .
Ah, how the senses flood at my repeating,
As once in her fire-lit heart I felt the furies
Beating, beating.

► *Palms*, October 1926; *Caroling Dusk*, ed. Countée Cullen, 1927.

Grapes: Still-Life

Snugly you rest, sweet globes,
Aged essence of the sun;
Copper of the platter
Like that you lie upon.

Is so well your heritage
You need feel no change
From the ringlet of your stem
To this bright rim's flange;

You green-white Niagara,
Cool dull Nordic of your kind,—
Does your thick meat flinch
From these . . . touch and press your rind?

Caco, there, so close to you,
Is the beauty of the vine;
Stamen red and pistil black
Thru the curving line;

Concord, the too peaceful one,
Purpling at your side,
All the colors of his flask
Holding high in pride. . . .

This, too, is your heritage,
You who force the plight;
Blood and bone you turn to them
For their root is white.

► *The Crisis*, April 1929.

Creed

If my garden oak spares one bare ledge
For a boughed mistletoe to grow and wedge;
And all the wild birds this year should know
I cherish their freedom to come and go;
If a battered worthless dog, masterless, alone,
Slinks to my heels, sure of bed and bone;
And the boy just moved in, deigns a glance-essay,
Turns his pockets inside out, calls, "Come and play!"

If I should surprise in the eyes of my friend
That the deed was *my* favor he'd let me lend;
Or hear it repeated from a foe I despise,
That I whom he hated was chary of lies;
If a pilgrim stranger, fainting and poor,
Followed an urge and rapped at my door,
And my husband loves me till death puts apart,
Less as flesh unto flesh, more as heart unto heart:
I may challenge God when we meet That Day,
And He dare not be silent or send me away.

► *Caroling Dusk*, ed. Countée Cullen, 1927.

[God never planted a garden]

God never planted a garden
But He placed a keeper there
And the keeper ever razed the ground
And built a city where
God cannot walk at the eve of day,
Nor take the morning air.

► Unpublished.

Substitution

Is Life itself but many ways of thought,
Does *thinking* furl the poets' pleiades,*
Is in His slightest convolution wrought
These mantled worlds and their men-freighted seas?
He thinks—and being comes to ardent things:
The splendor of the day-spent sun, love's birth,—
Or dreams a little, while creation swings
The circle of His mind and Time's full girth . . .
As here within this noisy peopled room
My thought leans forward . . . quick! You're lifted clear

Of brick and frame to moonlit garden bloom,—
Absurdly easy, now, our walking, dear,
Talking, my leaning close to touch your face . . .
His All-Mind bids us keep this sacred place!

*A group of seven brilliant French poets of the sixteenth century. In astrological terms, the Pleiades is a cluster of seven stars named after Atlas's seven daughters, who, in classical mythology, were placed in the celestial realm to save them from the pursuit of Orion, a hunter after whom a star constellation is also named.

► *Caroling Dusk*, ed. Countée Cullen, 1927.

Dunbar

Ah, how poets sing and die!
Make one song and Heaven takes it;
Have one heart and Beauty breaks it;
Chatterton, Shelley, Keats and I—*
Ah, how poets sing and die!

Paul Laurence Dunbar was the most important African American poet before the Harlem Renaissance. He was best known for his dialect poetry.

*Thomas Chatteron was an eighteenth-century English poet; Percy Bysshe Shelley and John Keats were nineteenth-century Romantic English poets.

► *The Crisis*, November 1920; *The Book of American Negro Poetry*, ed. James Weldon Johnson, 1922, 1931; *Caroling Dusk*, ed. Countée Cullen, 1927.

Clara Ann Thompson (1869–1949)

Hardly anything is known of this poet, who published two volumes of verse, *Songs from the Wayside* (1908) and *A Garland of Poems* (1926), but nothing in the period's journals or anthologies. Nevertheless, her poetry from the 1926 volume can be considered part of the Harlem Renaissance, and it is notable both for its witty use of the vernacular and for its commentary on issues of the era. Thompson was born to ex-slaves in Rossmoyne, Ohio, and became a full-time writer, speaker, and social worker in Cincinnati, where she was active in the NAACP, the YWCA, the Baptist Church, and St. Andrew's Episcopal Church. One of six children, Thompson had a brother and sister who were also published poets, Aaron Belford Thompson and Priscilla Jane Thompson. Thompson did not marry and evidently was close to her siblings and their children. She died in Cincinnati at the age of eighty.

The Flirt

No indeedy! I'm not caring,
    Let them hang around and pine,
If I didn't break their fool hearts,
    They would be a-breaking mine.

Men are mighty funny creatures,
    Keep things on the highest shelves,
Then they'll break their necks to get them,
    Jumpin' fit to kill themselves.

Keep things down where they can reach them,
    And just see them pass them by!
Still a-lookin' and a-jumpin'
    For the things they know's too high.

No indeedy! I ain't caring!
    Though they pine an' fume an' fret,
And just break their necks a-trying
    None of them have won me yet.

➤ *A Garland of Poems*, Clara Ann Thompson, 1926.

Aunt Mandy's Grandchildren

"Look here children! Who's this coming?
    Why it's old Aunt Mandy Payne,
With her basket and her bundle
    And that big old-fashioned cane.

"Come right in! Give me your basket;
    How've you been, you sweet old dear?"
"Oh I've had a sight uv trouble
    Chile, since last I wus here."

"You don't say! (Give me that bundle)
    (Now you children run and play)
And what were you saying Auntie?"
    "Why Nell's Jane has run away."

"You don't say so! What a pity!
    Nell was careless with that girl;
Let her run down there to Turner's;
    Wouldn't have done it for the world."

"Well, Jane was Nell's only gal child,
    An' she couldn't say her 'no';
But it wusn't 'cause Nell spilte her
    Dat made dat chile take on so.

"Run away wid dat low dawky,
    An' she's not yet turned sixteen;
Married to dat triflin' rascal—
    'Who'd she marry?' Turner's 'Gene!

"Yes done run away n' married,
    An' sich talk you never heard;
Turned to sassin' me an' Nellie,
    No! we couldn't say a word.

"Said she guessed she knew her bizness,
    Mother Turner wus her friend,
She had been more sympathetic
    Than we two had ever been.

"Umph! That jes' set Nellie crazy!
    An' it made me mighty sick,
But I seed as quick as lightnin'
    Somepin' else—the chile wus tricked!

"Yes indeed! Dat's what's de matter,
    An' I jes' tol' Nellie so;

Fust she tried to talk me out' it,
 But at last she let me go.

"An' I want to tell you honey!
 (Here Aunt Mandy's voice grew low)
Dah's a spell on all Nell's children
 Dat is whut I'd have you know!

"Fust 'twas Jim; he took to stealin';
 Den Bob took runnin' roun'
Wid dem triflin' low-life dawkies
 Dat you find in ev-ry town.

"Now it's Jennie—Nellie's baby,
 An' I spec' 'twill break her hawt;
Oh a spell is on dem children,
 Kinder b-lieved it frum de stawt.

"An' I jes' 'bout know who done it;
 I'm a-watching ev'ry sign;
An' I'll tell you all about it,
 When I've satisfied my mind."

Then, Aunt Mandy, nodding wisely,
 Went "to see de chaps a while,"
And the younger woman watched her,
 With a thoughtful, half-sad smile.

"Poor old fashioned, love blind granny!
 Any one outside could see
How they humored all those children
 What the consequence would be.

"So she thinks it's conjuration;*
 Hard to change when one is old;
Well, if that will help her bear it,
 Let her b'lieve it, dear old soul!"

*Conjuring is to cast a spell or put a hex on someone.

► *A Garland of Poems*, Clara Ann Thompson, 1926.

Our Heroes

*Written on the occasion of the return of the colored troops to Cincinnati,
Ohio, from the World War**

We crowded on the pavements,
   To see our boys march by;
Our soldier boys, with faces grave,
   But vict'ry in their eyes.

They left a few short months ago,
   For Europe's battle din;
They left us, jolly laughing boys,
   They came back grave faced men.

For theirs it was to blaze the way,
   On that dread field of blood;
They shrank not from the giant task,
   But fearlessly they stood,

And held their ground like iron men,
   And fought as demons fight,
Their foes were fiends for tyranny,
   But they were fiends for right!

Ah no! those black boys knew no fear;
   Knew no such word as "yield";
The German troops in terror fled
   Before their deadly steel.

They blazed the way to victory;
   We cheer till out of breath,
To see them marching, stalwart men
   Back from that field of death.

Yes, back again with laurels won;
    Our hearts are beating high;
We knew they'd fight as heroes fight,
    And die as heroes die.

We knew that when they fought in France,
    They'd gain an honored place,
For there they judge men by their deeds,
    Regardless of their race.

The whole world knows the story now,
    Then, will their homeland dare,
To still withhold the liberty,
    They fought so well to share?

Now let us pause, with faces bowed,
    While reverent silence reigns;
In mem'ry of those valiant boys,
    Who came not back again.

*World War I (1914–1918).

► *A Garland of Poems,* Clara Ann Thompson, 1926.

Lucy Mae Turner (1884 – ?)

The granddaughter of Nat Turner, who led the most famous slave revolt in American history in 1831, Lucy Mae Turner was a highly educated and talented poet whose single volume of verse, *'Bout Cullud Folkses* (1938), deserves greater attention. Like Zora Neale Hurston, Turner excelled at literary rendering of the working-class black vernacular and could create male as well as female voices. Going against the tide of literary history, both Hurston's *Their Eyes Were Watching God* (1937) and Turner's 1938 collection are among the last examples of black dialect to be produced by African American writers. Richard Wright, Ann Petry, James Baldwin, Margaret Walker, Ralph Ellison, and other black writers who came to the fore in the 1940s and 1950s created northern urban characters and eschewed dialect as an inappropriate throwback to plantation stereotypes. Poet Gwendolyn Brooks would continue to work in the vernacular, but it was a northern urban slang very different from that used by Hurston and Turner. Turner could write poems in standard English, and the one poem of hers included in Beatrice M. Murphy's *Negro Voices* (1938), "A Bird Is Singing," is representative of that style, but her wit, good ear, and political acumen shine through in the vernacular poems. There, she valorizes black working-class family men and hard-working women who earn their living in foundries, as waiters, and as laundresses while maintaining a sense of humor and healthy self-regard. Nonetheless, the vernacular Turner used made many people uncomfortable who lived through the era of minstrel stereotypes when such language was twisted and ridiculed by white performers. Even today, although we can see the wit and valorization embedded in most of this verse by Turner, a poem like "Matilda at the Tubs" comes uncomfortably close to reinforcing plantation myths of the Deep South. Turner's father, Gilbert, who was born a slave like his father, Nat, escaped from slavery to become a foundry worker in Zanesville, Ohio, where Lucy Mae was born. Her mother was the daughter of a Baptist minister. Although the family was poor, Gilbert and his wife encouraged their two daughters to attend college. Graduating from high school in 1903, Turner earned a degree from Wilberforce University in 1908, after which she taught in East St. Louis, Illinois, where she, her sister, and their mother lived together. East St. Louis was the site of the worst race riot in American history in 1917, which prompted a huge protest parade in Manhattan. Later, while still teaching in East St. Louis, Turner earned a BS from Ohio State University in 1934, a master's degree from the University of Illinois in

1942, and a law degree from St. Louis University in 1950. In 1955 she published a narrative about the Turner family after the 1831 revolt in *Negro History Bulletin*. Despite her sterling educational credentials, Turner was bitterly disappointed by her failure to be admitted to the Illinois Bar Association, which meant she could not practice law. Evidently, Lucy Mae Turner never married, and it is not known when or how she died.

Nat Turner, an Epitaph

Nat Turner was a slave who stood
For a supreme great brotherhood
Where men did not each other buy;
But, missing that, he chose to die!

The poet's grandfather, Nat Turner, led the largest slave revolt in American history on August 22, 1831, in Southampton County, Virginia. He led nearly two hundred slaves on a murderous rampage in which sixty-six whites were killed on the Turner plantation (where Nat was born) and elsewhere. The rebellion was put down violently with more than three hundred slaves killed in retaliation. Although Nat Turner escaped capture until October 30, he was finally caught, tried, and hanged.

► *'Bout Cullud Folkses*, Lucy Mae Turner, 1938.

A Bird Is Singing

A bird is singing at break of day,
Its heart is beating gladly,
The autos whiz along the way,
And life is flowing madly.

The earth thaws out from the winter cold,
And the grass is sprouting greenly;
The sky is tinted with blue and gold,
The breezes blowing keenly.

And my heart, that thought itself old for love,
Now finds that for love it is waiting.
Will he come tonight? Will he ask for my hand?
Ah, life! Ah, love! Ah, mating!

► *Negro Voices*, ed. Beatrice M. Murphy, 1938.

Pay Day

Pay day! Yo' fame hab ne'er been sung
By lofty bards and writers free,
Who hab not been enslaved as we
For sech a long an' weary time.

Dese free-breath folks look down on wealth,
Dey chiefly art an' culture crave,
Dey wants not muscles like a slave,
So dey eats scant an' daintily.

Dey sits retired on vast estates,
Deir gold an' jewels locked in chests,
Dey views hard times wid laugh an' jests;
Deir cattle browse on many hills.

But cullud folkses knows de pinch
Ob cold an' hunger, want an' pain,
Ob coverlets all wet wid rain,
An' wind a whistlin' through de chinks.

So Pay Day hab a blessed sound
Which thoughts ob food an' comfort bring,
Ob teakettles which boil and sing,
Ob soup bones, beans, and coffee brown;

Ob neck bone stew an' rich corn pone,
An' mustard greens and 'tater pie,*
An' toddies rich wid rock an' rye,
An' pig feet meltin' in de mouth;

An' at a lowly window pane,
A wife with radiant face is seen,
And little black boys clothed in jean,
Who run to welcome daddy home.

De foundry work is hot an' hard,
My hands is blistered so dey bleed,
But I must work so dey can feed
My brown-skinned wife an' little ones.

My tired face runs down in sweat,
My neck an' chest is seared wid heat,
But, oh! My family! Dey must eat,
An' so I toils through de day.

I see a fellow man fall out,
A kettle ob hot ore cooks his bones,
I hear his dying piteous tones
As his soul speeds onward up to God.

I straighten up my tired frame,
Oh, Lord! Make firm my footsteps slow.
Make safe for me the path I go
Among the tanks of red hot iron.

I sees before my tired eyes
My wife who bends in loving care.
She would my toil an' hardship share
For dese, our blessed little ones.

Pay Day will bring de needed check
To buy de food an' pay de rent,
An' get de little gifts that are sent
To Gran'ma Johnson, way down Sout'.

Pay Day in Pittsburgh where de smoke
Hangs in de air, a murky cloud!
Pay Day for cullud men who crowd
De stores, de restaurants, de bars!

Some throw deir money to de wind,
Ne'er takin' home a single dime,
Workin' all week in smoke an' grime
For a carousal[†] Saturday night.

But I looks forward to Pay Day
As the best day ob all the week
W'en I for food an' comforts seek,
An' take them home an' lay them down;

An' thank the Lord for this good earth,
For work and warmth, and love and friends,
For bounteous blessings what He sends
To a poor workin' cullud man.

God keep my muscles ever strong,
To be a sturdy workin' man,
Makin' a living as I can,
An' earning many an honest pay.

An' when at last my time is done,
May I hab lived an upright life,
Fum discord free, an' sin, an' strife,
So God calls me to Heaven's Pay Day!

*Sweet potato pie.

†Carousing; i.e., drinking, gambling, womanizing.

► 'Bout Cullud Folkses, Lucy Mae Turner, 1938.

Ebony

I was christened Ebenezer,
But dey calls me Ebony,
An' I'se like ole Julius Caesar,—
I'se a place in history.

Julius Caesar wrote 'bout battle,
'Bout de Gauls, deir ha'd fought war,—*
But I, Ebon, likes to rattle
On about ma' works an' car.

'Caze[†] I spins down to de hotel
In de morn, 'bout break o' day,
I don't t'ink to ring no doo'bell,
I'se well known all down dat way.

Sends ma' flivver to de garage,[‡]
Rolls ma' sleeves an' goes to work,
'Mongst de pots an' pans I forage,
Sta'ts t'ings up,—I ain't no shirk.

W'ite fo'ks beckon,—"Waiter, waiter,
Ain't you gwine to wait on me?"
Den wid grace polite I cater
To deir whim, does Ebony.

"Is it salt dey wants, or pepper,
Lobsta' stew, or chicken hash?"
I'se right dere, like a quick stepper,
Harsh words don't ma' grace abash.

An' soon all newcomers knows me,
Knows ma' smile so broad an' free,—
A few guests says, "Ebenezy,"
Mos' jes' says plain "Ebony."

Why it is a gran' position
To wait in de big hotels,
'Mongst de rich to hab admission,
Know de names ob all de swells.[§]

Know dey says, "Why Ebenezer
Is a waiter wuth a lot;
Tip him when he ope's de freezer
Fo' you w'en de day is hot."

"Don't he step wid graceful walkin',
Ain't he black as shinin' silk,
Ain't he awful good at talkin',
Eyes like di'monds, teef like milk!"

I'se as happy in my Ford car
As a multimillionaire,—
He can trabble to de lan's far,
I to de hotel, an' dere,—‖

Park ma' flivver in de garage,
Enter into rich fo'ks' lan',
Soothe ma' soul wid de mirage
Dat I'se wid dat lordly ban'.

If dey calls me "Ebenezer,"
Or jes' plain ole "Ebony,"
I feels still, like Julius Caesar,
Dat I'se a place in history.

*Their hard-fought war.

†Because.

‡Flivver is slang for automobile.

§Swells is slang for prominent members of the upper class.

‖There.

► 'Bout Cullud Folkses, Lucy Mae Turner, 1938.

Matilda at the Tubs

Yes, I goes down to Mis' Mary's,
Evah single Monday mawnin',
Sta'tin' 'long 'bout six or seben,
W'en de day is jes' a dawnin';
An' I takes de early street cah,*
'Long wid Marthy, Lize, an' Sally,
Who's all goin' to deir white fo'ks,
Hurryin' forth f'm cot an' alley.

Dey's a lot ob stylish creatures,
Ha'h† all pressed an' plumes a sweepin',
An' dey values deir importance,
An' dey feels deir oats an' keepin'.

For dey's high-toned cooks an' nursemaids,
Holdin' down de gran' positions,
Flyin' high,—but I, Matildy,
Glories in dese meek admissions,—

I'se a po' plain cullud pusson,
Not fixed up in silk an' satin,
But in cal'cer[‡] dress an' apern,
Flat heel shoes, an' jus' a fat'nin'
Off o' good hog jowl an' cabbage;
Ha'h done up in eight small bunches,
Plaited tight an' den tucked under;
An' I must confess I munches
Sometimes on a brown ol' snuffstick,—[§]
Sta'ted dat in ol' Kintucky,
Where tobaccy grows like rag weed.
Yes, chile, I'se been mighty lucky,
'Case I'se trabbled fa' an' widely,
Into Nof' an' Sout' Carliny,
Alabam, an' Mississippi,
Georgia where de woods is piney,
Up an' down de blue Ohio.
Now I'se here in ol' Missoury,
Scrabblin' ha'd to make a livin',
In dis lan' o' jedge an' jury.

So I goes down to Mis' Mary's
Evah single Monday mawnin',
Sta'tin' long 'bout six or seben
W'en de day is jes' a dawnin';
An' I puts de tubs to bilin',
An' I sta'ts dat washboard singin',
Soapsuds mountin' high an' highah,
Clothes advancin' white f'um wringin';
An' Mis' Mary says, "Why, Tildy,
You's jes' workin' lak' a young girl,
Sma'tness now is yo' meal ticket."
Now I weighs mos' nigh two hundred,

So dat makes me feel right spryly,
Sort o' kind a' young an' giddy,
An' I 'gins to sing right shyly:—

All about de ol' plantation,
Where I passed my early hours,
'Mid de sugah cane an' cotton,
An' de roses' leafy bowers;
While's de many lads an' lassies
Danced to chunes o' bones n' fiddles,‖
An' de little barefoot darkies
Listened open-mouthed to riddles;
An' Marse George an' Mis' Ophelia
Used to ride by in deir glory.
Horses steppin', bits a champin',
Lak' de kings an' queens o' story,—
An' I was de favored servant
'Mongst 'em on de whole plantation,
An' I 'joyed among my kinsmen,
An' in many a loved 'sociation.#

O, de change in times an' places
Since I passed dose happy hours,
'Midst de sugah cane an' cotton,
An' de roses' leafy bowers!
Dey are gone an' shall not come back,
Dey are vanished, ah, forebber!
Yet to me, in dreams an' mem'ry,
Dey shall pass away, no, nebber!
You may t'ink me plain an' sober,
Void o' eb'ry finer feelin',
As I toils, work-worn an' weary;
Yet dere comes a mem'ry stealin',
Liftin' me f'um out my harness,
An' f'um out my rough exterior,
An' f'um all my age an' worries,
An' my home rude an' inferior,
To pas' scenes so gay an' happy

Dat my heart fills up wid rapture,
An' my features lose deir sadness,
An' it seems de sunbeams capture.
An' dere is a light a shinin',
An' a growin' wide an' wider,
Shinin' roun' poor ol' Matildy,
Guidin' her whate'er betide her!
Even w'en I goes to washin',
Evah single Monday mawnin',
Sta'tin' 'long 'bout six or seben,
W'en de day is jes' a dawnin'!

*Streetcar.
†Hair.
‡Calico.
§A snuffstick is chewing tobacco.
‖Tunes of bones and fiddles.
#Association.
► *'Bout Cullud Folkses,* Lucy Mae Turner, 1938.

Evahbody's Got Trubbles

Evahbody's got trubbles,
I know dat, an' you know dat,
All us folkses got trubbles,
De lean's got deir's,* so has de fat.

Sam Browne made me trubble,
He saw me an' my gal passin' by,
So he butted into a'h biz'ness,
An' axed ha' jes' how come, an' why.

Well, den I picked up a bric' bat,
(You mus'nt try ma' tempah too fa')
An' I th'owed h'it at dat Sam'l,
But he came back wid a big crowba'.

Den Lucindy, de vixen,
Jes' drapped us bofe fum of'n ha' lis',[†]
'Caze we done disgraced ha' by fightin',
An' married a dude, hopin' to live in bliss.

But aftah dat drunkard done beat ha',
An' she wash an' iron mos' eb'ry day,[‡]
An' give dat rascal de money,
She wish she'd chose a diff'runt way.

So evahbody's got trubbles,
I know dat, an' you know dat,
Den let's wag along wid a'h burdens,
An' keep de blues fum undah a'h hat.

*Theirs.

†Just dropped us both from off of her list.

‡She is employed as a laundress by white women.

► 'Bout Cullud Folkses, Lucy Mae Turner, 1938.

Lucy Ariel Williams (1905–1973)
(a k a Ariel Williams Holloway)

Despite the small number of poems she published in journals or antholo-
gies and her single volume of verse, *Shape Them into Dreams* (1955),
Williams was a talented poet who tried very hard to get into print while earn-
ing her living as a music teacher. Her signature poem, "Northboun'," was pub-
lished in several anthologies, won a major prize in *Opportunity,* where it was
first published in 1926, and continues to be one of the best poems of the pe-
riod. Williams was the daughter of Fannie Brandon, a teacher and choir singer,
and a physician-pharmacist, Dr. H. Roger Williams of Mobile, Alabama, where
she was born. She earned a BA in music at Fisk University in Nashville, Ten-
nessee, in 1926, after which she attended the Oberlin Conservatory of Music,
where in 1928 she obtained a degree in music, with specialties in piano and
voice. Williams wanted to be a concert pianist, but opportunities for black con-
cert stage performers were extremely limited, and she ended up teaching mu-
sic at various high schools in the South after an initial position at North Caro-
lina College in Durham. From 1939 until 1973, when she died, Williams was
supervisor of music in the Mobile, Alabama, public school system. In 1936,
Williams married a postal worker, Joaquin M. Holloway, with whom she had a
son in 1937.

Prelude

I know how a volcano must feel
With molten lava
Smoldering in its breast.
Tonight thoughts, wild thoughts,
Are smoldering
In the very depths
Of my being.
I would hold them within me
If I could.
I would give them form
If I could.
I would make of them
Something beautiful
If I could.
But they will not be formed;
They will not be shaped.
I must pour them out thus,
Like molten lava.
Shape them into beautiful dreams
If you can.

I know how a volcano must feel.

► *The Crisis*, September 1929.

Northboun'

O' de wurl' ain't flat,
An' de wurl' ain't roun',
H'its one long strip
Hangin' up an' down—
Jes' Souf an' Norf;
Jes' Norf an' Souf.

Talkin' 'bout sailin' 'round de wurl'—
Huh! I'd be so dizzy my head 'ud twurl.
If dis heah earf wuz jes' a ball
You know the people all 'ud fall.

   O' de wurl' ain't flat,
   An' de wurl' ain't roun',
   H'its one long strip
   Hangin' up an' down—
   Jes' Souf an' Norf;
   Jes' Norf an' Souf.

Talkin' 'bout the City whut Saint John saw—
Chile, you oughta go to Saginaw;*
A nigger's chance is "finest kind,"
An' pretty gals ain't hard to find.

   Huh! de wurl' ain't flat,
   An' de wurl' ain't roun',
   Jes' one long strip
   Hangin' up an' down—
   Since Norf is up,
   An' Souf is down,
   An' Hebben is up,
   I'm upward boun'.

*Saginaw, Michigan, was one of the northern cities that recruited black laborers from the South to work in automobile plants and other industries during the World War I period.

► *Opportunity,* June 1926; *Caroling Dusk,* ed. Countée Cullen, 1927; *The Book of American Negro Poetry,* ed. James Weldon Johnson, 1931.

The Black Magician

Way down south, there's an old, old black man
   Who knows nothing of books or of pen,
But is skilled in the high art of living.
   A magician he's called by some men.

He can pour out a cupful of laughter
  From a kettle that's brimming with tears.
He can breathe forth a song of thanksgiving
  From a heart that has ached through the years.

▶ *The Brown Thrush*, ed. Lillian Voorhees and Charles O'Brien, 1932.

Glory

They stood, these two,
Against a mammoth wall . . .
So high
That neither could surmount it.
One brother stooped,
And on his back the other stood
And scaled the wall.
Men seeing him atop
Acclaimed him great.
They never saw his brother
Who lay prostrate
On the other side.

▶ *Opportunity*, January 1932.

J'ai Peur

I am afraid to laugh! . . .
For sorrow follows closely
In the wake of joy.

I am afraid to love . . .
For heartache comes too oft
When one loves dearly.

I am afraid to live! . . .
For death may take me captive
In the hour when life seems dearest.

Death! . . .
Then what! . . .
God! . . . I am afraid!

J'ai peur means "I am afraid."

► *Opportunity,* September 1929.

Octavia B. Wynbush (1898–ca. 1972)

Although Octavia Wynbush published only two poems, she was an accomplished short story writer, publishing several in *The Crisis* from 1931 through 1945. Not much is known about her beyond the fact that she was born in Washington, Pennsylvania, to Abraham and Mary Sheppard Wynbush and that she was well educated. In 1920 she obtained a BA in German from Oberlin College, and in 1934 she received an MA in English from Columbia University in New York. It was while she was in New York that she began publishing fiction in *The Crisis*. Self-supporting her entire life, Wynbush taught at colleges in New Orleans; Scottsville, Louisiana; and Pine Bluff and Little Rock, Arkansas. By 1936, she was a high school teacher in Kansas City, Missouri, where she stayed until her retirement in 1964. In 1963, when she was sixty-three, Wynbush married Lewis Strong. It is not known how or when she died.

Beauty

'Tis wondrous strange in what things men find beauty.
One sees it in the sun kissing the sleeping hills awake;
Another in the moon, trailing paths to fairy-land across the slow-
    moving water.
This man finds beauty in first youth; his friend, in mature women.
But beauty lurks for me in black, knotted hands,
Hands consecrated to toil that those who come
Behind them may have tender, shapely hands;
And beautiful are shoulders with bearing heavy burdens stooped
That younger shoulders may grow straight and proud.
And faces, dark, sad faces, too, are beautiful—
The patient, wistful faces of the many
Who have viewed their lands of promise from afar,
Turned from the mountain to the lonely path
Of sober duty, and gazed on
The promised land no more.
'Tis wondrous strange
In what things men find beauty.

► *Opportunity,* August 1930.

The Song of the Cotton

I sing of gleaming balls of down, rising from dark green stems,
Of bronzed men and women with tired arms, and aching backs,
Heart-breaking toil that binds and chains the mind—
My burden is, "Work, work, from rise to set of sun."
I sing of mellow song,
Sweet, dulcet, mournful melodies, born 'mid my blossoms white,
Woven into the softness of my down
A people's cries, sweet in their sadness.
I sing of tears that damp my silken balls,
Hot tears of hope deferred, "that maketh sick the heart."
Deep sighs, and unvoiced prayers, unuttered yearnings—
All these are woven into my song.

► *Opportunity,* June 1925.

APPENDIX: ANTHOLOGIES WITH WOMEN'S POETRY AND COLLECTIONS OF POETRY BY WOMEN OF THE HARLEM RENAISSANCE

Boelcskevy, Mary Anne Stewart, ed. *Voices in the Poetic Tradition: Clara Ann Thompson, J. Pauline Smith, Mazie Earhart Clark.* New York: G. K. Hall & Co., 1996.

Bontemps, Arna, and Langston Hughes, eds. *The Poetry of the Negro, 1746–1970.* New York: Doubleday & Co., 1970.

Braithwaite, William Stanley, ed. *Anthology of Magazine Verse.* Boston: B. J. Brimmer & Co., 1927, 1928.

Brown, Sterling, Arthur P. Davis, and Ulysses Lee, eds. *The Negro Caravan.* New York: Dryden Press, 1941.

Calverton, Victor, ed. *An Anthology of American Negro Literature.* New York: Modern Library, 1929.

Clifford, Carrie Williams. *Race Rhymes.* Washington, D.C.: R. L. Pendleton, 1911.

———. *The Widening Light.* Boston: Walter Reid Co., 1922.

Coleman, Anita Scott [Elizabeth Stapleton Stokes]. *Small Wisdom.* New York: Henry Harrison, 1937.

———. *Reason for Singing.* Prairie City, IL: Decker Press, 1948.

Cowdery, Mae V. *We Lift Our Voices and Other Poems.* Philadelphia: Alpress Pub., 1936.

Cromwell, Otelia, Lorenzo Dow Turner, and Eva B. Dykes. *Readings from Negro Authors.* New York: Harcourt Brace, 1931.

Cullen, Countée, ed. *Caroling Dusk: An Anthology of Verse by Negro Poets.* New York: Harper Bros., 1927.

Davis, Arthur, and Michael Peplow, eds. *The New Negro Renaissance.* New York: Harper & Row, 1975.

Fernandis, Sarah Collins. *Poems.* Boston: Gorham Press, 1925.

———. *Vision.* Boston: Gorham Press, 1925.

Fleming, Sarah Lee Brown. *Clouds and Sunshine.* Boston: Cornhill Pub., 1920.

Gates, Henry Louis, and Nellie Y. McKay, eds. *The Norton Anthology of African American Literature,* New York: W. W. Norton & Co., 1997.

Herron, Carolinia, ed. *Selected Works of Angelina Weld Grimké.* New York: G. K. Hall & Co., 1991.

Hill, Patricia Liggins, et al., eds. *Call and Response: The Riverside Anthology of the African American Literary Tradition.* Boston: Houghton Mifflin, 1998.

Holloway, Ariel Williams. *Shape Them into Dreams.* New York: Exposition Press, 1955.

Huggins, Nathan, ed. *Voices from the Harlem Renaissance.* New York: Oxford University Press, 1971.

Hull, Gloria, ed. *The Works of Alice Dunbar-Nelson.* New York: Oxford University Press, 1988.

Johnson, Charles S., ed. *Ebony and Topaz: A Collectanea.* New York: National Urban League, 1927.

Johnson, Georgia Douglas. *An Autumn Love Cycle.* Freeport, N.Y.: Books for Libraries Press, 1928.

———. *Bronze: A Book of Verse.* Boston: B. J. Brimmer Co., 1922.

———. *The Heart of a Woman and Other Poems.* Boston: Cornhill Co., 1918.

———. *Share My World: A Book of Poems.* Washington, D.C.: self-published, 1962.

Johnson, James Weldon, ed. *The Book of American Negro Poetry.* New York: Harcourt Brace and World, 1922, 1931.

Kerlin, Robert T., ed. *Negro Poets and Their Poems.* Washington, D.C.: Associated Pubs., 1923.

Lewis, David Levering, ed. *The Portable Harlem Renaissance Reader.* New York: Viking Press, 1994.

Locke, Alain, ed. *The New Negro.* New York: A. C. Boni, 1925.

McBrown, Gertrude Parthenia. *The Picture Poetry Book.* Washington, D.C.: Associated Pubs., 1935.

McLendon, Jacquelyn Y., ed. *Hope's Highway and Clouds and Sunshine by Sarah Lee Brown Fleming.* New York: G. K. Hall & Co., 1995.

Mitchell, Verner D., ed. *Helene Johnson: Poet of the Harlem Renaissance.* Amherst: University of Massachusetts Press, 2000.

Murphy, Beatrice M., ed. *Ebony Rhythm.* Freeport, N.Y.: Exposition Press, 1948.

———. *Love Is a Terrible Thing.* New York: Hobson Press, 1945.

———, ed. *Negro Voices: An Anthology of Contemporary Negro Verse.* New York: Henry Harrison Pub., 1938.

———. *The Rocks Cry Out.* Detroit: Broadside Press, 1969.

Murray, Pauli. *Dark Testament and Other Poems.* Norwalk, Conn.: Silvermine Press, 1970.

Newsome, Effie Lee. *Gladiola Gardens: Poems of Outdoors and Indoors for Second Grade Readers.* Washington, D.C.: Associated Pubs., 1940.

Patton, Venetria, and Maureen Honey, eds. *Double-Take: A Revisionist Harlem Renaissance Anthology.* Piscataway, N.J.: Rutgers University Press, 2001.

Popel, Esther. *A Forest Pool.* Washington, D.C.: Modernistic Press, 1934.

Roses, Lorraine Elena, ed. *Selected Works of Edythe Mae Gordon.* New York: G. K. Hall & Co., 1996.

Roses, Lorraine Elena, and Ruth Elizabeth Randolph, eds. *The Harlem Renaissance and Beyond: Literary Biographies of 100 Black Women Writers, 1900 – 1945.* Cambridge: Harvard University Press, 1990.

———, eds. *Harlem's Glory: Black Women Writing, 1900 – 1950.* Cambridge: Harvard University Press, 1996.

Rowland, Ida. *Lisping Leaves.* Philadelphia: Dorrance and Co., 1939.

Shockley, Ann Allen, ed. *Afro-American Women Writers, 1746 – 1933.* Boston: G. K. Hall, 1988.

Stetson, Erlene, ed. *Black Sister: Poetry by Black American Women, 1746 – 1980.* Bloomington: Indiana University Press, 1981.

Tate, Claudia, ed. *The Selected Works of Georgia Douglas Johnson.* New York: G. K. Hall & Co., 1997.

Thompson, Clara Ann. *A Garland of Poems.* Boston: Christopher Pub., 1926.

———. *Songs from the Wayside.* Rossmoyne, Ohio: self-published, 1908.

Turner, Lucy Mae. *'Bout Culled Folkses.* New York: Henry Harrison Pub., 1938.

Voorhees, Lillian, and Robert O'Brien, eds. *The Brown Thrush: The Anthology of Verse by Negro Students at Talladega College.* Bryn Athyn, Pa.: Lawson-Roberts Pub. Co., 1932.

White, Newman Ivey, and Walter Clinton Jackson, eds. *An Anthology of Verse by American Negroes.* Durham, N.C.: Trinity College, 1924.

Wilson, Sondra Kathryn, ed. *The Crisis Reader: Stories, Poetry, and Essays from the N.A.A.C.P.'s Crisis Magazine.* New York: Modern Library, 1999.

———, ed. *The Opportunity Reader: Stories, Poetry, and Essays from the Urban League's Opportunity Magazine.* New York: Modern Library, 1999.

ABOUT THE EDITOR

Maureen Honey is a professor of English and women's studies at the University of Nebraska–Lincoln. She is the coeditor of *Double-Take: A Revisionist Harlem Renaissance Anthology* (2001) and of *"Madame Butterfly" and "A Japanese Nightingale": Two Orientalist Texts by John Luther Long and Winnifred Eaton* (2002), both from Rutgers University Press. She is also the editor of *Bitter Fruit: African American Women in World War II* (University of Missouri Press, 1999) and the author of *Creating Rosie the Riveter: Class, Gender, and Propaganda during World War II* (University of Massachusetts Press, 1984).

PS 591
N 4
S 54
2006